PEARSON
Longman

Harlow, England • London • New York • Boston • San Francisco • Toronto
Sydney • Tokyo • Singapore • Hong Kong • Seoul • Taipei • New Delhi
Cape Town • Madrid • Mexico City • Amsterdam • Munich • Paris • Milan

New Era

Pitman New Era Shorthand

Pearson Education Limited
Edinburgh Gate
Harlow
Essex CM20 2JE
England

and Associated Companies throughout the world

Visit us on the World Wide Web at:
http://www.pearsoned.co.uk

First published 1975
Reprinted 1985, 1986, 1987, 1988, 1990, 1992, 1993
(all by Pitman Publishing)
Reprinted by Addison Wesley Longman 1996,
1997, 1998, 1999 (twice)
Reprinted by Pearson Education Limited, 2003 (twice)

British Library Cataloguing in Publication Data
A catalogue entry got this title is available from the British Library.

ISBN 0-582-29890-3

Produced by Pearson Education Asia Pte Ltd
Printed in Singapore (B&JO)

INTRODUCTORY NOTE

The present work is an abridgment of PITMAN SHORTHAND DICTIONARY, by SIR ISAAC PITMAN. It is designed to provide, in a size suitable for pocket use, a guide to the best shorthand outlines for approximately 20,000 of the more common words in the English language. The outlines are given in vocalized shorthand, except for short forms and any portions of derivative or compound words for which short forms are retained.

In addition, about 1,000 of the most useful words have been selected from the Appendix to PITMAN ENGLISH AND SHORTHAND DICTIONARY and entered in their appropriate alphabetical places.

A

a
aback′
aban′don
aban′doned
aban′doning
aban′donment
abash′
abashed′
abate′
aba′ted
abate′ment
abat′ing
abattoir′
ab′bot
abbre′viate
abbre′viated
abbre′viating
abbrevia′tion
ab′dicate
ab′dicated
ab′dicating
abdica′tion
abdo′men
abdom′inal
abduct′
abduct′ed
abduct′ing
abduc′tion
aberra′tion
abey′ance
abhor′
abhorred′
abhor′rence
abhor′rent
abhor′ring
abide′
abid′ing
abil′ity
ab′ject
ab′jectly

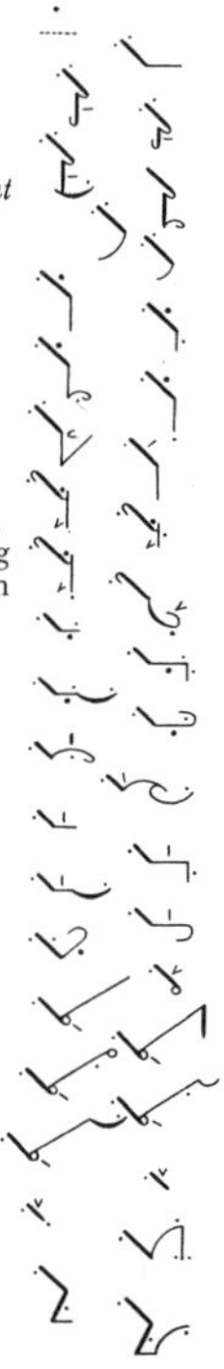

ablaze′
a′ble
a′ble-bodied
ablu′tion
a′bly
abnor′mal
abnormal′ity
aboard′
abode′
abol′ish
abol′ished
abol′ishing
abol′ishment
aboli′tion
abom′inable
abom′inate
abom′inated
abomina′tion
aborig′inal
abor′tive
abound′
abound′ed
abound′ing
about′
above′
abra′sion
abreast′
abridge′
abridged′
abridg′ing
abridg′ment
abroad′
ab′rogate
abroga′tion
abrupt′
abrupt′ly
abrupt′ness
ab′scess
abscond′
abscond′ed

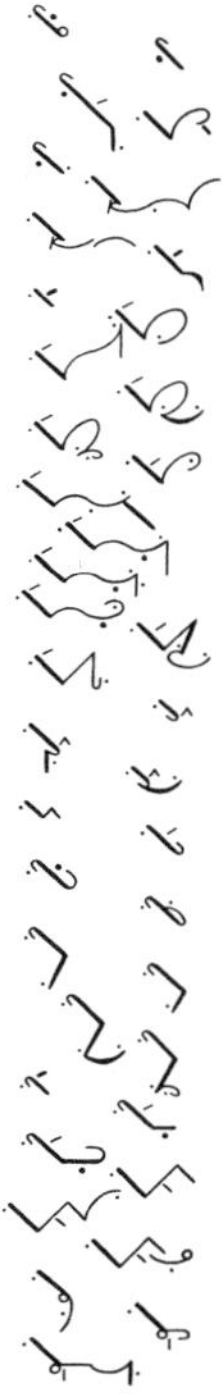

abscond′er
abscond′ing
ab′sence
{ab′sent, *a.*
{absent′, *v.*
absent′ed
absentee′
ab′solute
ab′solutely
absolu′tion
absolve′
absorb′
absorbed′
absorb′ent
absorb′ing
absorp′tion
abstain′
abstain′er
abstain′ing
abste′mious
absten′tion
ab′stinence
{abstract′, *v.*
{ab′stract,
{ *a.* & *n.*
abstract′ed
abstract′ing
abstrac′tion
abstruse′
absurd′
absurd′ity
absurd′ly
abun′dance
abun′dant
abun′dantly
abuse′
abused′
abus′ing
abu′sive
abu′sively
abut′
abyss′
academ′ic
academ′ical
acad′emy
accede′
acced′ed
acced′ing
accel′erate
accel′erated
accel′erating
accelera′tion
accel′erator
{ac′cent, *n.*
{accent′, *v.*
accent′ed
accent′ing
accent′uate
accent′uated
accentua′tion
accept′
accept′able
accept′ance
accept′ed
accept′ing
ac′cess
accessibil′ity
acces′sible
acces′sion
ac′cessory
ac′cident
acciden′tal
acclaim′
acclama′tion
accli′matize
accli′matized
accli′matizing
accom′modate
accom′modated
accom′modat-
ing
accommoda′-
tion
accom′panied
accom′pani-
ment
accom′panist
accom′pany
accom′panying
accom′plice
accom′plish
accom′plished
accom′plishing
accom′plish-
ment
accord′

accord'ance
accord'ed
accord'ing
accord'ingly
accord'ion
account'
account'able
account'ancy
account'ant
account'ed
account'ing
accred'ited
accre'tion
accrue'
accrued'
accru'ing
accu'mulate
accu'mulated
accu'mulating
accumula'tion
accu'mulator
ac'curacy
ac'curate
ac'curately
accusa'tion
accuse'
accused'
accus'ing
accus'tom
accus'tomed
ace
acerb'ity
acet'ylene
ache
ached
achieve'
achieved'
achieve'ment
achiev'ing
ach'ing
ac'id
acid'ity
acidos'is
acknowl'edge
*acknowl'edge*d
*acknowl'edg*ing
acknowl'edg-
ment

ac'me
a'corn
acous'tic
acquaint'
acquaint'ance
acquaint'ed
acquaint'ing
acquiesce'
acquies'cence
acquire'
acquired'
acquire'ment
acquir'ing
acquisi'tion
acquis'itive
acquit'
acquit'tal
acquit'ted
acquit'ting
a'cre
a'creage
ac'rid
acrimo'nious
ac'robat
acrobat'ic
ac'ronym
across'
act
act'ed
act'ing
actin'ium
ac'tion
ac'tionable
ac'tivate
ac'tive
ac'tively
activ'ity
act'or
act'ress
act'ual
act'ually
act'uary
acu'ity
acu'men
acute'
acute'ly
ad'age
ad'amant

adapt'
adaptabil'ity
adapt'able
adapta'tion
adapt'ed
adapt'ing
add
ad'ded
addict'
addic'ted
ad'ding
addi'tion
addi'tional
address'
addressed'
addressee'
address'ing
adept'
ad'equacy
ad'equate
ad'equately
adhere'
adhered'
adhe'rence
adhe'rent
adhe'ring
adhe'sion
adhe'sive
adhe'siveness
adieu'
adja'cent
adja'cently
ad'jective
adjoin'
adjoin'ing
adjourn'
adjourned'
adjourn'ing
adjourn'ment
adju'dicate
adjudica'tion
ad'junct
adjust'
adjust'ed
adjust'ing
adjust'ment
admin'ister
admin'istered

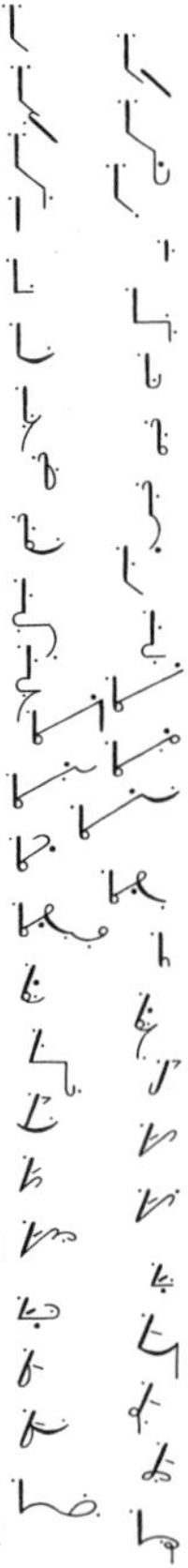

admin'istering
admin'istrate
administra'-
tion
admin'istra-
tive
admin'istrator
ad'mirable
ad'miral
ad'miralty
admira'tion
admire'
admired'
admir'er
admir'ing
admir'ingly
admis'sible
admis'sion
admit'
admit'tance
admit'ted
admit'ting
admon'ish
admon'ished
admon'ishing
admoni'tion
adoles'cence
adoles'cent
adopt'
adopt'ed
adopt'ing
adop'tion
ador'able
adora'tion
adore'
ador'ing
adorn'
adorned'
adorn'ing
adorn'ment
adre'nal
adren'alin
adult'
adul'terate
adul'terated
adultera'tion
adult'hood
advance'

advanced'
advance'ment
advan'cing
advan'tage
*advanta'*geous
advanta'ge-ously
adventi'tious
adven'ture
adven'turer
adven'turess
ad'verb
ad'versary
ad'verse
ad'versely
adver'sity
ad'vertise
ad'vertised
adver'tise-ment
ad'vertiser
*ad'vertis*ing
advice'
advisabil'ity
advis'able
advise'
advised'
advis'edly
advis'er
advis'ing
advis'ory
ad'vocacy
ad'vocate, *n.*
ad'vocate, *v.*
ad'vocated
ae'rial
aerobat'ics
aer'obus
aer'odrome
aer'ofoil
aeronau'tic
aer'oplane
aesthet'ic
aesthet'ics
affabil'ity
af'fable
af'fably
affair'
affect'
affecta'tion
affect'ed
affec'tion
affec'tionate
affec'tionately
affida'vit
affil'iate
affil'iated
affilia'tion
affirm'
affirm'ative
affirmed'
affirm'ing
affix', *v.*
af'fix, *n.*
affixed'
affix'ing
afflict'
afflict'ed
afflict'ing
afflic'tion
af'fluently
afford'
afford'ed
afford'ing
affloresta'tion
affront'
affront'ed
afloat'
afore'said
afraid'
afresh'
Af'rican
Afrikaans'
Afrikan'der
aft'er
aft'ermath
afternoon'
aft'erwards
again'
against'
age
a'ged
a'gency
agen'da
a'gent

aggrand'ize-ment
ag'gravate
ag'gravated
ag'gravating
aggrava'tion
ag'gregate
ag'gregated
ag'gregating
aggrega'tion
aggres'sion
aggress'ive
aggress'or
aggrieve'
aggrieved'
aghast'
ag'ile
agil'ity
ag'itate
ag'itated
ag'itating
agita'tion
ag'itator
agita'to
agnos'tic
ago'
ag'onizing
ag'ony
agree'
agree'able
agreed'
agree'ing
agree'ment
agricul'tural
ag'riculture
agricul'turist
aground'
a'gue
ah
ahead'
aid
aid'ed
aide-mém'oire
aid'ing
ail
ailed
ail'ing
ail'ment
aim
aimed
aim'ing
aim'less
aim'lessly
aim'lessness
air
air'borne
air'craft
air'field
air'force
air'-hole
air'-lift
air'line
air'mail
air'minded
air'plane
air'port
air-shaft
air'ship
air'strip
air'tight
air'way
air'worthi'ness
air'worthy
aisle
akin'
à la carte'
alac'rity
alarm'
alarmed'
alarm'ing
alarm'ingly
alas'
al'bum
al'cohol
alcohol'ic
al'derman
ale
alert'
alert'ness
al'gebra
a'lias
al'ibi
a'lien
a'lienate
a'lienated

a'lienating
aliena'tion
alight'
alight'ed
alight'ing
align', aline'
align'ment
alike'
aliment'ary
al'imony
alive'
al'kali
al'kaline
all
allay'
allayed'
allay'ing
allega'tion
allege'
alleged'
alle'giance
alleg'ing
all'ergy
alle'viate
alle'viated
alle'viating
allevia'tion
al'ley
al'leyway
alli'ance
al'lied
al'lies
al'locate
al'located
al'locating
alloca'tion
allot'
allot'ment
allot'ropism
allot'ted
allot'ting
allow'
allow'able
allow'ance
allowed'
allow'ing
alloy'
allude'
allud'ed
allud'ing
allure'
allur'ing
allur'ingly
allu'sion
allu'via
al'ly
al'manac
*al*might'y
a'lmond
al'most
aloft'
alone'
along'
along'side
aloof'
aloud'
al'phabet
alphabet'ic
alphabet'ical
Alp'ine
*al*read'y
al'so
al'tar
al'ter
altera'tion
alterca'tion
al'tered
al'tering
al'ternate, *v.*
altern'ate, *a.*
al'ternated
altern'ately
al'ternating
alter'native
altern'atively
al'ternator
although'
al'titude
altogeth'er
al'truism
altruis'tic
alumin'ium
alu'minum
*al'*ways
am
amal'gamate

*amal'gamat*ed
*amal'gamat*ing
amalgama'tion
amanuen'sis
amass'
amassed'
amass'ing
am'ateur
amaze'
amazed'
amaze'ment
amaz'ing
amaz'ingly
Am'azon
ambas'sador
am'ber
ambigu'ity
ambig'uous
ambig'uously
ambi'tion
ambi'tious
ambi'tiously
ambiv'alence
ambiv'alent
am'bulance
am'bush
ame'liorate
ameliora'tion
amen'
ame'nable
ame'nably
amend'
amend'ed
amend'ment
amen'ity
Amer'ican
Amer'icanism
a'miable
am'icable
am'icably
amid'
amidst'
amiss'
am'ity
ammo'nia
ammuni'tion
amoe'bic
amok'
among'
amongst'
amo'ral
amoral'ity
amortiza'tion
amor'tize
amor'tizement
amount'
amount'ed
amount'ing
amp'
amper'age
amphib'ian
amphithe'atre
am'ple
amplifica'tion
am'plified
am'plifier
am'plify
am'plifying
am'ply
am'poule
am'putate
am'putated
am'putating
amputa'tion
amuse'
amused'
amuse'ment
amus'ing
an
anach'ronism
anae'mia
anaem'ic
anaesthet'ic
analges'ic
anal'ogous
anal'ogy
an'alyse
an'alysed
an'alysing
anal'ysis
an'alyst
analyt'ic
analyt'ical
an'archist
an'archy
anath'ema

anatom'ical
anat'omy
an'cestor
ances'tral
anch'or
anch'ored
anch'oring
an'cient
and
an'ecdote
ane'mic
  anae'mic
anesthet'ic
  anaesthet'ic
anew'
an'gel
angel'ic
an'ger
an'gered
an'gle
Ang'lophil
Ang'lophile
Ang'lophobe
ango'ra
an'grily
an'gry
an'guish
an'gular
angular'ity
an'iline
an'imal
an'imate
an'imated
an'imating
anima'tion
animos'ity
an'iseed
an'kle
an'nals
annex'
annexa'tion
annexed'
annex'ing
anni'hilate
anni'hilated
anni'hilating
annihila'tion
anniver'sary

an'notate
an'notated
an'notating
annota'tion
announce'
announced'
announce'-
  ment
announc'er
announc'ing
annoy'
annoy'ance
annoyed'
annoy'ing
an'nual
an'nually
annu'ity
annul'
annul'ling
an'num
anom'alous
anom'aly
anonym'ity
anon'ymous
anon'ymously
anoph'eles
anoth'er
an'swer
an'swerable
an'swered
an'swering
antag'onism
antag'onist
antagonist'ic
antag'onize
Antarc'tic
antece'dent
an'tedate
an'tedated
antenat'al
an'them
anthol'ogist
anthol'ogy
an'thracite
an'thrax

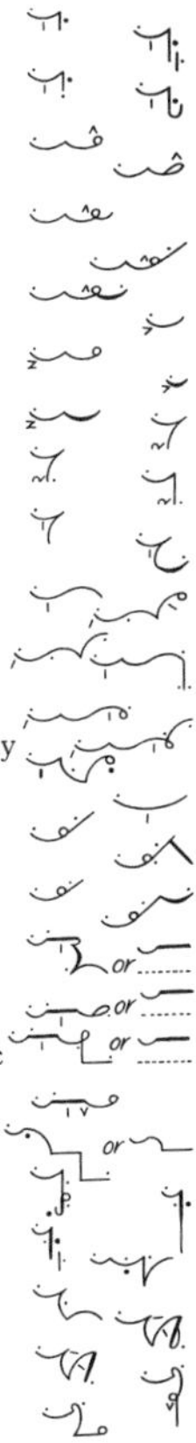

anti-air'craft
antibiot'ic
an'tic
antic'ipate
antic'ipated
antic'ipating
anticipa'tion
an'tidote
antihist'amine
an'tiquated
antique'
antiq'uity
anti-semit'ic
antisep'tic
antith'esis
anti-vivisec'tion
ant'ler
an'vil
anxi'ety
anx'ious
anx'iously
an'y
*an'y*body
*an'y*how
*an'y*one
*an'y*time
an'ything
*an'y*way
*an'y*where
apart'
apart'heid
apart'ment
apathet'ic
ap'athy
ape'ritif
ap'erture
a'pex
aph'orism
aphrodis'iac
apiece'
apologet'ic
apolo'gia
apol'ogize
apol'ogized
apol'ogizing
apol'ogy
apos'tle
appal'

appalled'
appall'ing
appara'tus
appar'el
appa'rent
appa'rently
appeal'
appealed'
appeal'ing
appear'
appear'ance
appeared'
appear'ing
appease'
appel'lant
appel'late
appella'tion
append'
append'age
append'ed
appen'dices
appendici'tis
append'ing
appen'dix
appen'dixes
appertain'
appertained'
appertain'ing
ap'petite
ap'petize
ap'petizing
applaud'
applaud'ed
applaud'ing
applause'
ap'ple
appli'ance
ap'plicable *or*
ap'plicant
applica'tion
applied'
apply'
apply'ing
appoint'
appoint'ed
appoint'ing
appoint'ment

appor'tion
appor'tioned
appor'tioning
appor'tion-
ment
ap'posite
apprais'al
appraise'
appraised'
appre'ciable
appre'ciate
appre'ciated
appre'ciating
apprecia'tion
appre'ciative
apprehend'
apprehend'ed
apprehend'ing
apprehen'sion
apprehen'sive
appren'tice
appren'ticed
appren'tice-
ship
approach'
approach'able
approached'
approach'ing
approba'tion
appro'priate
appro'priated
appro'priately
appro'priate-
ness
appro'priating
appropria'tion
approv'al
approve'
approved'
approv'ing
approv'ingly
approx'imate
approx'imated
approx'imately
approx'imat-
ing
approxima'-
tion

A'pril
a'pron
apropos'
apt
apt'itude
apt'ly
apt'ness
a'qualung
aquamarine'
a'qua-planing
aqua'rium
aquat'ic
a'queduct
Ar'ab
Ara'bian
Ar'abic
ar'able
ar'biter
arb'itrage
*ar'bitrar*ily
ar'bitrary
ar'bitrate
*ar'bitrat*ed
*ar'bitrat*ing
arbitra'tion
ar'bitrator
arbor'eal
ar'bour, ar'bor
arc
arcade'
arch
archa'ic
archbish'op or
ar'chitect
architect'ural
ar'chitecture
arc'-lamp
Arc'tic
ar'dent
ar'dently
ar'dour, ar'dor
ar'duous
are
a'rea
are'na
Ar'gentine
ar'gosy

ar'gue
ar'gued
ar'guing
ar'gument
argumen'ta-
tive
ar'id
arid'ity
aright'
arise'
aris'en
aris'ing
aristoc'racy
ar'istocrat
aristocrat'ic
arith'metic
arithmet'ical
arm
Armagedd'on
ar'mament
ar'mature
arm'*chair*
armed
arm'ing
arm'istice
ar'mour,
ar'mor
arms
ar'my
aro'ma
arose'
around'
arouse'
aroused'
arous'ing
arraign'
arraigned'
arrange'
arranged'
arrange'ment
arrang'ing
array'
arrayed'
arrear'
arrears'
arrest'

arrest'ed
arrest'ing
arri'val
arrive'
arrived'
arriv'ing
ar'rogance
ar'rogant
ar'rogantly
ar'row
ar'senal
ar'senic
ar'son
art
ar'tery
arte'sian
art'ful
ar'ticle
art'ifact
art'ifice
artifi'cial
artil'lery
ar'tisan
art'ist
artist'ic
ar'tistry
art'less
as
asbes'tos
ascend'
ascen'dancy
ascend'ency
ascertain'
ascertained'
ascet'ic
ascor'bic
ascribe'
ascribed'
ascrib'ing
ash
ashamed'
ashore'
A'sian
Asiat'ic
aside'
asinin'ity
ask
askance'

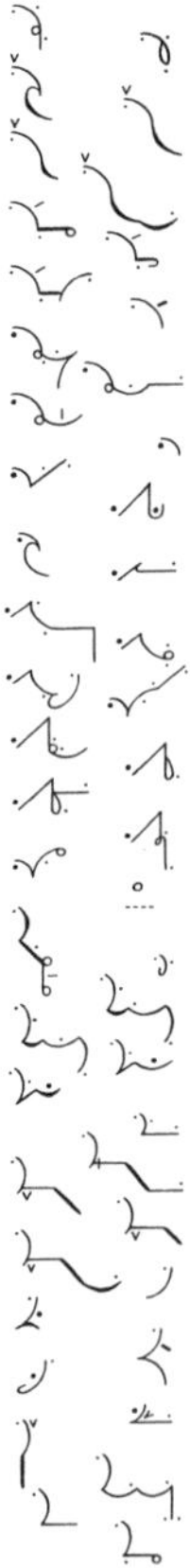

asked
asleep'
as'pect
asper'sion
as'phalt
asphyxia'tion
aspi'rant
as'pirate, *n.*
as'pirate, *v.*
aspira'tion
aspire'
aspired'
aspir'in
aspir'ing
assail'
assail'ant
assailed'
assail'ing
assas'sin
assas'sinate
assas'sinated
assault'
assault'ed
assault'ing
assay'
assayed'
assay'er
assay'ing
assem'ble
assem'bled
assem'bling
assem'bly
assent'
assent'ed
assent'ing
assert'
assert'ed
assert'ing
asser'tion
assess'
assessed'
assess'ing
assess'ment
assess'or
as'sets
assidu'ity
assid'uous
assid'uously
assign'
assigned'
assignee'
assign'ment
assignor'
assigns'
assim'ilate
assim'ilated
assim'ilating
assimila'tion
assist'
assist'ance
assist'ant
assist'ed
assist'ing
assize'
assiz'es
asso'ciate
asso'ciated
asso'ciating
associa'tion
assort'
assort'ed
assort'ing
assort'ment
assuage'
assume'
assumed'
assum'ing
assump'tion
assur'ance
assure'
assured'
assur'edly
assur'ing
as'ter
as'terisk
asth'ma
astir'
aston'ish ... or ...
aston'ished ... or ...
aston'ishing ... or ...
aston'ishment ... or ...
astound'
astound'ed
astrakhan'

astray'
astrin'gent
as'trodome
astrol'ogy
as'tronaut
astronaut'ics
astron'omer
astron'omy
astute'
asun'der
asy'lum
at
ate
a'theist
ath'lete
athlet'ic
athlet'ics
Atlan'tic
At'las, at'las
at'mosphere
atmospher'ic
atmosphe'rics
at'om
at'omizer
aton'al
atone'
atoned'
atone'ment
atro'cious
atro'ciously
atroc'ity
at'rophy
attach'
attached'
attach'ing
attach'ment
attack'
attacked'
attack'ing
attain'
attain'able
attained'
attain'ing
attain'ment
attempt'
attempt'ed
attempt'ing
attend'
attend'ance
attend'ant
attend'ed
attend'ing
atten'tion
atten'tive
atten'tively
atten'uate
attest'
attesta'tion
attest'ed
attest'er, attest'or
attest'ing
at'tic
attire'
attired'
at'titude
attor'ney
Attor'ney-*Gen'eral*
attract'
attract'ed
attract'ing
attrac'tion
attract'ive
attract'ively
attrib'utable
{at'tribute, *n.*
{attrib'ute, *v.*
attrib'uted
attrib'uting
au'burn
auc'tion
auc'tioneer'
auda'cious
auda'ciously
audac'ity
audibil'ity
au'dible
au'dience
au'dio
au'dit
au'dited
au'diting
au'ditor
audito'rium
aught

augment'
augment'ed
augment'ing
au'gur
au'gured
{Au'gust, *n.*
{august', *adj.*
aunt
au'ral
au'spices
auspi'cious
auspi'ciously
Australa'sian
Austra'lian
Aus'trian
aut'archy
authen'tic
authen'ticate
authen'ticated
authentic'ity
au'thor
au'thoress
authoritar'ian
authori-
tar'ianism
author'itative
author'ita-
tively
author'ity
authoriza'tion
au'thorize
au'thorized
au'thorizing
au'thorship
aut'o
autobiograph'-
ical
autobiog'raphy
autoc'racy
au'tocrat
autocrat'ic
au'tograph
aut'omate
automat'ic
automa'tion
autom'aton
automobile'

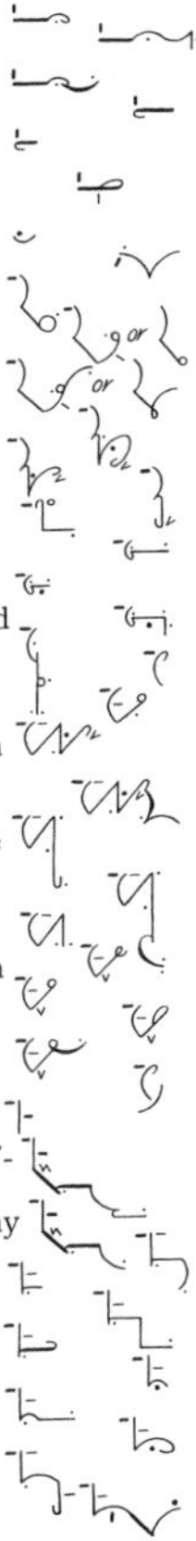

automot'ive
auto-sugges'tion
au'tumn
autum'nal
auxil'iary
avail'
avail'able
availed'
avail'ing
av'alanche
av'arice
avari'cious
avenge'
avenged'
av'enue
aver'
av'erage
av'eraged
av'eraging
averse'
aver'sion
avert'
avert'ed
avert'ing
avia'tion
a'viator
a'viatrix
av'id
av'idly
avoca'do
avoca'tion
avoid'
avoid'able
avoid'ance
avoid'ed
avoid'ing
avoirdupois'
avow'
avow'al
await'
await'ed
await'ing
awake'
awa'ken
awa'kened
awa'kening
award'
award'ed

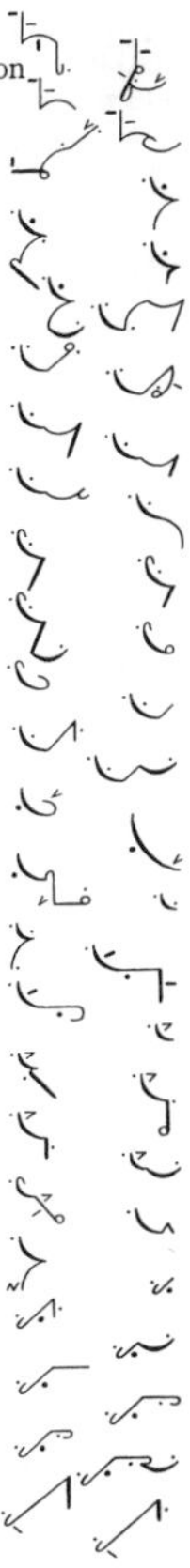

award'ing
aware'
aware'ness
away'
awe
awed
aw'ful
aw'fully
awhile'
awk'ward
awk'wardly

awl
awn'ing
awoke'
axe
axe'head
ax'iom
ax'is
ax'le
ay (yes)
aye
az'ure

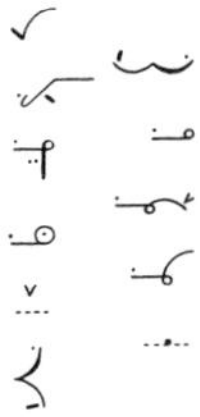

B

bab'ble
ba'by
bab'y-sitt'er
bach'elor
bacil'lus
back
back'ben'cher
back'bone
back'chat
back'cloth
back'fire
back'ground
back'log
back'marker
back'*num'ber*
back'scratch'er
back'wards
ba'con
bacte'ria
bacteriol'ogist
bad
bade
badge
bad'ly
baf'fle
baf'fled
baf'fling
bag
bag'gage
bag'pipe
bail
bailed
bai'liff
bait
bait'ing
bake
bak'er
bak'ery
bak'ing
bal'ance

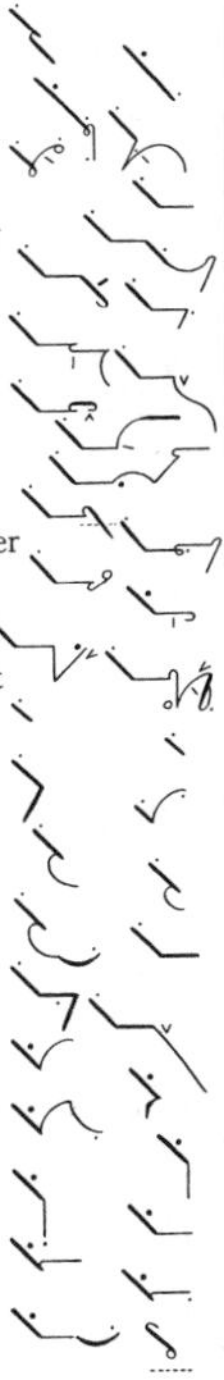

bal'anced
bal'ance-sheet
*bal'anc*ing
bal'cony
bald
bald'headed
bald'ly
bale
baled
balk
ball
bal'lad
bal'last
ballerin'a
balletomane'
balletoma'nia
balloon'
bal'lot
bal'loted
ballyhoo'
balm'y
bal'sa
bamboo'
ban
bana'na
band
band'age
band'aging
band'ed
band'master
band'saw
band'wag'on
bang
banged
ban'ish
ban'ished
ban'ishment
bank
bank'book
banked

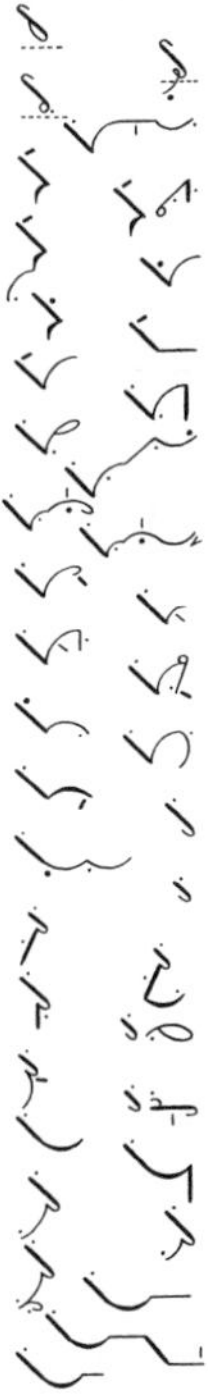

bank'er
bank'ing
bank'rupt
bank'ruptcy
ban'ner
ban'quet
ban'ter
bap'tism
Bap'tist
baptize'
baptized'
bar
barathe'a
barbar'ic
bar'barous
bar'ber
barb'itone
barbiturate'
bare
bared
bare'faced
bare'ly
bar'est
bar'gain
bar'gaining
barge
bar'ing
bark
bark'ing
bar'ley
barn
barom'eter
baromet'ric
baroque'
bar'rage
barred
bar'rel
bar'ren
barricade'
barrica'ded
barrica'ding
bar'rier
bar'ring
bar'row

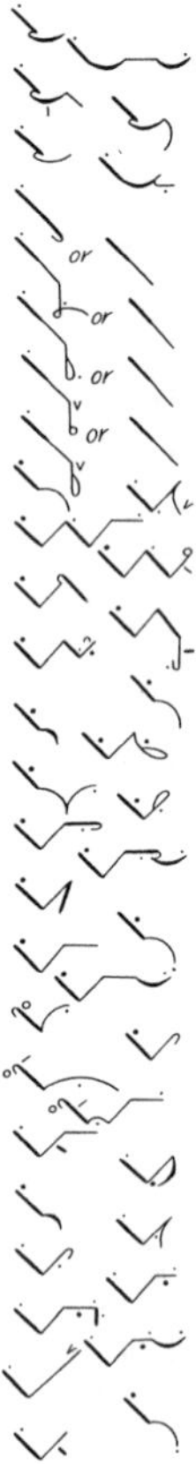

bar'ter
bar'tered
bar'tering
bas'cule
base
base'ball
based
base'less
base'ment
bash'ful
ba'sic
bas'ically
ba'sin
ba'sing
ba'sis
bas'ket
bas'ketball
bat
batch
bath
bathe
bath'er
bath'ing
bath'room
bath'yscaphe
bath'ysphere
bat'tery
bat'tle
bat'tleship
baulk
baux'ite
Bava'rian
bay
bazaar
be
beach
beach'-comber
bea'con
bead
beak
beam
beamed
bean
bean'o
bear
bear'able
beard
beard'ed

bear'er
bear'ing
beast
beast'ly
beat
beat'en
beat'ing
beau'tified
beau'tiful
beau'tify
beau'tifying
beau'ty
bea'ver
became'
because'
beck'on
beck'oned
beck'oning
become'
*be*com'ing
bed
bed'ding
bed'pan
bedrag'gle
bedrag'gled
bed'rock
bed'room
bed'sit'ter
bed'spread
bed'stead
bed'time
bee
beech
beef
bee'hive
been
beer
beet
beet'le
befall'
befal'len
befell'
befit
befit'ted
befit'ting
before'
before'*hand*
befriend'

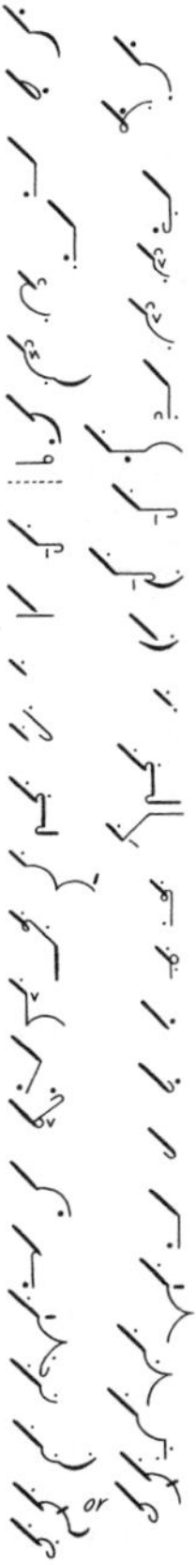

befriend'ed
befriend'ing
beg
began'
beg'gar
beg'ging
begin'
begin'ner
begin'ning
begrudge'
begrudg'ing
beguile'
beguiled'
begun'
behalf'
behave'
beha'ving
behav'iour,
behav'ior
behav'iourism
behav'iourist
beheld'
behind'
behold'
behoove'
beige
be'ing
belat'ed
bel'fry
Bel'gian
belief'
*believ'*able
believe'
believed'
believ'er
*believ'*ing
belit'tle
belit'tled
bell
bellig'erent
bel'low
bel'lowing
bell'push
belong
belonged'
belong'ing
beloved'
belov'ed

below'
belt
bench
bend
bend'able
bend'ing
beneath'
benedic'tion
benefac'tor
benefac'tress
benef'icence
benef'icent
benef'icently
benefi'cial
benefi'ciary
ben'efit
ben'efited
ben'efiting
benev'olence or
benev'olent or
benign'
benig'nant or
benign'ly
bent
ben'zine
bequeath'
bequeathed'
bequeath'ing
bequest'
bereave'
bereaved'
bereave'ment
bereft'
ber'et
ber'ry
ber'serk
berth
beseech'
beseech'ing
beset'
beset'ting
beside'
besides'
besiege'
besieg'ing
best
bestow'
bestowed'
bet
bête-noire
betray'
betray'al
betroth'
betroth'al
betrothed'
bet'ter
bet'tering
bet'terment
bet'ting
between'
betwixt'
bev'el
bev'elled,
bev'eled
bev'erage
beware'
bewil'der
bewil'dered
bewil'dering
bewil'derment
beyond'
bian'nual
bi'as
bi'ased
Bi'ble
Bib'lical
bibliog'raphy
bi'cycle
bid
bid'der
bid'ding
bien'nial
bifo'cal
bifo'cals
big
big'amist
big'amous
big'amy
big'ger
big'gest
big'ot
big'oted
big'otry

bikin'i
biling'ualism
bil'ious
bil'iousness
bill
billed
bil'let
bill'iards
bil'lion
bil'low
bimet'allism, bimet'alism
bind
bind'er
bind'ery
bind'ing
bing'o
binoc'ular
biochem'ical
biochem'ist
biochem'istry
biog'rapher
biograph'ic
biograph'ical
biog'raphy
biolog'ical
biol'ogy
bi'plane
birch
bird
bird's'-eye
birth
birth'-control'
birth'day
birth'mark
birth'place
birth'rate
birth'right
bis'cuit
bisect'
bisect'ed
bisect'ing
bish'op
bis'muth
bit
bite
bit'ing

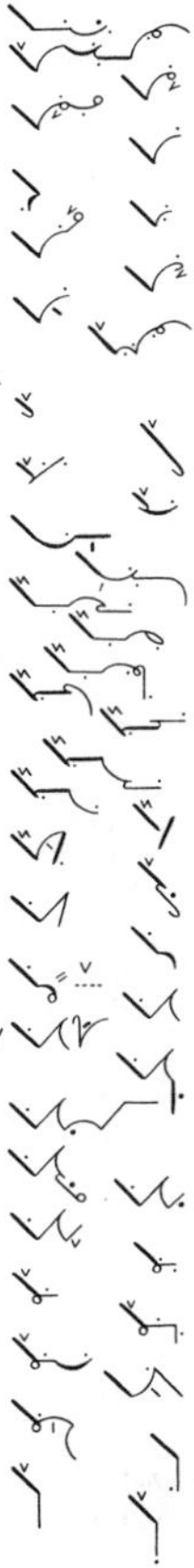

bit'ten
bit'ter
bit'terness
bitu'minous
bizarre'
black
black'berry
black'bird
black'board
black'en
black'ened
black'ening
black'*guard*
black'mail
black'smith
blad'der
blade
blame
blamed
blame'less
blame'worthy
blank
blank'et
blaspheme'
blasphemed'
blas'phemous
blas'phemy
blast
blast'ed
blast'ing
bla'tant
blaze
blazed
blaz'er
bleach
bleach'ing
bleak
bled
bleed
bleed'ing
blem'ish
blend
blend'ed
bless
blessed
bless'ed
bless'ing
blest

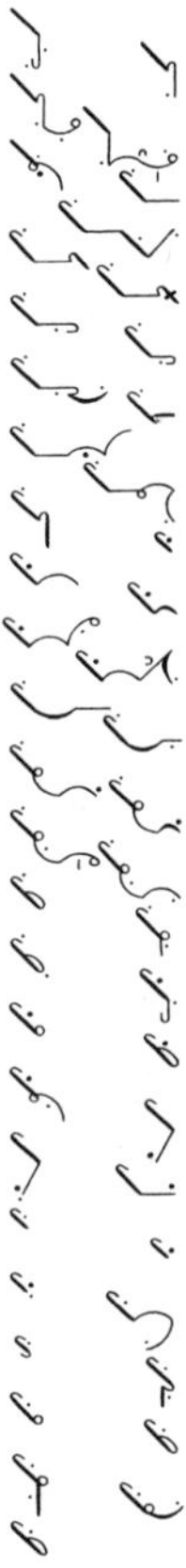

blew
blight
blight'ed
blight'ing
blind
blind'ed
blind'fold
blind'folded
blind'ing
blind'ly
blind'ness
blindspot
blink'ered
bliss
bliss'ful
bliss'fulness
blis'ter
blis'tered
blis'tering
blithe
blitz
bliz'zard
block
blockade'
blockad'ed
blockad'ing
blocked
block'head
blond, blonde
blood
blood'-group
blood'shed
bloom
bloomed
blos'som
blos'somed
blot
blotch
blot'ter
blouse
blow
blow'ing
blow'lamp
blown
blue
blue'berry
blue'-chip
bluff

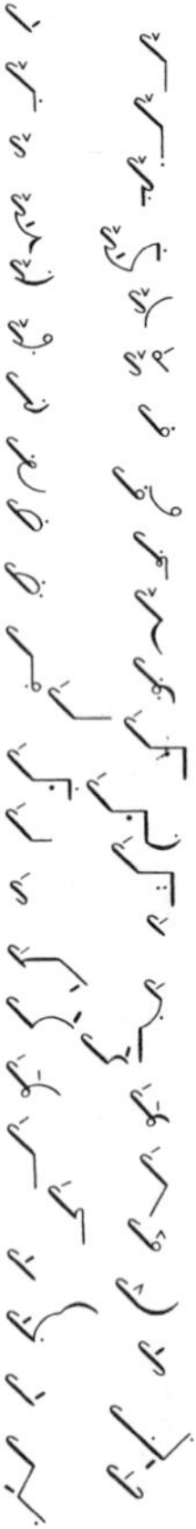

blun'der
blun'dered
blun'dering
blunt
blunt'ed
blunt'ly
blur
blurred
blur'ring
blurt
blurt'ed
blush
blushed
blush'ing
blus'ter
blus'tered
blus'tering
blus'tery
board
board'ed
board'er
board'ing
board'ing-house
boast
boast'ed
boast'ful
boast'fulness
boast'ing
boat
boat'house
boat'swain
bob
bobbed
bob'sleigh
bod'ily
bod'y
bod'y-*guard*
boff'in
bo'gus
Bohe'mian
boil
boiled
boil'er
bois'terous
bois'terously
bold
bold'er

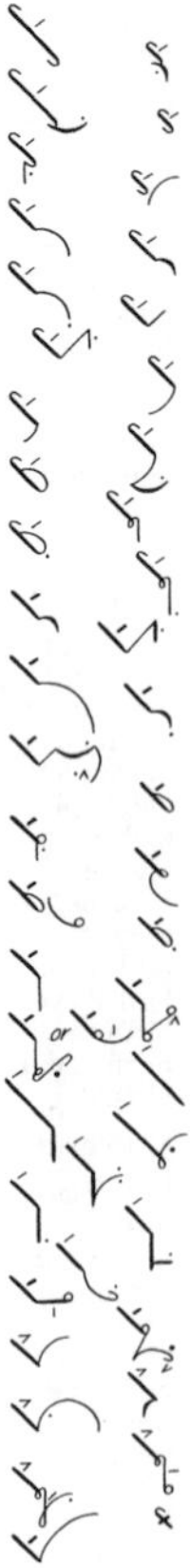

bold'ly
bold'ness
Bol'shevik
bol'ster
bol'stered
bol'stering
bolt
bolt'ed
bomb
bom'bard, *n.*
bombard', *v.*
bombard'ed
bombard'ing
bombard'ment
bombast'ic
bomb'proof
bomb'shell
bond
bond'age
bond'ed
bond'holder
bone
bon'fire
bon'net
bo'nus
book
book'binder
book'binding
book'case
book'-keeper
book'-keeping
book'let
book'seller
book'shelf
book'stall
book'store
book'worm
boom
boomed
boon
boost
boost'er
boot
booth
bor'der
bor'dering
bor'derline
bore
bored
bore'dom
bo'ring
born
borne
bor'ough
bor'row
bor'rowed
bor'rower
bor'rowing
bos'om
boss
bot'anist
bot'any
both
both'er
both'ered
both'ering
bot'tle
bot'tleneck
bot'tling
bot'tom
boudoir'
bough
bought
boul'der
boul'evard
bounce
bounced
bounc'ing
bound
bound'ary
bound'ed
bound'ing
bound'less
boun'tiful
boun'ty
bouquet'
bourgeois'
bour'geois
bout
boutique'
bow (part of violin; a weapon)
bow (part of a ship; to bend the body)

bowed
bow'els
bow'er
bow'ing
bowl
bowled
bowl'er
bow'line
box
boxed
box'er
box'-office
boy
boy'cott
boy'hood
boy'ish
boy'ishly
bra
brace
braced
brace'let
bra'ces
brack'et
brack'eted
brag
bragged
braid
braid'ed
braid'ing
Braille
brain
brain'less
brain'wash
brain'wave
brake
branch
branch'ing
brand
brand'ed
bran'dish
bran'dished
bran'dy
brass
brass'erie
brass'ière
brava'do
brave
brave'ly

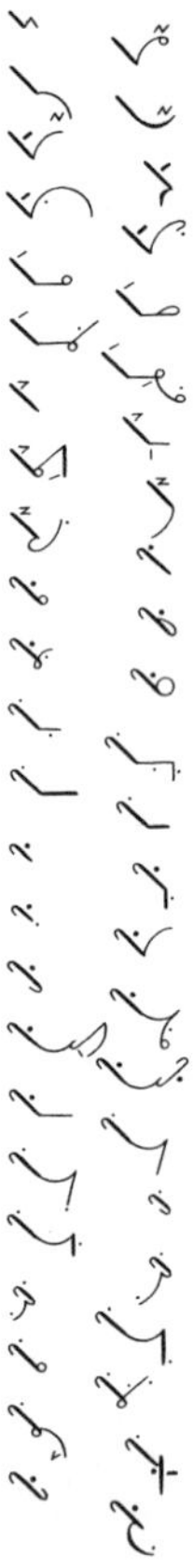

brav'ery
brav'est
brawl
brawled
brawn
bra'zen
Brazil'ian
breach
bread
breadth
bread'winner
break
break'able
break'age
break'down
break'fast
break'ing
break'neck
break'water
breast
breath
breathe
breath'less
bred
breech
breed
breed'er
breed'ing
breeze
breez'y
breth'ren
brev'ity
brew
brew'ing
bribe
bribed
brib'ery
brick
brick'layer
brick'work
brick'yard
bri'dal
bride
bridge
bri'dle
bri'dled
brief
brief'est

brief'ly
brigade'
brigadier'
brig'and
bright
bright'en
bright'er
bright'ly
bright'ness
bril'liance
bril'liancy
bril'liant
bril'liantly
brim
brim'ful
brine
bring
brink
brisk
bris'tle
bris'tled
Britan'nic
Brit'ish
brit'tle
brit'tleness
broach
broach'ing
broad
broad'cast
broad'caster
broad'casting
broad'en
broad'er
broad'ly
broad'mind'ed
brocade'
brocad'ed
bro'chure
brogue
broke
bro'ken
brok'en-
heart'ed
bro'ker
bro'mide
bron'chial
bronchi'tis
bronze
bronzed
bronz'ing
brooch
brood
brood'ed
brood'ing
brook
broom
broth
broth'er
broth'erhood *or*
broth'er-in-law
brought
brow
brown
bruise
bruised
brunette'
brunt
brush
brushed
brush'wood
brusque
bru'tal
brutal'ity
bru'tally
brute
bub'ble
bub'bled
buck
buck'et
buc'kle
buck'ram
buck'wheat
bucol'ic
bud
bud'ding
budg'erigar'
budg'et
budg'eting
buff
buf'falo
buf'fet
buf'feted
bug'bear
bug'gy
bu'gle
bu'gler

build
build'er
build'ing
built
bulb
bulge
bulk
bulk'y
bull
bull'doze
bull'dozer
bul'let
bul'letin
bul'let-proof
bul'lied
bul'lion
bul'lock
bul'ly
bul'lying
bul'wark
bump
bumped
bump'er
bump'ing
bump'tious
bump'tious-
ness
bun
bunch
bun'dle
bun'galow
bun'gle
bunk
bunk'er
buoy
buoy'ancy
buoy'ant
buoy'antly
buoyed
bur'den
bur'densome
bureau'
bur'eaucrat
bureaucrat'ic
burg
burg'lar

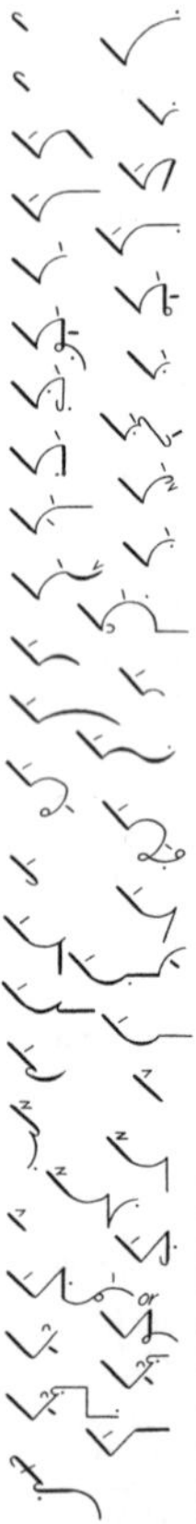

burg'lary
bur'ial
bur'ied
burlesque'
bur'ly
burn
burned
burn'er
burn'ing
burnt
bur'row
bur'rowed
bur'rowing
burst
burst'ing
bur'y
bur'ying
bus
bush
bush'el
bus'ier
bus'iest
bus'ily
bus'iness
bus'inesslike
bus'inessman'
bust
bus'tle
bus'tled
bus'y
but
butch'er
but'ler
butt
butt'ed
but'ter
but'ton
but'tonhole
buy
buy'er
buy'ing
buzz
by, bye
by'pass
by'-prod'uct
by'stander
by'*word*

C

cab
cab'bage
cab'in
cab'inet
ca'ble
ca'blegram
cack'le
cadet'
Caesa'rean
ca'fé
cafete'ria
cage
cajole'
cake
caked
calam'itous
calam'ity
cal'culable
cal'culate
cal'culated
cal'culating
calcula'tion
Caledo'nian
cal'endar,
cal'ender
cal'endered
calf
cal'ibre,
cal'iber
cal'ico
calk, caulk
call
called
call'er
call'-girl
*call'*ing
cal'lous
cal'lousness
calm
calmed

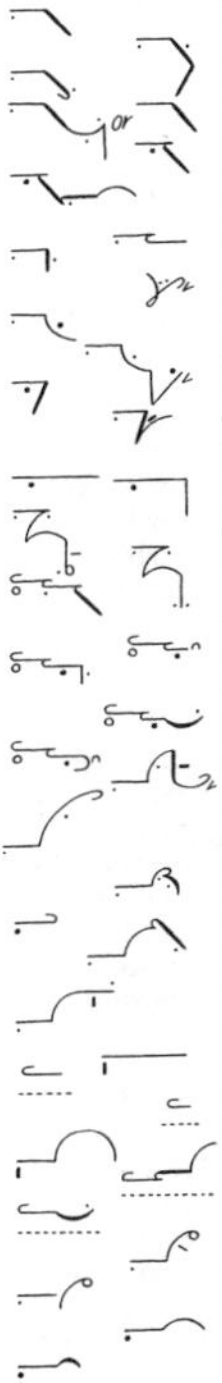

calm'er
calm'ly
cal'orie
calum'niate
cal'umny
calyp'so
camaraderie
cam'ber
cam'bric
came
cam'el
cam'eo
cam'era
cam'ouflage
camp
campaign'
camp'-bed
camped
cam'phor
cam'phorated
camp'ing
cam'pus
can
can
Cana'dian
canal'
can'apé
cana'ry
can'cel
cancella'tion
can'celled
can'celling
can'cer
can'did
can'didacy
can'didate
can'didly
can'dle
can'dlestick

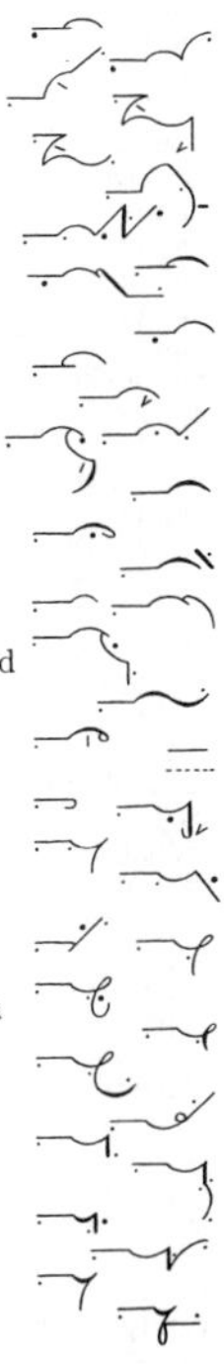

can'dour,
can'dor
can'dy
cane
can'ine
can'ister
can'ker
can'kered
canned
can'nery
can'ning
can'non
can'not
canoe'
can'on
cañ'on
can'opy
cant
cantan'kerous
canteen'
can'ter
can'tered
can'ton
can'vas, *adj.*, *n.*
can'vass, *v.*
can'vassed
can'vasser
can'yon
cap
capabil'ity
ca'pable
ca'pably
capa'cious
capac'itance
capac'itor
capac'ity
cape
cap'ital
cap'italism
cap'italist
capitalis'tic
capitaliza'tion
cap'italize
Cap'itol
capit'ulate
capitula'tion
caprice'
capri'cious
capsize'
capsized'
cap'stan
cap'sule
cap'tain
cap'tion
cap'tivate
cap'tivated
captiva'tion
cap'tive
captiv'ity
cap'tor
cap'ture
cap'tured
car
car'amel
car'at
car'avan
car'bide
carbohy'drate
carbol'ic
car'bon
carbon'ic
car'bonizer
car'burate
car'burettor,
car'buretter
car'cass
carcinogen'ic
card
card'board
car'diac
car'digan
car'dinal
card'-in'dex
car'diogram
car'diograph
care
cared
career'
career'ist
*care'*free
*care'*ful
*care'*fully
*care'*less
*care'*lessness
caress'

caressed'
car'et
*care'*worn
car'go
car'icature
car'icatured
*car'*ing
car'mine
carna'tion
car'nival
carn'ivore
carniv'orous
car'ol
carp
car'penter
car'pentry
car'pet
car'riage
car'ried
car'rier
car'rot
car'ry
car'rying
cart
cart'age
carte blanche'
cart'ed
car'ton
cartoon'
cartoon'ist
car'tridge
carve
carved
carv'er
carv'ing
cascade'
case
cash
cashed
cashier'
cash'ing
cash'mere
cash'-register
cask
cas'ket
cassette
cast
caste
cas'tigate
castiga'tion
cast'ing
cast'-iron
cas'tle
cas'tor
cas'ual
cas'ually
cas'uals
cas'ualty
cat
cat'aclysm
cat'alogue
cat'apult
cat'aract
catarrh'
catarrh'al
catas'trophe
catastroph'ic
catch
catch'-phrase
catch'ing
cat'echism
categor'ical
cat'egory
ca'ter
ca'tering
cat'erpillar
cathe'dral
Cath'olic, cath'olic
Cathol'icism
cat'tle
caught
caul'dron
cau'liflower
caulk
cause
caused
caus'ing
caus'tic
cau'terize
cau'tion
cau'tionary
cau'tioned
cau'tioning

cau'tious
cau'tiously
cavalcade'
cavalier'
cav'alry
cave
cav'ern
cav'il
cav'ity
cease
ceased
cease'less
cease'lessly
ceas'ing
ce'dar
cede
ce'ded
ceil'ing
cel'ebrate
cel'ebrated
cel'ebrating
celebra'tion
celeb'rity
celer'ity
cel'ery
celes'tial
cel'ibacy
cel'ibate
cell
cel'lar
cell'ophane
cel'luloid
cel'lulose
Celt'ic
cement'
cement'ed
cement'ing
cem'etery
cen'otaph
cen'sor
cen'sorship
cen'sure
cen'sured
cen'suring
cen'sus
cen'suses
cent
cen'tenary
cen'tigrade
cen'tral
centraliza'tion
cen'tralize
cen'tralized
cen'tre
cen'tred
cen'tring
cen'tury
ceram'ics
ce'real
ceremo'nial
ceremo'nious
cer'emony
cer'tain
cer'tainly
cer'tainty
cert'ifiable
certif'icate
certif'icated
certifica'tion
cer'tified
cer'tify
cessa'tion
chafe
chafed
chaff
cha'fing
chagrin'
chain
chair
*chair'*man
*chair'*manship
chalk
chal'lenge
chal'lenged
chal'lenger
cham'ber
cham'berlain
chame'leon
champagne'
cham'pion
cham'pioned
cham'pionship
chance
chanced
chan'cellor
chan'cery

change
change'able
changed
chan'ging
chan'nel
chant
chant'ed
cha'os
chaot'ic
chap
chap'el
chap'eron
chap'lain
chap'ter
char
char'-à-banc
char'acter
characterist'ic
characteris'tic-
ally
char'coal
charge
charge'able
charged
charg'ing
char'itable
char'ity
char'la'dy
char'latan
charm
charm'ing
charred
chart
char'ter
char'tered
char'woman
cha'ry
chase
chased
chasm
chas'sis
chaste
chastise'
chastised'
chas'tisement
chastis'ing
chas'tity
chat

chat'ted
chat'tel
chat'ter
chauf'feur
cheap
cheap'en
cheap'ly
cheat
cheat'ed
cheat'ing
check
check'ing
check'-up
cheek
cheer
cheered
*cheer'*ful
*cheer'*fulness
*cheer'*ing
*cheer'*less
cheese
chef
chem'ical
chem'ist
chem'istry
cheque
cheque'-book
cher'ish
cher'ished
cher'ry
ches'nut
chess
chest
chest'nut
chew
chewed
chew'ing
chic
chick'en
chic'ory
chief
chief'ly
chil'blain
child
*child'*hood
*child'*ish
*child'*ishly
chil'dren

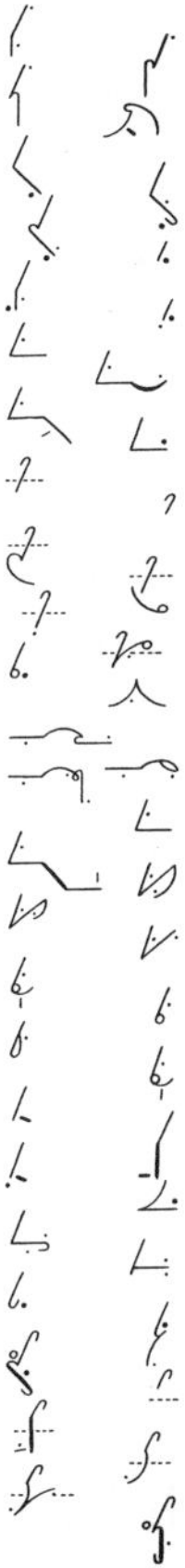

chill
chilled
chime
chimed
chim'ney
chimpan'zee
chin
chi'na
Chinese'
chintz
chip
chirop'odist
chirop'ody
chiroprac'tor
chirp
chis'el
chis'el(l)er
chiv'alrous
chiv'alry
chlor'inate
chlo'roform
choc'olate
choice
choi'cest
choir
choke
chol'era
choose
choos'ing
chop
chopped
chop'per
chop'ping
cho'ral
chord
chore
choreog'rapher
choreog'raphy
cho'rus
chose
chos'en
Christ
chris'ten
Chris'tendom
chris'tened
Chris'tian
Christian'ity

Christ'mas
chromat'ic
chrome
chro'mium
chrom'osome
chron'ic
chron'icle
chronolog'-ical-ly
chrysan'the-mum
chum
church
church'*yard*
churl'ish
churl'ishly
churn
chute
chut'ney
ci'der
cigar'
cigarette'
cinch
cin'der
cin'e
cine-cam'era
cin'ema
cinemat'o-graph
cin'namon
ci'pher
cir'ca
cir'cle
cir'cuit
cir'cuited
circu'itous
cir'cular
circulariza'tion
cir'cularize
cir'culate
cir'culated
cir'culating
circula'tion
circum'ference
circumscribe'
circumscribed'
cir'cumspect

circumspec'tion
cir'cumstance
cir'cumstanced
circumstan'tial
circumvent'
cir'cus
cis'tern
cit'adel
cita'tion
cite
ci'ted
cit'izen
cit'izenship
cit'rus
cit'y
civ'ic
civ'il
civil'ian
civil'ity
civiliza'tion
civ'ilize
civ'ilized
clad
claim
claim'ant
claimed
claim'ing
clam'ber
clam'bered
clam'our, clam'or
clam'orous
clamp
clandes'tine
clang
clanged
clap
clar'ify
clash
clashed
clasp
class
classed
clas'sic
clas'sical
classifica'tion
classifi'able
clas'sify
class'room
clat'ter
clause
claustrophob'ia
claw
clawed
clay
clean
cleaned
clean'er
clean'est
clean'ing
clean'liness
clean'ly, *adj.*
clean'ly, *adv.*
cleanse
cleans'er
cleans'ing
clear
clear'ance
cleared
clear'er
clear'est
clear'ing
clear'ing-house *or*
clear'ly
clear'ness
clear'-sighted
clear'way
clem'ency
clench
clench'ing
cler'gy
cler'gyman
cler'ic
cler'ical
clerk
clerk'ship
clev'er
clew
cliché
click
cli'ent
clientele'
cliff
cli'mate

climat'ic
cli'max
climb
climbed
climb'er
climb'ing
clinch
cling
cling'ing
clin'ic
clinic'ian
clink
clink'er
clip
clipped
clip'ping
clique
cloak
clock
clock'work
clog
clogged
clois'ter
close
closed
close'ly
clos'est
clos'et
close'up
clo'sure
clot
cloth
clothe
cloth'ier
cloth'ing
cloud
cloud'burst
cloud'ed
clo'ver
clo'verleaf
clown
club
club'-house
clue
clump
clum'sily
clum'sy
clung

clus'ter
clus'tered
clus'tering
clutch
clutch'ing
coach
coach'ing
coach'work
coal
coal'face
coal'-gas
coali'tion
coal'-tar
coarse
coars'en
coarse'ness
coars'est
coast
coast'al
coast'*-guard*
.coast'ing
coast'line
coat
coat'ed
coax
coax'ial
cob'bler
co'caine
cock
co'co
co'coa
cocoon'
cod
code
cod'icil
cod'ify
co'ed'
coed'ucate
coeduca'tional
coerce'
coer'cion
cof'fee
cof'fer
cof'fin
cog
co'gency *or*
co'gent

cog'itate
cogita'tion
co'gnac
cohere'
coher'ence
coher'ency
coher'ent
cohe'sion
cohe'sive
coiffeuse'
coiffure
coif'fured
coil
coin
coin'age
coincide'
coin'cidence
coke
cold
cold'er
cold'est
cold'-hearted
cold'ly
cold'ness
collab'orate
collabora'tion
collab'orator
collage'
collapse'
collapsed'
collaps'ible
col'lar
col'lared
collate'
colla'ted
collat'eral
col'league
col'lect, *n.*
collect', *v.*
collect'ed
collec'tion
collect'ive
collect'ively
collect'or
col'lege
colle'giate
collide'
colli'ded
colli'ding
col'lier
col'liery
colli'sion
collo'quial
collo'quialism
collu'sion
co'lon
col'onel
colo'nial
col'onist
coloniza'tion
col'onize
col'ony
col'or, col'our
col'ored,
col'oured
col'ourful
col'oring,
col'ouring
colos'sal
colt
Colum'bian
col'umn
col'umnist
comb
com'bat
com'batant
combed
combina'tion
combine'
combin'ing
combus'tible
combus'tion
come
come'dian
com'edy
comely
com'et
com'fort
com'fortable
com'forted
com'forter
com'forting
com'ic
com'ical

*com'*ing
command'
command'ed
command'er
command'-ment
commem'orate
commem'-orated
commemora'-tion
commence'
commenced'
commence'-ment
commend'
commend'able
commenda'-tion
commen'-datory
commend'ed
commen'surate
com'ment
com'mentary
com'mented
com'merce
commer'cial
commer'cialize
commer'cially
commissar'
commissa'riat
commis'sion
commis'sioner
commit'
commit'ment
commit'ted
commit'tee
commit'ting
commo'dious
commod'ity
com'mon
com'moner
com'monest
com'monly
com'monplace
com'mon-wealth
commo'tion
{com'mune, *n.*
{commune', *v.*
commu'nicate
commu'ni-cated
communica'-tion
commun'ion
commu'niqué
com'munism
com'munist
commu'nity
commuta'tion
commute'
{com'pact, *n.*
{compact', *v.*,*adj.*
compan'ion
compan'ion-ship
com'pany
com'parable
compar'ative
compar'atively
compare'
compared'
compar'ing
compar'ison
compart'ment
com'pass
compas'sion
compas'sionate
compatibil'ity
compat'ible
compat'riot
compel'
compelled'
compen'dium
com'pensate
com'pensated
com'pensating
compensa'tion
compete'
compet'ed
com'petence
com'petent
com'petently
compet'ing

competi'tion
compet'itive
compet'itor
compila'tion
compile'
compiled'
compi'ler
compla'cency
compla'cent
compla'cently
complain'
complain'ant
complained'
complain'ing
complaint'
complais'ant
com'plement
complement'-
ary
complete'
comple'ted
complete'ly
complete'ness
complet'ing
comple'tion
com'plex
complex'ion
complex'ity
compli'ance
compli'ant
com'plicate
com'plicated
complica'tion
complic'ity
complied'
com'pliment
compliment'-
ary
com'plimented
comply'
comply'ing
compo'nent
compose'
composed'
compo'ser
com'posite
composi'tion
compos'itor
compo'sure
com'pound, *n.*
compound', *v.*
compound'ed
comprehend'
comprehend'ed
comprehend'-
ing
comprehen'-
sible
comprehen'-
sion
comprehen'-
sive
com'press, *n.*
compress', *v.*
compressed'
compres'sion
comprise'
comprised'
com'promise
com'promised
comptrol'ler
compul'sion
compul'sorily
compul'sory
compunc'tion
computa'tion
compute'
compu'ter
com'rade
con'cave
conceal'
concealed'
conceal'ment
concede'
conce'ded
conceit'
conceit'ed
conceiv'able
conceive'
conceived'
con'centrate
con'centrated
con'centrating
concentra'tion

concep'tion
concern'
concerned'
concern'ing
{con'cert, *n.*
{concert', *v.*
concer'to (or)
conces'sion
concessionnaire'
concil'iate
concil'iated
concilia'tion
concise'
concise'ly
concise'ness
conclude'
conclu'ded
conclu'ding
conclu'sion
conclu'sive
conclu'sively
concoct'
concoct'ed
concoct'ing
concoc'tion
concom'itant
con'cord
con'course
con'crete
concur'
concurred'
concur'rence
concur'rent
concur'rently
concus'sion
condemn'
condemna'tion
condemned'
condemn'ing
condensa'tion
condense'
condensed'
condens'er
condens'ing
condescend'
condescend'ed
condescend'ing
condescen'sion
condi'tion
condi'tional
condole'
condo'lence
condomin'ium
condu'cive
{con'duct, *n.*
{conduct', *v.*
conduct'ed
conduct'or
con'duit
cone
confec'tion
confec'tioner
confec'tionery
confed'erate
confedera'tion
confer'
con'ference
conferred'
confess'
confessed'
confes'sion
confide'
confi'ded
con'fidence
con'fident
confiden'tial
con'fidently
confine'
confined'
confine'ment
confirm'
confirma'tion
confirmed'
con'fiscate
con'fiscated
confisca'tion
conflagra'tion
{con'flict, *n.*
{conflict', *v.*
conflict'ed
conflict'ing
conform'
conformed'
conform'ity
confound'

confound'ed
confront'
confront'ed
confront'ing
confuse'
confused'
confu'sion
congeal'
conge'nial
congen'ially
congen'ital
conges'tion
conglomera'-
tion
congrat'ulate
congrat'ulated
congratula'tion
con'gregate
con'gregated
con'gregating
congrega'tion
congrega'-
tional
con'gress
congres'sional
con'gressmen
conjec'ture
conjec'tured
con'jugal
conjunc'tion
conjure'
con'jure
conjured'
con'jured
con'jurer
connect'
connect'ed
connec'tion,
connex'ion
conni'vance
connive'
con'quer
con'quered
con'queror
con'quest
con'science
conscien'tious
conscien'-
tiously
con'scious
con'sciously
con'sciousness
{con'script,
adj.
conscript', *v.*
conscrip'tion
con'secrate
con'secrated
consecra'tion
consec'utive
consec'utively
consen'sus
consent'
consent'ed
con'sequence
con'sequent
con'sequently
conserva'tion
conserv'ative
conserv'atively
conserve'
consid'er
consid'erable
consid'erably
consid'erate
consid'erately
considera'tion
consid'ered
consid'ering
consign'
consigned'
consignee'
consign'er
consign'ment
consignor'
consist'
consist'ed
consist'ency
consist'ent
consist'ently
consist'ing
consola'tion
console'
consoled'
consol'idate

consol'idated
consol'idating
consolida'tion
con'sonant
consonan'tal
con'sort, *n.*
consort', *v.*
consort'ed
consor'tium
conspic'uous
conspic'uously
conspir'acy
conspir'ator
conspire'
conspired'
con'stable
constab'ulary
con'stant
con'stantly
consterna'tion
constit'uency
constit'uent
con'stitute
con'stituted
con'stituting
constitu'tion
constitu'tional
constitu'tion-
ally
constrain'
constraint'
constrict'
constrict'ed
constric'tion
construct'
construct'ed
construc'tion
construct'ive
construct'ively
con'strue
con'strued
con'sul
con'sular
consult'
consult'ant
consulta'tion
consult'ed
consult'ing

consume'
consumed'
consu'mer
consum'mate
consumma'-
tion
consump'tion
consump'tive
con'tact
conta'gion
conta'gious
contain'
contained'
contain'er
contam'inate
contam'inated
contam'inat-
ing
contamina'-
tion
con'template
con'templated
con'templating
contempla'tion
contempora'-
neous
contem'porary
contempt'
contempt'ible
contemp'tuous
contemp'tu-
ously
contend'
contend'ed
contend'er
con'tent,
content'
content'ed
content'edly
conten'tion
content'ment
con'tents,
contents'
con'test, *n.*
contest', *v.*
contest'ant
contest'ed
contest'ing

con'text
contig'uous
con'tinent
continen'tal
contin'gency
contin'gent
contin'gently
contin'ual
contin'ually
contin'uance
continua'tion
contin'ue
contin'ued
contin'uing
continu'ity
contin'uous
contin'uously
contin'uum
con'tour
con'tra
con'traband
contracep'tion
contracep'tive
{con'tract, *n.*
{contract', *v.*
contract'ed
contrac'tion
contract'or
contradict'
contradict'ed
contradic'tion
contradict'ory
contrap'tion
con'trary
{con'trast, *n.*
{contrast', *v.*
contrast'ed
contrast'ing
contravene'
contraven'tion
contrib'ute
contrib'uted
contrib'uting
contribu'tion
contrib'utor
contrib'utory
contri'vance
contrive'

control'
control'lable
controlled'
control'ler
controver'sial *or*
con'troversy *or*
conun'drum
conurba'tion
convales'cence
convales'cent
convec'tor
convene'
convened'
conve'nience
conve'nient
conve'niently
con'vent
conven'tion
conven'tional
con'versant
conversa'tion
conversa'tional
{con'verse, *n., adj.*
{converse', *v.*
conversed'
con'versely
conver'sion
{con'vert, *n.*
{convert', *v.*
convert'ed
convert'ible
con'vex
convey'
convey'ance
convey'or
{con'vict, *n.*
{convict', *v.*
convict'ed
convict'ing
convic'tion
convince'
convinced'
convin'cing
conviv'ial

{con'voy, *n.*
{convoy', *v.*
convulse'
convul'sion
convul'sive
cook
cooked
cook'er
cook'ery
cook'ing
cool
cool'ant
cooled
cool'er
cool'est
coo'lie
cool'ly
co-op'erate
co-op'erated
co-op'erating
co-opera'tion
co-op'erative
co-op'erator
co-opt'
co-or'dinate, *v.*
co-or'dinate, *n.a.*
co-ordina'tion
co-ord'inator
copart'nership
cope
cop'ied
co'-pi'lot
co'ping
co'pious
cop'per
cop'y
cop'yholder
cop'ying
cop'yright
copy-*wri'ter*
cor'al
cord
cor'dial
cordial'ity
cor'don
cor'duroy
core
cork
cork'screw
corn
cor'ner
cor'nice
corol'lary
corona'tion
cor'oner
cor'porate
corpora'tion
corps
corpse
cor'pulence
cor'pulency
cor'pulent
cor'puscle
correct'
correct'ed
correct'ing
correc'tion
correct'ive
correct'ly
correct'ness
cor'relate
cor'related
correla'tion
correspond'
correspond'ed
correspond'-ence
correspond'ent
correspond'ing
cor'ridor
corrob'orate
corrob'orated
corrob'orating
corrobora'tion
corrob'orative
corrob'oratory
corrode'
corro'ded
corro'sion
corro'sive
corrupt'
corrup'tion
cort'isone
co'sily

cosmet'ic
cos'monaut
cosmop'olis
cosmopol'itan
cost
cost'liness
cost'ly
cos'tume
co'sy
co'terie
cot'tage
cot'ton
couch
cough
coughed
cough'ing
could
coun'cil
coun'cillor, coun'cilor
coun'sel
coun'selled, coun'seled
coun'sellor, coun'selor
count
count'ed
coun'tenance
count'er
counteract'
counteract'ed
counter-*bal'ance*
counter-*bal'ance*d
counter*bal'-ancing*
coun'terblast
count'erclaim
count'erfeit
count'erfeited
count'erfeiter
count'erfoil
countermand'
counter-mand'ed
count'erpart
count'ess
count'ing
count'ing-house
count'less
count'ry
count'ryman
coun'tryside
count'y
coupé'
coup'le
cou'pon
cour'age
coura'geous
course
coursed
court
court'eous
court'esy
court-mar'tial
cous'in
couture'
couturier'
cov'enant
cov'er
cov'er-charge
cov'ered
cov'ering
cov'et
cov'etous
cow
cow'ard
cow'ardice
coy
co'zily
co'zy
crab
crack
cracked
cra'dle
craft
craft'ily
craft'iness
crafts'man
craft'y
cram
cramp

cramped
cran'berry
crane
crank
crash
crashed
crash'-landing
crate
cra'ter
crave
craved
cra'ving
crawl
crawled
cray'on
craze
crazed
cra'zy
creak
creaked
cream
crease
creased
create'
crea'ted
crea'tion
crea'tive
creativ'ity
crea'tor
crea'ture
cre'dence
creden'tial
credibil'ity
cred'ible
cred'it
cred'itable
cred'ited
cred'iting
cred'itor
credu'lity
cred'ulous
creed
creek
creep
creep'ing
cre'ole
crêpe
crept

cres'cent
crest
cretonne'
crev'ice
crew
crib
crick'et
crick'eter
cried
crime
crim'inal
crim'son
crip'ple
cri'sis
crisp
crite'rion
crit'ic
crit'ical
crit'icism
crit'icize
crit'icized
cro'chet
cro'cheted
crock'ery
crook
crook'ed
crop
crop'per
croquette'
cross
crossed
cross-examina'tion
cross-exam'ine-d
cross-exam'ining
cross'-ref'erence
cross'roads
cross'-sec'tion
cross'*word*
crowd
crowd'ed
crowd'ing
crown
crowned
cru'cial

cru'cifix
crucifix'ion
cru'cify
crude
cru'dity
cru'el
cru'elly
cru'elty
cru'et
cruise
cruis'er
crumb
crum'ble
crum'ple
crusade'
crush
crushed
crust
crust'ed
crutch
crux
cry
cry'ing
crypt'ic
crys'tal
crys'tallize
Cu'ban
cube
cu'bic
cu'cumber
cue
cuff
cul'minate
cul'minated
culmina'tion
culottes'
cul'pable
cul'prit
cul'tivate
cul'tivated
cultiva'tion
cul'tural
cul'ture
cul'tured
cul'vert
cum'bersome
cum'brous

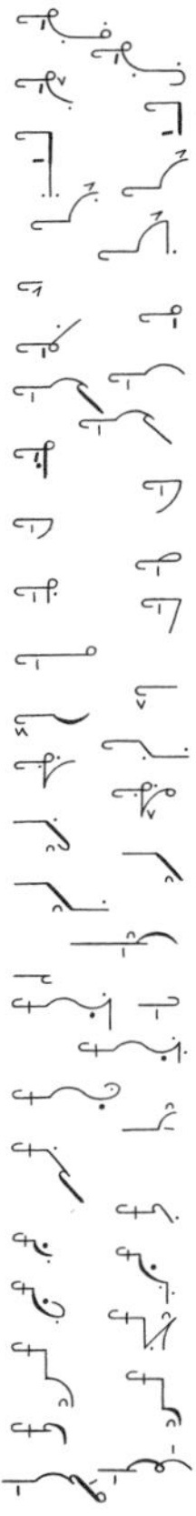

cu'mulative
Cunard'er
cun'ning
cun'ningly
cup
cup'board
cu'pro-nick'el
cur'able
curb
cure
cured
cur'ing
cu'rio
curios'ity
cu'rious
cu'riously
curl
curled
curl'y
cur'rant
cur'rency
cur'rent
cur'rently
curric'ula
curric'ulum
curse
cursed
curs'ed
cur'sive
curs'or
cur'sorily
cur'sory
curt
curtail'
curtailed
curtail'ment
cur'tain
curt'ly
curv'ature
curve
curved
curv'ing
cush'ion
cus'tard
custo'dian
cus'tody
cus'tom

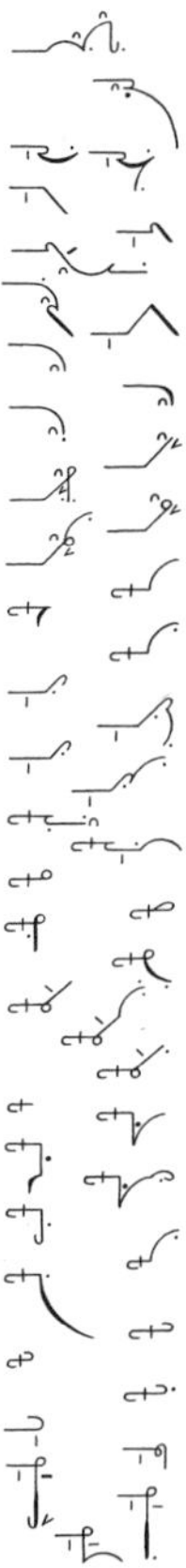

cus'tomarily
cus'tomary
cus'tomer
cus'tom-house
cus'toms
cut
cute
cu'test
cut'lery
cut'ter
cybernet'ics
cy'cle

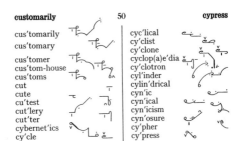

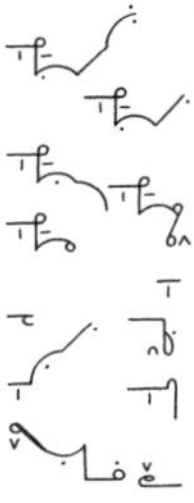

cyc'lical
cy'clist
cy'clone
cyclop(a)e'dia
cy'clotron
cyl'inder
cylin'drical
cyn'ic
cyn'ical
cyn'icism
cyn'osure
cy'pher
cy'press

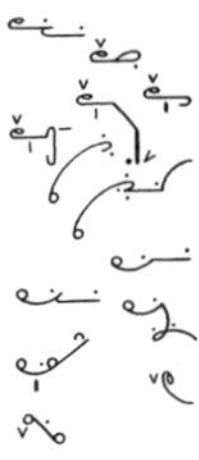

D

dab'ble
dad
dad'dy
dai'ly
dain'ty
dai'ry
da'is
dai'sy
dam
dam'age
dam'aged
dam'aging
dam'ask
dame
damn
damp
damp'en
damp'er
damp'ness
dance
danced
dan'cer
dan'cing
dan'dy
dan'ger
dan'gerous
*dan'ger*ously
Da'nish
dare
dared
dar'ing
dar'ingly
dark
dark'en
dark'er
dar'ling
darn
darned
dart
dart'ed

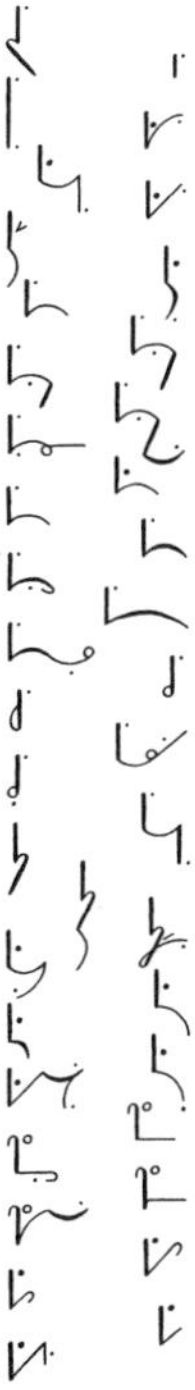

dash
dash'board
dashed
das'tardly
da'ta
date
da'ted
date'-line
daugh'ter
daunt
daunt'ed
daunt'less
dav'it
dawn
day
day'break
day'light
day'time
daze
daz'zle
daz'zled
dead
dead'beat
dead'en
dead'ened
dead'lock
deaf
deaf'-aid
deaf'en
deaf'ened
deal
deal'er
dealt
dean
dear
*dear'*er
*dear'*est
dearth
death
débâc'le

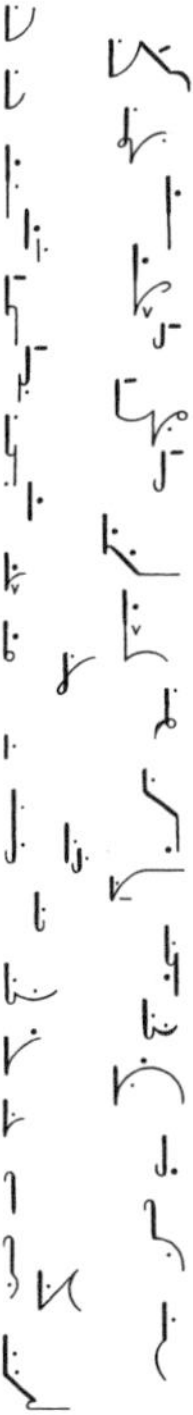

debag'
debar'
debarred'
debar'ring
debase'
debased'
deba'table
debate'
deba'ted
deba'ting
deben'ture
debil'ity
deb'it
deb'ited
deb'iting
debonair'
débris'
debt
debt'or
debunk'
début'
déb'utant
déb'utante
dec'ade
dec'adence
decay'
decayed'
decay'ing
decease'
deceased'
deceit'
deceit'ful
deceit'fulness
deceive'
decel'erate
Decem'ber
de'cency
de'cent
de'cently
decentraliza'tion
decen'tralize
decep'tion
decep'tive
de'cibel
decide'
deci'ded
deci'dedly
dec'imal
dec'imate
decima'tion
deci'pher
deci'phered
deci'sion
deci'sive
deci'sively
deck
declara'tion or
declare'
declared'
declar'ing
declen'sion
decline'
decli'ning
decliv'ity
declutch'
decode'
decompose'
decomposed'
decomposi'tion
decompress'
decontam'inate
decontrol'
dec'orate
dec'orated
decora'tion
dec'orative
dec'orator
deco'rous
deco'rum
de'coy
decoyed'
decoy'ing
decrease'
decreased'
decree'
decreed'
decrep'it
decried'
decry'
ded'icate
ded'icated
dedica'tion
deduce'
deduced'

deduct'
deduct'ed
deduct'ing
deduc'tion
deduct'ive
deed
deem
deemed
deep
deep'en
deep'er
deep'est
deep'ly
deer
deface'
defaced'
deface'ment
defal'cate
defalca'tion
defama'tion
defam'atory
defame'
default'
default'ed
default'er
default'ing
defeat'
defeat'ed
defeat'ing
defeat'ist
defect'
defect'ive
defence'
defend'
defend'ant
defend'ed
defen'sible
defen'sive
defer'
def'erence
deferen'tial
defer'ment
deferred'
defer'ring
defi'ance
defi'ant
defi'ciency
defi'cient
defi'ciently
def'icit
defied'
define'
defined'
def'inite
def'initely
defini'tion
deflate'
defla'tion
deflect'
deflect'ed
deform'
deformed'
deform'ity
defraud'
defraud'ed
defraud'ing
defray'
defrayed'
defray'ing
de'frost'
deft
deft'ly
defunct'
defy'
degen'erate, *n.* & *a.*
de'generate, *v.*
degen'erated
degrada'tion
degrade'
degra'ded
degree'
dehyd'rate
deign
deigned
de'ity
deject'
deject'ed
dejec'tion
delay'
delayed'
delay'ing
del'egate, *n.*
dele'gate, *v.*

del'egated
del'egating
delega'tion
delete'
delete'rious
dele'tion
delib'erate, *adj.*
delib'erate, *v.*
delibera'tion
del'icacy
del'icate
delicatess'en
deli'cious
delight'
delight'ed
delight'ful
delin'eate
delinea'tion
delin'quency *or*
delin'quent *or*
delir'ious
delir'ium
deliv'erance
deliv'er-ed
deliv'ering
deliv'ery
del'ta-wing
delude'
del'uge
delu'sion
delve
demand'
demand'ed
demand'ing
demarca'tion
demean'our, demean'or
demerar'a
demo'bilize
democ'racy *or*
dem'ocrat
democrat'ic *or*
demol'ish
demol'ished
demoli'tion
demonetiza'-tion
dem'onstrate
dem'onstrated
dem'onstrating
demonstra'tion
demon'strative
dem'onstrator
demor'alize
demor'alized
demor'alizing
demo'tion
demur'
demure'
demur'rage
demurred'
demy'
deni'al
denied'
de'nim
denom'inating
denomina'tion
denomina'tional
denote'
deno'ted
deno'ting
denounce'
denounced'
dense
dense'ly
den'sity
dent
den'tal
den'tifrice
den'tist
den'tistry
denuncia'tion
deny'
deo'dorize
depart'
depart'ed
depart'ing
depart'ment
department'al
depar'ture

depend′
depend′able
depend′ed
depend′ence
depend′ent
deplete′
deple′ted
deple′ting
deple′tion
deplor′able
deplore′
deplored′
deplor′ing
deport′
deport′ed
deport′ment
depose′
deposed′
depos′it
depos′itary
depos′ited
depos′iting
deposi′tion
depos′itor
depos′itory
dep′ot
depraved′
deprav′ity
dep′recate
dep′recated
depre′ciate
depre′ciated
depre′ciating
deprecia′tion
depress′
depressed′
depres′sion
depriva′tion
deprive′
depth
deputa′tion
depute′
depu′ted
depu′ting
dep′utize
dep′uty
derange′

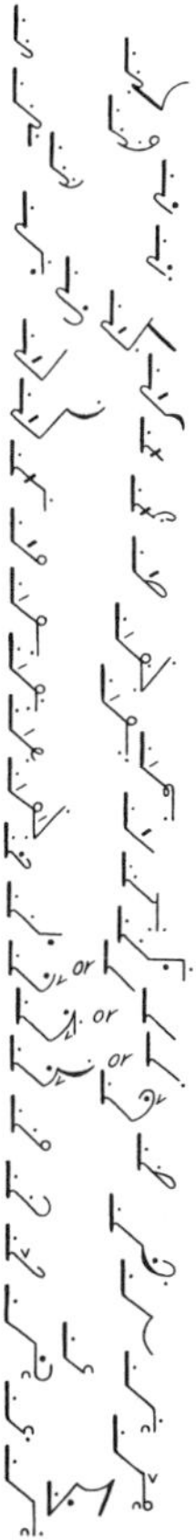

derange′ment
der′elict
derelic′tion
deride′
deri′ded
deri′sion
deri′sive
deriva′tion
deriv′ative
derive′
deri′ving
descend′
descend′ant
descend′ed
descent′
describe′
descri′bing
descried′
descrip′tion
descrip′tions
descrip′tive
descry′
des′ecrate
desecra′tion
des′ert, *n.*, *adj.*
desert′, *v.*
desert′ed
desert′er
desert′ing
deser′tion
deserve′
deserv′edly
deserv′ing
desidera′tum
design′
des′ignate
des′ignated
designa′tion
designed′
design′er
desirabil′ity
desir′able
desire′
desired′
desir′ing
desir′ous
desist′

desist'ed
desist'ing
desk
des'olate, *adj.*
des'olate, *v.*
desola'tion
despair'
despaired'
despair'ing
despair'ingly
despatch'
despera'do
des'perate
despera'tion
des'picable
despise'
despised'
despite'
despoil'
despoiled'
despoil'er
despond'ency
despond'ent
des'pot
dessert'
destina'tion
des'tine
des'tiny
des'titute
destitu'tion
destroy'
destroy'er
destroy'ing
destruc'tion
destruc'tive
destruc'tively
des'ultory
detach'
detach'ing
detach'ment
de'tail, *n.*
detail', *v.*
detailed'
detain'
detained'
detect'
detect'ed
detec'tion
detec'tive
deten'tion
deter'
dete'riorate
dete'riorated
deteriora'tion
determina'tion
deter'mine
deterred'
deter'rent
deter'ring
detest'
detest'able
detesta'tion
detest'ed
detest'ing
det'onate
det'onated
detona'tion
det'onator
detour'
detract'
detract'ed
detract'or
detrain'
det'riment
detrimen'tal
deval'uate
dev'astate
dev'astated
devasta'tion
devel'op
devel'oped
devel'oping
devel'opment
de'viate
de'viated
devia'tion
devia'tionist
device'
dev'il
de'vious
devise'
devised'
devoid'
devolve'
devolved'

devolv'ing
devote'
devo'ted
devo'tedly
devotee'
devo'ting
devo'tion
devour'
devoured'
devour'ing
devout'
dew
dexter'ity
dex'terous
diabe'tes
diabol'ic
diagnose'
diagno'sis
diag'onal
di'agram
di'al
di'alect
di'alling, di'aling
di'alogue
diam'eter
diamet'ric
diamet'rical
di'amond
di'aphragm
di'arist
di'ary
dic'tate, *n.*
dictate', *v.*
dicta'ted
dicta'ting
dicta'tion
dicta'tor
dictato'rial
dicta'torship
dic'tion
dic'tionary
dic'tum
did
die
died
die'hard
di'et
di'etary
di'eted
dietet'ics
di'eting
dif'fer
dif'fered
dif'ference
dif'ferent
differen'tiate
dif'ferently
dif'ficult
dif'ficulty
dif'fidence
dif'fident
diffuse'
diffused'
diffu'sion
dig
di'gest, *n.*
digest', *v.*
digest'ed
digest'ible
digest'ing
diges'tion
digest'ive
dig'it
dig'nify
dig'nity
digress'
digres'sion
dike
dilap'idate
dilap'idated
dilapida'tion
dilate'
dil'atory
dilem'ma
dil'igence
dil'igent
dil'igently
dilute'
dilu'ted
dilu'tion
dim

dimen'sion
dimin'ish
dimin'ished
diminu'tion
dimin'utive
dimmed
din
dine
di'ner
din'gey,
din'ghy
din'gy
di'ning
di'ning-room
din'ner
dint
di'ocese
di'ode
dip
di'phone
diphthe'ria
diph'thong
diplo'ma
diplo'macy
dip'lomat
diplomat'ic
dire
direct'
direct'ed
direc'tion
direct'or
direct'orate
direct'ory
dirn'dl
dirt
dirt'y
disabil'ity
disa'ble
disa'blement
disa'bling
dis*advan'tage*
dis*advanta'-*
geous
dis*advanta'-*
geously
disagree'
disagree'able
disagreed'
disagree'ing
disagree'ment
disallow'
disappear'
disappear'ance
disappeared'
disappear'ing
disappoint'
disappoint'ed
disappoint'ing
dis*appoint'-*
ment
disapproba'-
tion
disapprov'al
disapprove'
disapprov'ing
disarm'
disarm'ament
disarmed'
disarrange'
disarranged'
disas'ter
disas'trous
disas'trously
disband'
disband'ed
disbelief'
disbelieve'
disbelieved'
disburse'
disbursed'
disburse'ment
disc
discard'
discard'ed
discard'ing
discern'
discerned'
discern'ible
discern'ing
discern'ment
discharge'
discharged'
*discharg'*ing
disci'ple
disciplina'rian
dis'ciplinary

dis'cipline
disc'-jock'ey
disclaim
disclose'
disclosed'
disclo'sure
discol'our,
  discol'or
discol'oured
discom'fit
discom'fited
discom'fiture
discom'fort
disconcert'
disconcert'ed
disconnect'
discontent'
discontent'ed
discontin'ue
discontin'ued
dis'cord
discord'ant
{dis'count, *n.*
{discount', *v.*
discount'ed
discour'age
discour'age-
  ment
discourse
discov'er
discov'ered
discov'ering
discov'ery
discred'it
discred'itable
discred'ited
discreet'
discrep'ancy
discre'tion
discrim'inate,
  a.
discrim'inate,
  v.
discuss'
discussed'
discus'sion
disdain'
disease'

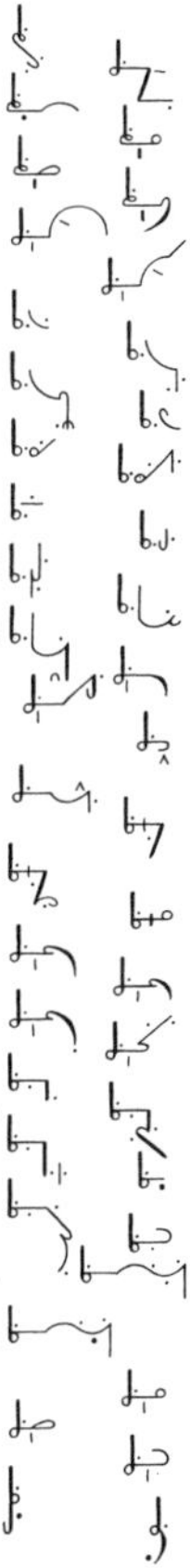

diseased'
disembark'
disembarka'-
  tion
{dis*estab'lish*
{dis*estab'-*
  lished
{dis*estab'lish-*
  ment
disfa'vour,
  disfa'vor
disfig'ure
disfig'urement
disfig'uring
disfran'chise
disgorge'
disgrace'
disgraced'
disgrace'ful
disgrace'fully
disgrun'tled
disguise'
disguised'
disgust'
disgust'ed
disgust'ing
dish
disheart'en
disheart'ened
disheart'ening
dishev'el
dishev'elled,
  dishev'eled
dishon'est
dishon'estly
dishon'esty
dishon'our,
  dishon'or
dishon'ourable
dishon'oured
disillu'sion
disincen'tive
disinclina'tion
disinclined'
disinfect'
disinfect'ant
disinfect'ed

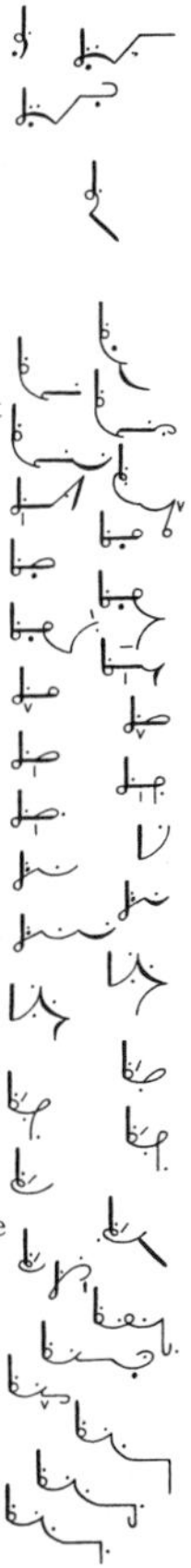

disinher'it
disinher'itance
disinher'ited
disin'tegrate
disin'tegrated
disintegra'tion
dis*in'terested*
disjoint'ed
dislike'
disliked'
dis'locate
dis'located
dis'locating
disloca'tion
disloy'al
dis'mal
disman'tle
disman'tled
dismay'
dismiss'
dismiss'al
dismissed'
dismiss'ing
dismount'
dismount'ed
disobe'dience
disobe'dient
disobey'
disor'der
disor'derly
dis*organiza'-tion*
dis*or'ganize*
dis*or'ganized*
disown'
disowned'
dispar'age
dispar'age-ment
dispatch'
dispatch'ing
dispen'sary
dispensa'tion
dispense'
dispensed'
dispen'sing
dispers'al
disperse'
dispersed'
dispers'ing
displace'
displaced'
displace'ment
display'
displayed'
display'ing
displease'
displeased'
dis*pleas'ure*
dispo'sal
dispose'
disposed'
disposi'tion
dispossess'
dispossessed'
dis*propor'-tionate*
disprove'
disput'able
dis'putant
dispute'
dispu'ted
dispu'ting
disqualifica'-tion
disqual'ify
disqual'ifying
disregard'
disregard'ed
disrep'utable
disrepute'
dis*respect'*
dis*respect'*ful
disrup'tion
dis'*satisfac'tion*
dissat'isfied
dissect'
dissec'tion
dissent'
dissim'ilar (or)
dis'sipate
dis'sipated
dissipa'tion
dissolu'tion
dissolve'

dissuade′
dissua′ded
dis′tance
dis′tant
dis′tantly
distaste′
distaste′ful
distem′per
distil′, distill′
distilled′
distil′lery
distinct′
distinc′tion
distinct′ive
distinct′ively
distinct′ly
distin′guish
distin′guish-
able
distin′guished
distin′guishing
distort′
distort′ed
distor′tion
distract′
distract′ed
distrac′tion
distrain′
distress′
distressed′
distress′ful
distrib′ute
distrib′uted
distrib′uter
distrib′uting
distribu′tion
distrib′utor
dis′trict
distrust′
distrust′ed
distrust′ful
disturb′
disturb′ance
disturbed′
disturb′ing
disuse′, *n.*
disuse′, *v.*
disused′

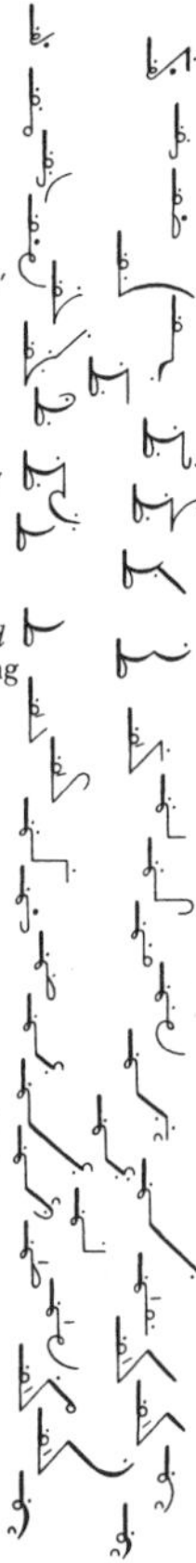

ditch
dit′to
divan′
dive
di′ver
diverge′
diver′gent
di′vers
diverse′
diver′sified
diver′sion
diver′sity
divert′
divert′ed
divide′
divi′ded
div′idend
divi′ding
divine′
divine′ly
divin′ity
divis′ible
divi′sion
divi′sional
divorce′
divorced′
divorcee′
divulge′
diz′zy
do
do′cile
dock
docker
dock′et
dock′yard
doc′tor
doc′trine
doc′ument
documen′tary
dod′derer
dodge
does, *v.*
dog
dog′ma
dogmat′ic
do′ing
dole
dole′ful

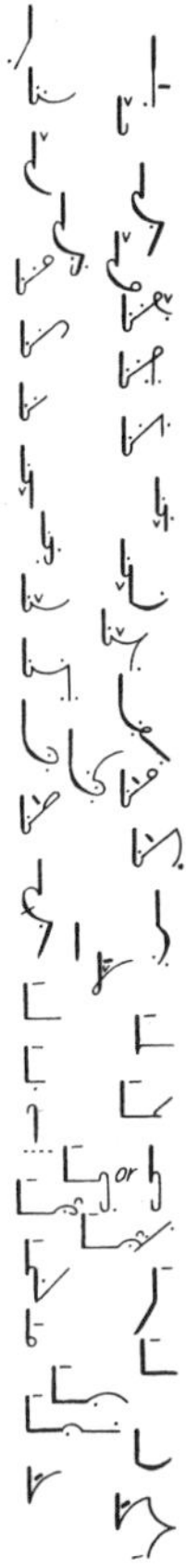

doll
dol'lar
domain'
dome
domes'tic
domes'ticate
domes'ticated
dom'icile
dom'inant
dom'inate
dom'inated
domina'tion
domineer'ing
Domin'ican
domin'ion
donate'
dona'ted
dona'ting
dona'tion
done
do'nor
doo'dle
doom
door
door'step
door'way
dope
dor'mant
dor'mitory
dose
dot
dot'ted
dot'ting
doub'le
doubt
doubt'ed
doubt'ful
doubt'fully
doubt'ing
doubt'ingly
doubt'less
doubts
douche
dough
dough'nut
dove'tail
dove'tailed
down

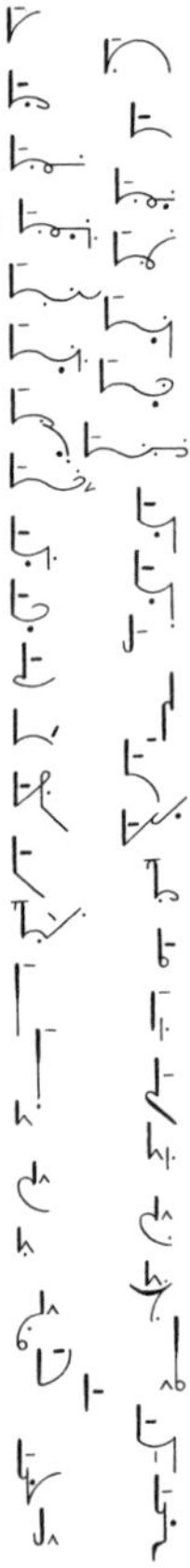

down'cast
down'fall
down'hearted
down'hill
down'pour
down'right
down'stairs
down'wards
doze
dozed
doz'en
drab
drachm
draft
draft'ed
drag
drain
drain'age
drake
dram
dra'ma
dramat'ic
dram'atist
drank
drape
dra'per
dras'tic
dras'tically
draught
draughts'man
draught'y
draw
drawee'
draw'er
draw'ing
drawl
drawn
dray
dread
dread'ed
dread'ful
dread'ing
dread'nought
dream
dreamed
dreamt'
drear'y
dredge

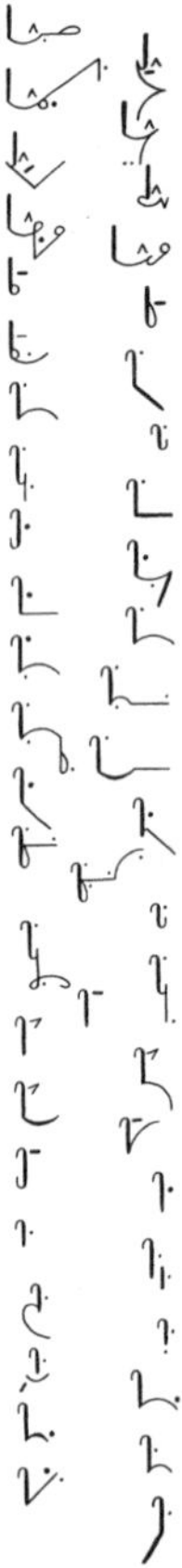

dredg'er
dregs
drench
Dres'den
dress
dress'er
dress'maker
dried
dri'er
drift
drift'ed
drift'ing
drill
drilled
drink
drink'er
drip
drive
driv'el
driv'en
dri'ver
dri'ving
driz'zle
drom'edary
drone
droop
drop
dross
drought
drouth
drove
drown
drow'siness
drow'sy
drudge
drudg'ery
drug
drug'gist
drum
drum'mer
drunk
drunk'ard
drunk'en
drunk'enness *or*
dry
dry'clean
dry'-rot
du'al

dubi'ety
du'bious
du'cal
duch'ess
duch'y
duck
duc'tile
due
du'el
duet'
dug
duke
dull
du'ly
dumb
dumbfound'
dumbfound'ed
dump
dun
dunce
dune
dun'ning
duoden'al
dupe
du'plex
du'plicate, *n.* & *a.*
du'plicate, *v.*
du'plicated
duplica'tion
du'plicator
duplic'ity
durabil'ity
du'rable
dural'umin
dura'tion
dur'ing
dusk
dusk'y
dust
dust'ed
dust'er
Dutch
du'tiable
du'tiful
du'ty
dwarf

dwarfed
dwell
dwell'er
dwell'ing
dwell'ing-
house
dwelt
dwin'dle
dwin'dled
dwin'dling
dye
dye'ing

dy'er
dy'ing
dynam'ic
dy'namite
dy'namo
dy'namotor
dy'nasty
dys'entery

dyspep'sia
dyspep'tic

E

each
ea'ger
ea'gerly
ea'gle
ear
ear'-ache
earl
ear'lier
ear'liest
ear'ly
earn
earned
earn'er
ear'nest
ear'nestly
earn'ing
ear'-phone
earth
earth'en
earth'enware
earth'ly
earth'quake
ear'wig
ease
ea'sel
eas'ier
eas'iest
eas'ily
east
East'er
east'erly
east'ern
east'ward
east'wards
eas'y
eas'y-*chair*
eat
eat'en
eat'ing
ebb

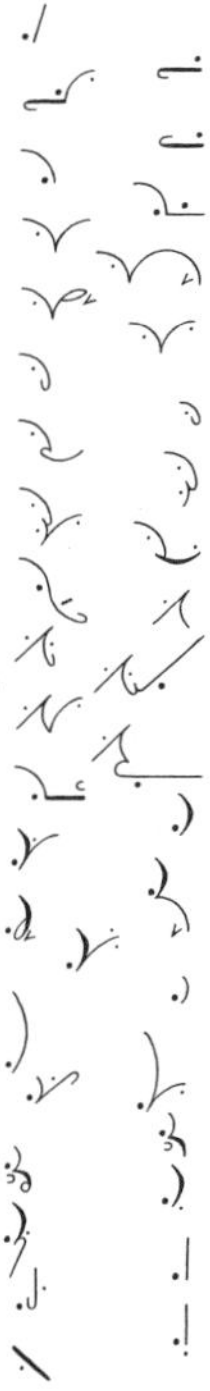

ebbed
ebb'tide
eb'ony
eccen'tric
eccentric'ity
ecclesias'tic
ech'o
ech'oed
éc'lair
eclipse'
econom'ic
econom'ical
econom'ics
econ'omist
econ'omize
econ'omy
ec'stasy
ecstat'ic
ec'toplasm
edge
edg'y
ed'ible
e'dict
edifica'tion
ed'ifice
ed'ified
ed'ify
ed'it
ed'ited
ed'iting
edi'tion
ed'itor
edito'rial
ed'itorship
ed'ucate
ed'ucated
educa'tion
educa'tional
educa'tionalist

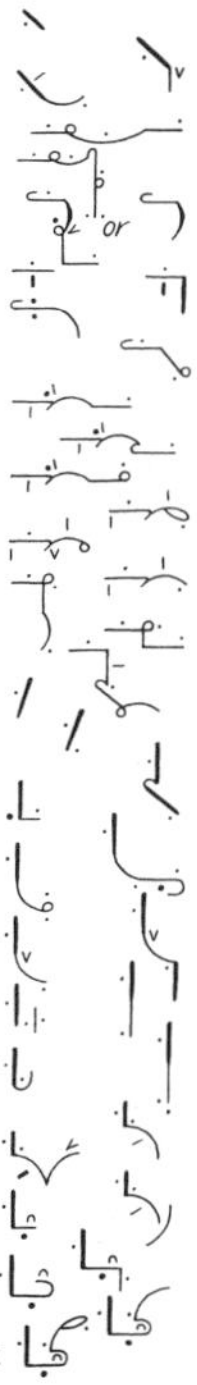

educa'tionist
ed'ucator
eel
ee'rie, ee'ry
efface'
efface'ment
effect'
effect'ed
effect'ing
effect'ive
effect'ively
effects'
effec'tual
effem'inate
effervesce'
efferves'cent
effica'cious
ef'ficacy
{*effi'ciency*
{*effi'cient-ly*
ef'fort
ef'fortless
egg
Egyp'tian
eh
ei'derdown
eight
eighteen
eighteenth
eighth
eight'ieth
eight'y
ei'ther
ejac'ulate
ejac'ulated
ejacula'tion
eject'
eject'ed
ejec'tion
elab'orate, *adj.*
elab'orate, *v.*
elab'orately
elabora'tion
elapse'
elas'tic
elastic'ity
el'bow
el'der
el'derly
el'dest
elect'
elect'ed
elec'tion
elect'or
elect'oral
elect'orate
elec'tric
elec'trical
*elec'trical*ly
electri'cian
electric'ity
electrifica'tion
elec'trified
elec'trify
elec'trocute
elec'trocuted
electrol'ysis
elec'tron
electron'ic
electron'ics
el'egance
el'egant
el'egantly
el'ement
elemen'tary
el'ephant
el'evate
el'evated
eleva'tion
el'evator
elev'en
elev'enth
elic'it
elic'ited
eligibil'ity
el'igible
elim'inate
elim'inated
elim'inating
elimina'tion
Elizabe'than
elm
elocu'tion
elocu'tionist
e'longate
e'longated

elonga'tion
elope'
elope'ment
el'oquence
el'oquent
el'oquently
else
else'where
elu'cidate
elu'cidated
elucida'tion
elude'
elu'sive
elu'sively
ema'ciate
ema'ciated
em'anate
em'anating
eman'cipate
emancipa'tion
embalm'
embalmed'
embank'ment
embar'go
embark'
embarka'tion
embar'rass
embar'rass-
ment
em'bassy
embed'
embed'ded
embel'lish
embel'lished
embel'lish-
ment
embez'zle
embez'zled
embez'zlement
embez'zler
embit'ter
em'blem
embod'ied
embod'iment
embod'y
emboss'
embrace'

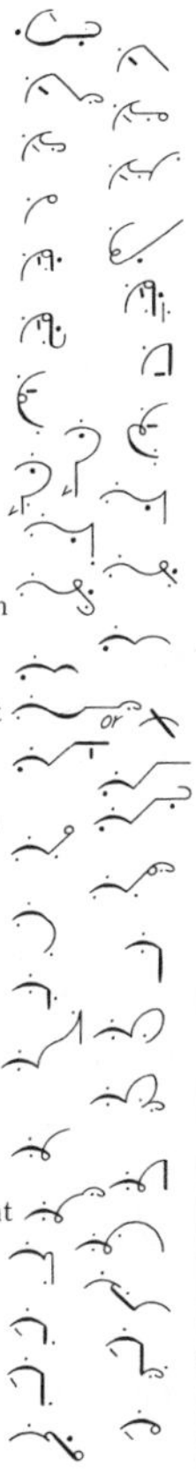

embroca'tion
embroid'er
embroid'ery
em'bryo
emend'
emenda'tion
em'erald
emerge'
emer'gency
em'ery
emet'ic
em'igrant
em'igrate
em'igrated
emigra'tion
em'inence
em'inent
em'inently
em'issary
emis'sion
emit'
emol'ument
emo'tion
emo'tional
em'pathy
em'peror
em'phasis
em'phasize
em'phasized
emphat'ic
emphat'ically
em'pire
empir'ical
employ'
employ'able
employee'
employees'
employ'er
employ'ing
employ'ment
empo'rium
empow'er
empow'ered
em'press
emp'tied
emp'ty
emp'tying
em'ulate

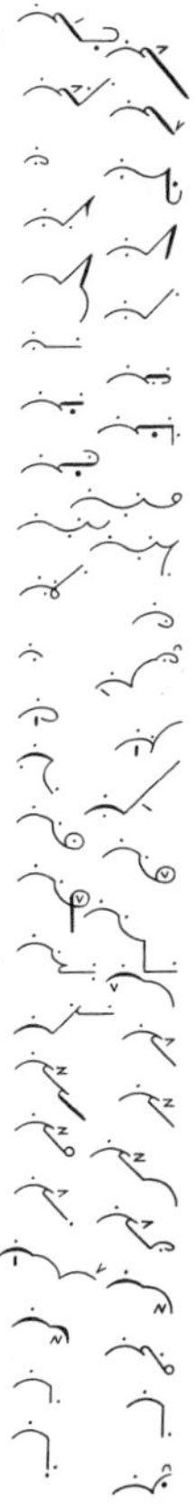

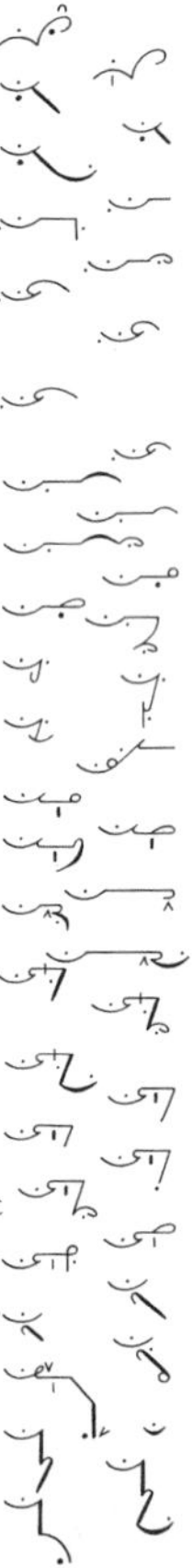

emula'tion
emul'sion
ena'ble
ena'bled
ena'bling
enact'
enact'ed
enact'ment
enam'el
enam'elled, enam'eled
enam'our, enam'or
enam'oured
encamp'
encamped'
encamp'ment
encase'
encased'
encash'ment
enchant'
enchant'ed
enchant'ment
encir'cle
enclose'
enclosed'
enclo'sure
encoun'ter
encoun'tered
encount'ering
encour'age
encour'age-ment
encour'aging
encroach'
encroached'
encroach'ing
encroach'ment
encrust'
encrust'ed
encum'ber
encum'bered
encum'brance
encyclope'dia
end
en*dan'ger*
en*dan'ger*ing
endear'

endeav'our, endeav'or
end'ed
end'less
end'lessly
endorse'
endorse'ment
endow'
endowed'
endow'ment
endur'able
endur'ance
endure'
endured'
en'emy
energet'ic
en'ergy
en'ervate
en'ervated
enfold'
enfold'ed
enfold'ing
enforce'
enforced'
enforce'ment
enforc'ing
enfran'chise
enfran'chise-ment
engage'
engage'ment
engen'der
engen'dered
en'gine
engineer'
engineered'
engineer'ing
Eng'lish
Eng'lishman
*Eng'lish*woman
engrave'
engraved'
engra'ver
engra'ving
engross'
engrossed'
enhance'
enhanced'

enhance'ment
enhan'cing
enig'ma
enigmat'ic
enjoin'
enjoy'
enjoy'able
enjoy'ment
enlarge'
enlarged'
*enlarge'*ment
enlar'ger
*enlar'*ging
enlight'en
enlight'ened
enlight'enment
enlist'
enlist'ed
enlist'ing
enlist'ment
enli'ven
enli'vened
en'mity
enor'mity
enor'mous
enough'
enquire'
enquired'
enquir'y
enrage'
enrich'
enrol', enroll'
enrolled'
enrol'ment
enshrine'
en'sign
ensue'
ensued'
ensu'ing
ensure'
entail'
entailed'
entan'gle
entan'gled
entan'glement
en'ter
en'tered
en'terprise
entertain'
entertained'
entertain'er
entertain'ment
enthuse'
enthu'siasm
enthu'siast
enthusias'tic
*enthusias'tic-*ally
entice'
enticed'
entice'ment
entire'
entire'ly
entire'ty
enti'tle
enti'tled
enti'tling
en'trance, *n.*
entrance', *v.*
entranced'
entranc'ing
en'trant
entreat'
entreat'ed
entreat'y
entrust'
entrust'ed
entrust'ing
en'try
enu'merate
enu'merated
enumera'tion
enun'ciate
enun'ciated
enuncia'tion
envel'op
en'velope
en'viable
en'vied
en'vious
envi'ronment
envis'age
en'voy
en'vy
en'zyme
ep'ic

epicen'tre
epidem'ic
ep'ilogue
epis'copal
ep'isode
epis'tle
ep'itaph
ep'ithet
epit'ome
ep'och
e'quable
e'qual
equalitar'ian
equal'ity
*equal*iza'tion
*e'qual*ize
*e'qual*ized
e'qualled,
e'qualed
*e'qual*ling,
*e'qual*ing
e'qually
equa'tor
eq'uerry
eques'trian
equilib'rium
e'quine
equip'
equip'ment
equipped'
eq'uitable
eq'uity
equiv'alent
equiv'ocal
e'ra
erad'icatė
erase'
era'ser
era'sure
ere
erect'
erec'tion
ergonom'ics
er'mine
erode'
ero'sion
err
er'rand

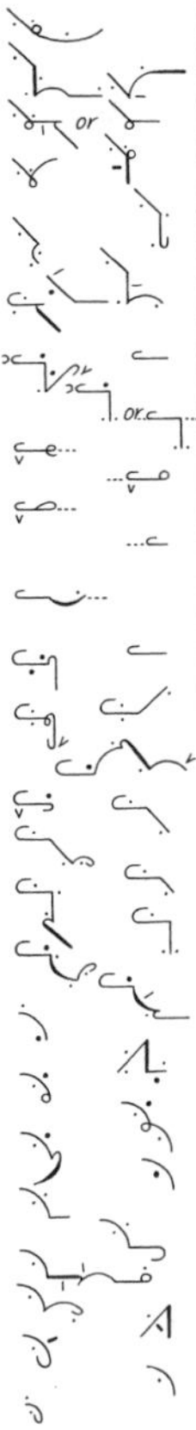

erra'ta
errat'ic
erra'tum
erred
err'ing
erro'neous
erro'neously
er'ror
erst'while
er'udite
erudi'tion
erup'tion
es'calator
escape'
eschew'
eschewed'
es'cort, *n.*
escort', *v.*
escort'ed
espe'cial
espe'cially
espy'
esquire'
es'say
essayed'
es'sayist
es'sence
essen'tial
estab'lish
estab'lished
*estab'lish*ing
estab'lishment
estate'
esteem'
esteemed'
es'timable
es'timate, *n.*
es'timate, *v.*
es'timated
estima'tion
estrange'
estrange'ment
es'tuary
et cet'era, etc.
etch
etch'er
etch'ing
eter'nal

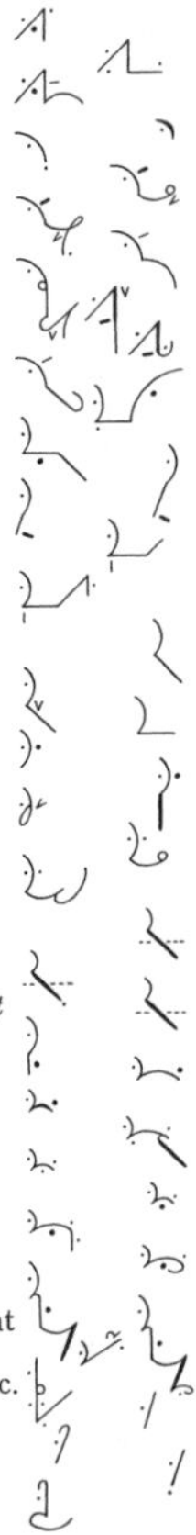

eter'nity
e'ther
ethe'real
eth'ical
eth'ics
eth'yl
et'iquette
etymolog'ical
etymol'ogy
Euclid
eugen'ic
eu'logy
euphor'ia
Europe'an
evac'uate
evacua'tion
evade'
eval'uate
evalua'tion
evan'gelist
evap'orate
evap'orated
evapora'tion
eva'sion
eva'sive
eve
e'ven
eve'ning
e'venly
e'vensong
event'
event'ful
even'tual
eventual'ity
even'tually
ev'er
everlast'ing
everlast'ingly
ev'ery
ev'erybody
ev'erything
everywhere
evict'
evic'tion
ev'idence
ev'ident
ev'idently
e'vil

evince'
evoke'
evoked'
evolu'tion
evolve'
ewe
ew'er
exact'
exact'ly
exag'gerate
exaggera'tion
exalt'
exalt'ed
exalta'tion
examina'tion
exam'ine
exam'iner
exam'ining
exam'ple
exas'perate
exas'perated
exaspera'tion
ex'cavate
ex'cavated
excava'tion
exceed'
exceed'ingly
excel'
excelled'
ex'cellence
ex'cellent
ex'cellently
excel'sior
except'
except'ed
except'ing
excep'tion
excep'tional
ex'cerpt
excess'
excess'ive
excess'ively
{*exchange'*
{*exchanged'*
*exchang'*ing
excise'
excite'
excite'ment

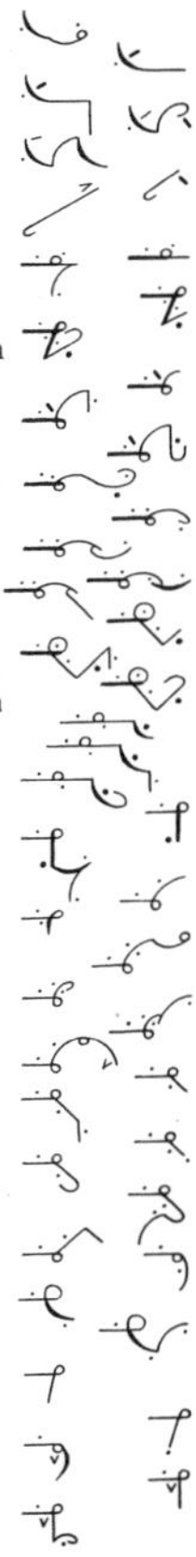

exclaim′
exclaimed′
exclama′tion
exclude′
exclu′sion
exclu′sive
exclu′sively
excru′ciate
excur′sion
excu′sable
{excuse′, *n.*
{excuse′, *v.*
excused′
ex′ecute
ex′ecuted
execu′tion
exec′utive
exec′utor
exec′utrix
exem′plary
exem′plify
exempt′
exemp′tion
ex′ercise
ex′ercised
exert′
exert′ed
exer′tion
exhale′
exhaled′
exha′ling
exhaust′
exhaust′ed
exhaust′ing
exhaustion
exhaust′ive
exhaust′ively
exhib′it
exhib′ited
exhib′iting
exhibi′tion
exhibi′tionist
exhib′itor
exhil′arate
exhil′arated
exhilara′tion
exhort′
exhorta′tion
exhort′ed
ex′igency
ex′ile
ex′iled
exist′
exist′ed
exist′ence
exist′ent
existen′tial
exist′ing
ex′it
exor′bitant
expand′
expand′ed
expanse′
expan′sion
expan′sionist
expan′sive
{*expect′*
{*expect′ed*
expect′ant
expect′antly
expecta′tion
*expect′*ing
expe′diency
expe′dient
expe′diently
ex′pedite
ex′pedited
expedi′tion
expel′
expelled′
expend′
expend′ed
expend′iture
expense′
expen′sive
*expen′sive*ly
expe′rience
expe′riencing
exper′iment
experimen′tal
ex′pert
expertise′
expira′tion
expire′
expired′

expi'ry
explain'
explained'
explana'tion
explan'atory
explic'it
explode'
explo'ded
exploit'
exploita'tion
explora'tion
explore'
explored'
explor'er
explo'sion
explo'sive
expo'nent
{ex'port, *n.*
{export', *v.*
export'ed
export'er
export'ing
expose'
exposi'tion
expo'sure
express'
expres'sion
express'ive
express'ly
expul'sion
ex'quisite
ex'tant
extempora'-
neous
extend'
extend'ed
exten'sion
exten'sive
extent'
exten'uate
exten'uating
extenua'tion
exte'rior
exter'minate
exter'minated
extermina'tion
exter'nal
extinct'

extinc'tion
{*extin'guish*
{*extin'guished*
extin'guisher
extol'
extolled'
extor'tion
ex'tra
{ex'tract, *n.*
{extract', *v.*
extract'ed
extrac'tion
ex'tradite
ex'tradited
ex'traditing
extradi'tion
extra'neous
extraor'din-
arily
extraor'dinary
extrav'agance
extrav'agant
extrav'agantly
extreme'
extrem'ity
ex'tricate
ex'tricated
ex'trovert
exu'berance
exu'berant
exude'
exult'
exulta'tion
exult'ed
eye
eye'ball
eye'brow
*eye*d
eye'ing, *ey*'ing
eye'lash
eye'lid
eye'-op'ener
*eye*s
eye'sight
eye'sore
eye'wash
eye'-witness

F

fa'ble
fab'ric
fab'ricate
fabrica'tion
fab'ulous
façade'
face
fac'et
face'tious
face'tiously
fa'cial
fac'ile
facil'itate
facil'itated
facil'ity
facsim'ile
fact
fac'tion
fac'tious
fac'tor
fac'tory
fac'tual
fac'ulty
fad
fad'dist
fade
fade'-out
fag
Fah'renheit
fail
failed
fail'ing
fail'ure
faint
faint'ed
faintheart'ed
faint'ly
fair
fair'er

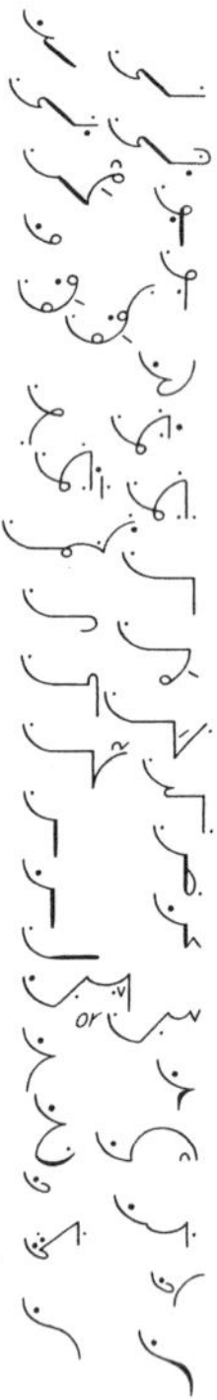

fair'est
fair'ly
fair'ness
fair'y
faith
faith'ful
faith'fully
faith'fulness
faith'lessness
fake
faked
fall
falla'cious
fal'lacy
fall'en
fall'ing
fall'-out
false
false'hood
false'ly
falset'to
falsifica'tion
fal'sified
fal'sify
fal'ter
fal'tered
fal'tering
fame
famed
famil'iar
familiar'ity
familiariza'-tion
famil'iarize
famil'iarized
famil'iarizing
famil'iarly
fam'ily
fam'ine
fam'ish

fam'ished
fam'ishing
fa'mous
fan
fanat'ic
fanat'ical
fanat'icism
fan'cied
fan'ciful
fan'cifully
fan'cy
fantas'tic
fantas'tical
fantas'tically
fan'tasy
far
farce
far'cical
fare
fared
farewell'
farina'ceous
farm
farmed
farm'er
farm'house
far'sighted
far'ther
far'thest
farth'ing
fas'cinate
fascina'tion
fash'ion
fash'ionable
fash'ioned
fast
fast'en
fast'ened
fast'ener
fast'er
fast'est
fastid'ious
fast'ing
fat
fa'tal
fa'talism
fa'talist

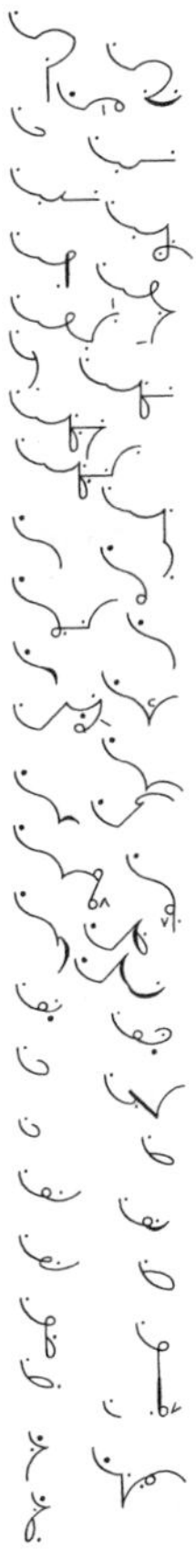

fatal'ity
fa'tally
fate
fate'ful
fa'ther
fa'ther-in-law
fa'therland
fa'therless
fath'om
fatigue'
fat'ten
fatu'ity
fat'uous
fault
fault'less
fault'y
fau'na
fa'vour, fa'vor
fa'vourable
fa'voured
fa'vourite
fa'vouritism
fawn
fear
feared
fear'ful
fear'ing
fear'less
feasibil'ity
fea'sible
fea'sibly
feast
feast'ing
feat
feath'er
feath'ery
fea'ture
fea'tured
fea'tureless
Feb'ruary
fed
fed'eral
fed'eralism
fed'eralist
federa'tion
fee
fee'ble
feed

feed'er
feed'ing
feel
feel'ing
feel'ingly
feet
feign
feint
felic'itate
felic'itated
felicita'tion
felic'itous
felic'ity
fe'line
fell
felled
fel'low
fel'lowship
fel'on
felo'nious
felo'niously
fel'ony
felt
fe'male
fem'inine
fem'inism
fence
fenced
fen'cer
fend'er
{fer'ment, *n.*
{ferment', *v.*
fermenta'tion
ferment'ed
fern
fero'cious
feroc'ity
ferroconc'rete
fer'ry
fer'tile
fertil'ity
fertiliza'tion
fer'tilize
fer'tilizer
fer'vent
fer'vently
fer'vid
fer'vour, fer'vor
fes'ter
fes'tered
fes'tival
fes'tive
festiv'ity
fetch
fetch'ing
fet'ter
fet'tered
feud
feu'dal
feuds
fe'ver
fe'verish
fe'verishly
few
few'er
fiancé, fiancée
fias'co
fi'at
fib
fi'bre
fi'breglass
fibrosit'is
fi'brous
fick'le
fic'tion
ficti'tious
fid'dle
fidel'ity
fidg'et
fidg'ety
fidu'ciary
field
fiend
fiend'ish
fierce
fierc'est
fi'ery
fi'es'ta
fifteen'
fifteenth'
fifth
fif'ty
fig

fight
fight'er
fight'ing
fig'ment
fig'urative
fig'uratively
fig'ure
fig'urehead
figurine'
fil'ament
filch
file
filed
fil'ial
fi'ling
fill
filled
fill'er
fil'let
fil'leted
fill'ing
fill'ip
film
fil'ter
fil'tered
filth
fil'trate
filtra'tion
fin
fi'nal
final'ity
fi'nally
finance'
financed'
finan'cial
finan'cially
finan'cier
find
find'er
find'ing
fine
fined
fine'drawn
fine'ly
fi'ner
fi'nery
finesse'
fi'nest

fin'ger
fin'gered
fin'ical
fi'nis
fin'ish
fin'ished
fin'ishing
fir
fire
fire'arms
fire'brand
fire'clay
fire'-damp
fired
fire'-engine
fire'man
fire'place
fire'proof
fire'side
fire'wood
fire'works
fir'ing
firm
fir'mament
firm'er
firm'ly
firm'ness
first
first'-class
first'-hand
first'ly
first'-rate
firth
fis'cal
fish
fished
fish'er
fish'ery
fish'-hook
fis'sure
fis'sured
fist
fit
fit'ful
fit'ly
fit'ness

fit'ted
fit'ter
fit'test
fit'ting
fit'tingly
five
fiv'er
fix
fixa'tion
fixed
fix'edly
fix'ture
fiz'zle
fiz'zled
flab'by
flac'cid
flag
flag'on
fla'grant
fla'grantly
flag'-ship
flake
flaked
flamboy'ant
flame
flan
flange
flank
flan'nel
flannelette
flap
flap'per
flare
flared
flash
flashed
flask
flat
flat'ly
flat'ten
flat'tened
flat'ter
flat'tered
flat'terer
flat'tery
flat'ulence
flat'ulent
flaunt
flaunt'ed
fla'vour, fla'vor
fla'voured
fla'vouring
flaw
flaw'less
flax
flay
flea
fled
flee
fleece
fleet
flesh
flew
flexibil'ity
flex'ible
flick
flick'er
flick'ered
fli'er
flight
flight'y
flim'sily
flim'sy
flinch
fling
flint
flip'pancy
flip'pant
flip'pantly
flirt
flirt'ing
flit
flit'ted
flit'ting
float
float'ed
flock
flocked
flog
flogged
flood
flood'ing
flood'light
floor
floor'ing

flop
flo'ral
flor'id
flor'in
flor'ist
floss
flota'tion
flotil'la
flot'sam
flounce
floun'der
floun'dered
flour
flour'ish
flour'ished
flour'ishing
flout
flout'ed
flow
flowed
flow'er
flow'ered
flow'ery
flow'ing
flown
fluc'tuate
fluc'tuated
fluc'tuating
fluctua'tion
flue
flu'ency
flu'ent
flu'ently
fluff
fluff'y
flu'id
fluke
flung
flunk'ey
fluores'cent
flur'ried
flur'ry
flush
flushed
flus'ter
flus'tered
flute
flut'ter

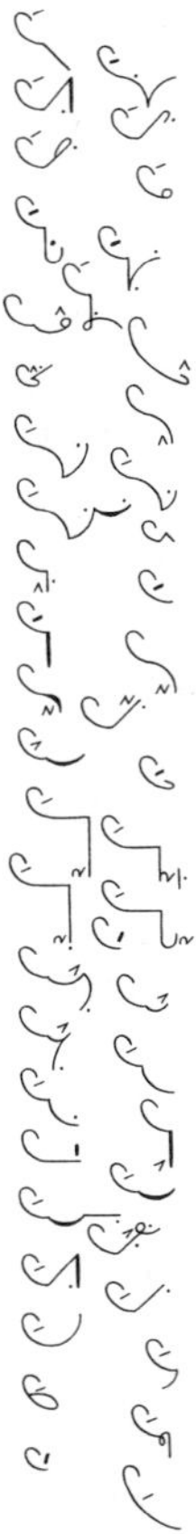

flut'tered
flux
fly
fly'er
fly'leaf
fly'*over*
fly'-wheel
foam
fob
fo'cus
fo'cus(s)ed
fod'der
foe
fog
fogged
fog'gy
foil
foiled
foist
fold
fold'ed
fold'er
fold'ing
fo'liage
fo'lio
folk
folk'lore
fol'low
fol'lowed
fol'lower
fol'lowing
fol'ly
foment'
fomenta'tion
fond
fond'er
fond'est
fon'dle
fon'dled
fond'ly
food
food'stuff
fool
fooled
fool'hardy
fool'ish
fool'ishly
fools'cap

foot
foot'ball
foot'board
foot'hold
foot'ing
foot'lights
foot'mark
foot'note
foot'print
foot'sore
foot'step
foot'stool
for
for'age
for'ay
forbad', forbade'
for'bear, *n.*
forbear', *v.*
forbear'ance
forbid'
forbid'den
force
forced
force'ful
for'ceps
for'cible
ford
ford'ed
fore
fore'arm
forebo'ding
fore'cast, *n.*
forecast', *v.*
foreclose'
foreclo'sure
fore'court
fore'father
forego'
forego'ing
foregone'
fore'ground
fore'*hand*
fore'head
for'eign
for'eigner
fore'man
fore'*most*

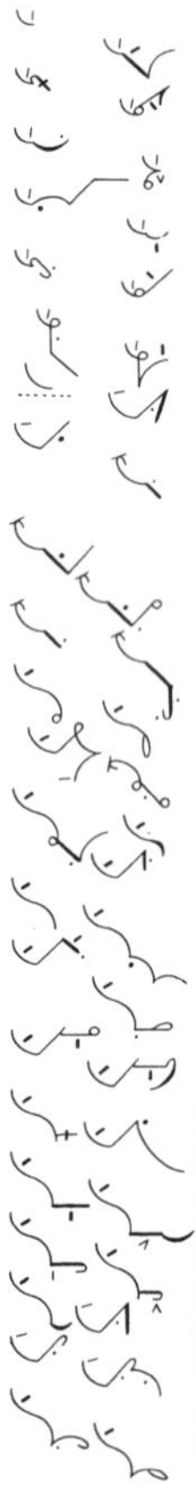

fore'noon
forerun'ner
foresee'
foresee'able
foreseen'
foreshad'ow
fore'sight
for'est
forestall'
forestalled'
for'ester
for'estry
fore*tell'*
fore'thought
foretold'
forev'er
forewarn'
forewarned'
fore'*word*
for'feit
for'feited
for'feiture
forgave'
forge
for'ger
for'gery
forget'
forget'ful
forget'fulness
for*give'*
for*give'*ness
for*giv'*ing
forgo'
forgot'
forgot'ten
fork
forlorn'
form
form'al
formal'ity
forma'tion
formed
for'mer
for'merly
for'midable
for'mula
for'mulate
forsake'

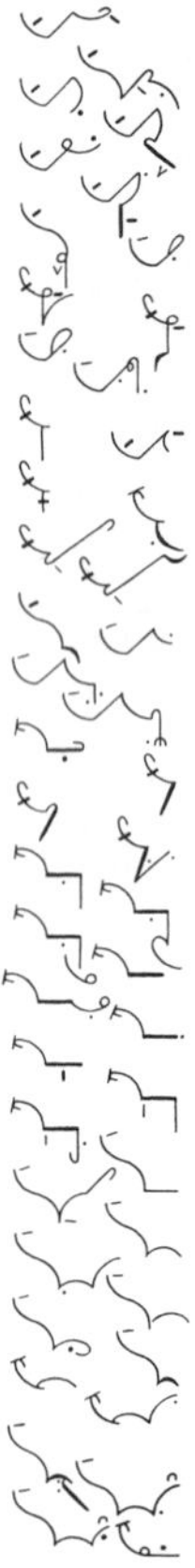

forsa'ken
forsook'
fort
forth
forth'coming
forth'right
forthwith'
for'tieth
fortifica'tion
for'tified
for'tify
for'titude
fort'night
fort'nightly
for'tress
fortu'itous
for'tunate
for'tunately
for'tune
for'ty
fo'rum
for'ward
for'warded
for'warding
for'wards
fos'sil
fos'ter
fos'tered
fos'tering
fought
foul
fouled
foul'ly
found
founda'tion
found'ed
foun'der
foun'dered
foun'dry
fount
foun'tain
foun'tain-head
four
four'some
fourteen'
fourteenth'
fourth
fowl

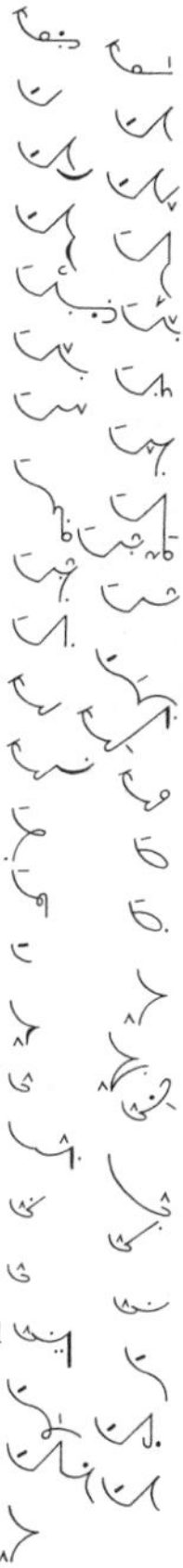

fox
fracas
frac'tion
frac'tious
frac'ture
frac'tured
frag'ile
fragil'ity
frag'ment
frag'mentary
fra'grance
fra'grant
frail
frail'ty
frame
framed
fra'mer
frame'work
franc
fran'chise
fran'chisement
frank
frank'ly
frank'ness
fran'tic
frater'nal
frater'nity
fraud
fraud'ulent
fraud'ulently
fraught
fray
frayed
freak
freck'le
free
freed
free'dom
free'hold
free'lance
free'ly
fre'er
freeze
freez'ing
freight
freight'age
freight'ed

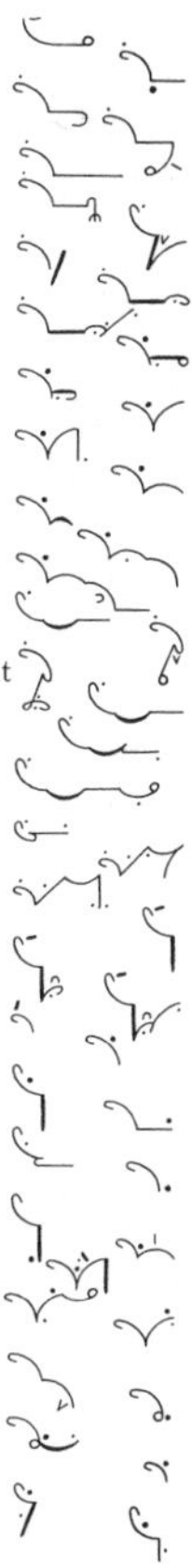

French
French'man
fren'zied
fren'zy
fre'quency
fre'quent, *adj.*
frequent', *v.*
frequent'ed
frequent'ing
fre'quently
fres'co
fresh
fresh'en
fresh'ened
fresh'ening
fresh'er
fresh'est
fresh'ly
fret
fret'ful
fret'ted
fret'ting
fri'ar
fric'tion
Fri'day
fried
friend
friend'less
friend'lier
friend'liest
friend'liness
friend'ly
friend'ship
frieze
fright
fright'en
fright'ful
fright'fulness
frig'id
frigid'ity
frill
frilled
fringe
frisk
frit'ter
frit'tered
frivol'ity
friv'olous

friv'olously
frock
frog
frol'ic
from
front
front'age
fron'tal
fron'tier
fron'tispiece
frost
frost'bite
frost'ed
frost'y
froth
frown
frowned
frown'ing
froze
fro'zen
fru'gal
frugal'ity
fruit
fruit'ful
fruit'fulness
frui'tion
fruit'less
fruit'lessness
frus'trate
frus'trated
frustra'tion
fry
fuch'sia
fudge
fu'el
fu'gitive
fulfil'
fulfilled'
fulfil'ment
full
full'est
full'-length
full'ness
full'y
ful'some
fum'ble
fum'bled
fume

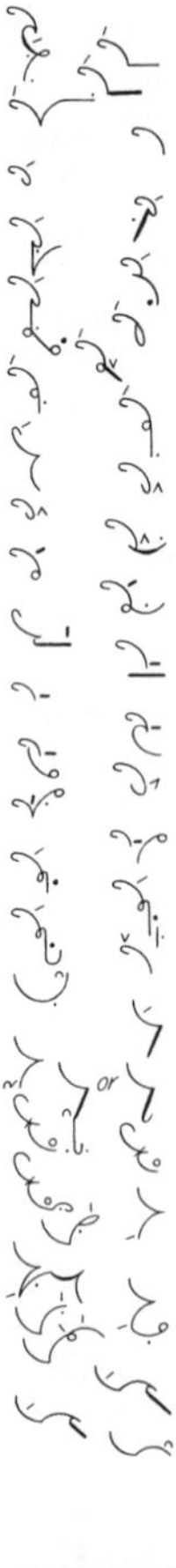

fumed
fu'migate
fu'migated
fumiga'tion
fun
func'tion
func'tioned
fund
fundamen'tal-
-ly
fu'neral
fune'real
fun'gus
fun'nel
fun'niest
fun'ny
fur
fu'rious
fu'riously
furl
furled
fur'long
fur'lough
fur'nace
fur'nish
fur'nisher
fur'niture
fur'rier
fur'row
fur'rowed
fur'ther
fur'therance
fur'thered
fur'ther*more*
fur'ther*most*
fur'thest
fur'tive
fur'tively
fu'ry
fuse
fused
fu'selage
fu'sible
fusillade'
fu'sion
fuss
fuss'y
fust'y
fu'tile
futil'ity
fu'ture
fu'turist
futuris'tic
futu'rity

G

gab'erdine
ga'ble
Gael'ic
gadg'et
gaffe
gag
gage
gagged
gai'ety, gay'ety
gai'ly, gay'ly
gain
gained
gain'ing
gait
ga'la
gale
gall
gal'lant,
gallant'
gal'lantry
gal'lery
gal'lon
gal'lop
galore'
galvan'ic
gal'vanize
gal'vanized
gam'ble
gam'bler
gam'bling
gam'bol
game
ga'mut
gan'der
gang
gang'ster
gang'way
gaol
gaol'er

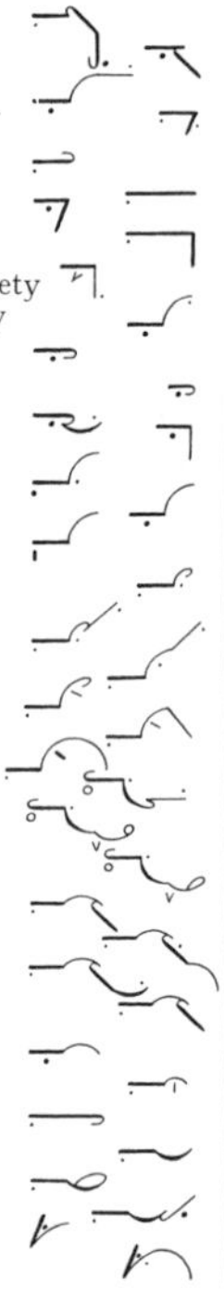

gap
gape
garage
garb
gar'bage
gar'den
gar'dener
gar'gle
gar'land
gar'ment
gar'ner
gar'nered
gar'nish
garnishee'
gar'ret
gar'rison
gar'rulous
gar'ter
gas
gash
gashed
gas'-meter
gas'olene
gasom'eter
gasp
gas'tric
gate
gâ'teau
gath'er
gath'ered
gath'ering
gauge
gaunt
gaunt'let
gauze
gave
gay
gay'est
gaze

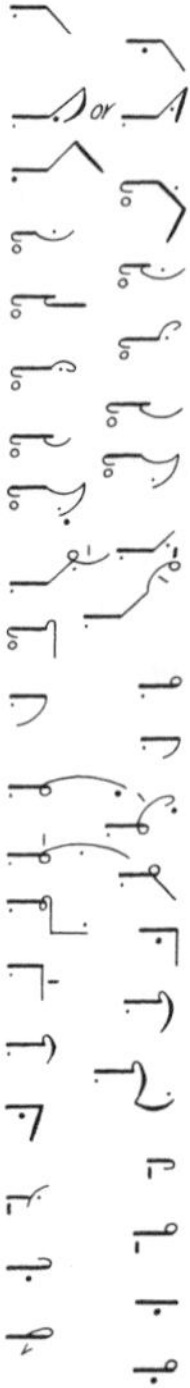

gazed
gazette'
gazetteer'
gear
geared
geese
gel'atine
gem
gen'der
gen'eral
general'ity
generaliza'tion
gen'eralize
gen'eralized
gen'erally
gen'erate
gen'erated
gen'erating
genera'tion
gen'erator
generosity
gen'erous
gen'erously
gen'esis
ge'nial
genial'ity
ge'nius
gen'ocide
genteel'
Gen'tile
gen'tle
gen'tleman
*gen'tleman*ly
gen'tlemen
gen'tleness
gen'tly
gen'uine
gen'uinely
geograph'ic
geograph'ical
geog'raphy
geolog'ical
geol'ogist
geol'ogy
geomet'ric
geomet'rical
geomet'rically
geom'etry

geriat'ric
germ
Ger'man
germane'
gestic'ulate
gestic'ulated
ges'ture
get
get'ting
gey'ser
ghast'ly
ghost
gi'ant
gibe
gid'dy
gift
gift'ed
gigan'tic
gild
gild'ed
gill (of a fish)
gill (a measure)
gilt
gimm'ick
gin
gin'ger
gip'sy, gyp'sy
gird
gird'ed
gird'er
gir'dle
girl
girl'hood
girth
gist
give
giv'en
giv'er
gives
*giv'*ing
glacé
gla'cial
glac'ier
glad
glad'den
glade
glad'ly
glad'ness

glam′orous
glam′our, glam′or
glance
glanced
glan′cing
gland
glare
glared
glass
glass′ful
glass′ware
glass′y
glaze
glazed
gleam
gleamed
glean
gleaned
glee
glen
glib
glide
glim′mer
glimpse
glint
glis′ten
glis′tened
glit′ter
glit′tered
global
globe
gloom
gloom′y
glorifica′tion
glo′rify
glo′rious
glo′ry
gloss
glos′sary
gloss′y
glove
glow
glu′cose
glue
glu′ey
glum
glut
glut′ton
glut′tonous
glyc′erine
gnash
gnaw
gnawed
go
goad
go′-ahead
goal
goat
gob′ble
gob′let
God
god′ly
go′ing
gold
gold′en
gold′smith
golf
golosh′
gone
gong
good
good-bye′
good-hu′moured
goodna′ture
goodna′tured
good′ness
good-night′
goods
good′-sized
goodwill′
goose
gore
gored
gorge
gorged
gor′geous
goril′la
gos′pel
gos′sip
got
Goth′ic
gouge

gov'ern
gov'erned
gov'erning
gov'ernment
*govern*men'tal
gov'ernor
gov'ernorship
gown
grab
grace
grace'ful
grace'fully
gra'cious
gra'ciously
grada'tion
grade
gra'ded
gra'dient
gra'ding
grad'ual
grad'ually
grad'uate
grad'uated
gradua'tion
graft
graft'ed
graft'er
graft'ing
grain
gram'mar
gramma'rian
grammat'ical
gram'ophone
gran'ary
grand
grand'-daughter
grand'est
gran'deur
grand'father
grand'mother
grand'parent
grand'son
grange
gran'ite
grant
grant'ed
gran'ulate
gran'ulated
grape
graph'ic
graph'ically
graph'ite
grap'ple
grap'pled
grap'pling
grasp
grasped
grasp'ing
grass
grass'y
grate
grate'ful
gratifica'tion
grat'ified
grat'ify
gra'tis
grat'itude
gratu'itous
gratu'ity
grave
grav'el
grave'ly
gravita'tion
grav'ity
gra'vy
gray, grey
graze
grazed
grease
greas'y
great
*great'*er
great'est
*great'*ly
*great'*ness
Gre'cian
greed
greed'ily
greed'y
Greek
green
green'house
greet

greet'ed
greet'ing
grega'rious
grew
grey'hound
grid
grief
griev'ance
grieve
grieved
griev'ous
griev'ously
grill, grille
grilled
grim
grimace'
grime
grin
grinned
grin'ning
grind
grind'er
grind'ing
grip
gripe
grit
groan
groaned
groan'ing
gro'cer
gro'cery
groom
groove
grooved
grope
gross
grotesque'
ground
ground'less
ground'-nut
ground'-plan
ground'work
group
grouped
group'ing
grove
grov'el
grow

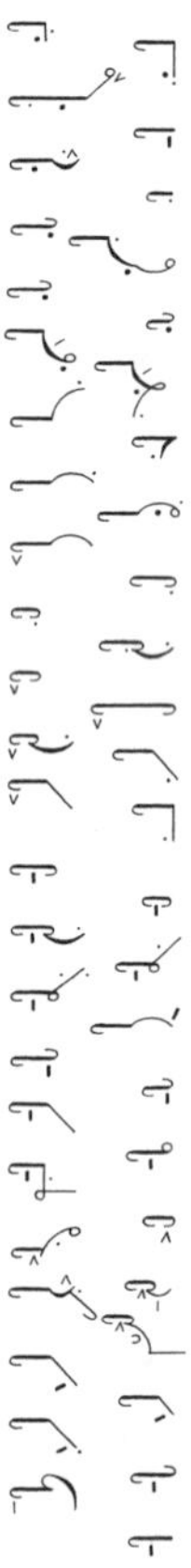

grow'er
growl
growled
grown
growth
grub
grudge
grudg'ingly
grue'some
gruff
gruff'ly
grum'ble
grum'bled
grunt
grun'ted
guarantee'
guaranteed'
guarantee'ing
guarantor'
guaranty
guard
guard'ed
guard'ian
guard'ianship
guard'ing
guess
guessed
guess'work
guest
guid'ance
guide
guild
guild'hall
guile
guillotine'
guilt
guilt'y
guin'ea
guise
guitar'
gulf
gull
gulled
gul'let
gul'lible
gulp
gum
gummed

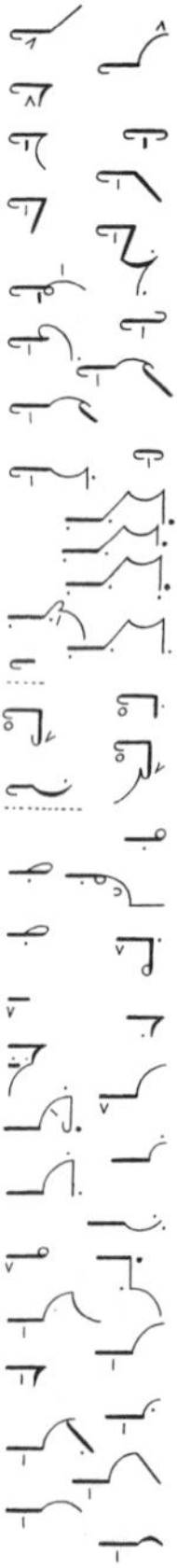

gump'tion
gun
gun'man
gun'ner
gun'nery
gun'powder
gun'smith
gun'wale
gur'gle
gush
gushed
gust
gust'y
gut
gut'ta-per'cha
gut'ted
gut'ter
gut'tural
guy
gymna'sium
gym'nast
gymnas'tic
gymnas'tics
gyrate'
gyra'ted
gyra'ting
gyra'tion
gy'ratory
gy'roscope

H

hab'it
hab'itable
habita'tion
habit'ual
habit'uate
hack
hack'ney
hack'neyed
had
haem'orrhage,
hem'orrhage
hag
hag'gard
hag'gle
hail
hailed
hair
hair'dresser
hair'y
hale
half
half'-caste
half-heart'ed
half'pence
half'penny
hall
hall'mark
hal'low
halt
halt'ed
hal'ter
halve
halved
ham
ham'hand'ed
ham'let
ham'mer
ham'mered
ham'mock
ham'per

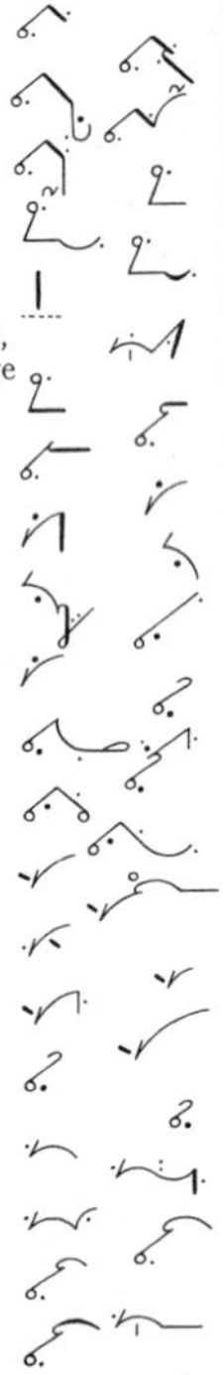

ham'pered
hand
*hand'*book
hand'ed
*hand'*ful
*hand'*icap
*hand'*icraft
*hand'*ing
hand'iwork
hand'kerchief
*hand'*le
*hand'*led
*hand'*ling
hand'-made
hand'-out
*hand'*some
*hand'*work
*hand'*writing
hand'y
hang
hang'ar
hanged
hang'er
hang'over
hank'er
haphaz'ard
hap'pen
hap'pened
hap'pening
hap'pier
hap'piest
hap'pily
hap'piness
hap'py
harangue'
harangued'
har'ass
har'bour,
har'bor

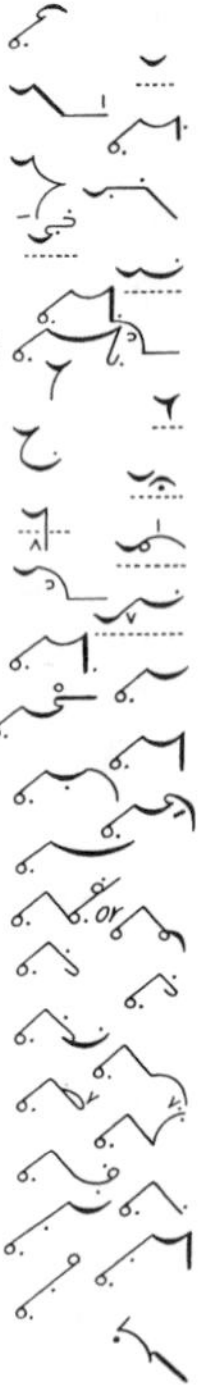

hard
hard'board
hard'en
hard'ened
hard'er
hard'est
hard'-hearted
hard'ly
hard'ness
hard'ship
hard'ware
hard'y
hare
harm
harmed
harm'ful
harm'less
harmon'ics
harmo'nious
har'monize
har'mony
har'ness
harp
harpoon'
har'row
har'rowed
har'rowing
harsh
harsh'ly
har'vest
har'vested
har'vesting
has
hash
haste
ha'sten
ha'stened
ha'stily
ha'sty
hat
hatch
hatched
hatch'et
hatch'ing
hate
hate'ful
hate'fully
ha'tred

haugh'ty
haul
haul'age
hauled
haunt
haunt'ed
Havan'a
have
ha'ven
hav'ing
hav'oc
hawk
hawk'er
haw'thorn
hay
hay'stack
haz'ard
haz'ardous
haze
ha'zel
ha'ziness
ha'zy
he or
head
head'ache
head'light
head'line
head'long
headmast'er
head'quart'ers or
head'strong
head'way
heal
healed
health
health'ful
health'ier
health'iest
health'y
heap
hear
heard
hear'er
hear'ing
hear'say
heart

heart'en
heart'ening
heart'felt
hearth
heart'ily
heart'y
heat
heat'ed
heat'er
heath
heath'en
heat'ing
heave
heav'en
heav'enly
heav'ily
heav'y
Hebra'ic
He'brew
heck'le
hec'tic
hedge
heed
heed'ful
heed'less
heel
heif'er
height
height'en
hei'nous
heir
heir'ess
held
hel'icopter
hel'iport
hell
helm
helm'et
help
help'er
help'ful
help'fulness
help'less
help'lessness
hem
hem'isphere
hemp
hemp'en

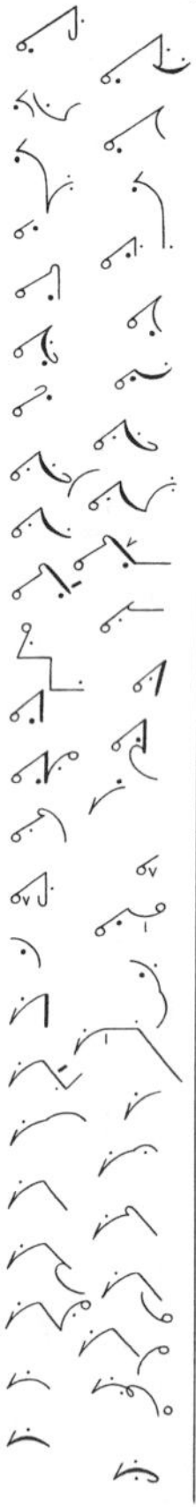

hen
hence
henceforth'
hencefor'ward
her
her'ald
her'alded
her'aldry
herb
Hercu'lean
herd
herd'ed
here
hereaf'ter
hereby'
hered'itary
hered'ity
here***in'***
hereof'
hereon'
here*to'*
heretofore'
here*un'der*
herewith'
her'itage
her'mit
he'ro
hero'ic
he'roin
her'oine
her'oism
her'ring
hers
herself'
hes'itancy
hes'itant
hes'itate
hes'itated
hes'itating
hes'itatingly
hesita'tion
hew
hewed
hewn
hex'agon
hia'tus
hid

hid'den
hide
hid'eous
hi'ding
hieroglyph'ic
hi'fi
high
high'brow
high'er
high'est
high-hand'ed
high'land
high'ly
high'ness
high'road
high'way
hi'-jacker
hike
hi'ker
hila'rious
hilar'ity
hill
hill'side
hilt
him
himself'
hin'der
hin'dered
hin'dering
hin'drance
Hin'du
hinge
hint
hint'ed
hint'ing
hip
hire
hired
hire'-pur'chase
hir'ing
his
hiss
hissed
hist'amine
histo'rian
histor'ic
histor'ical
his'tory

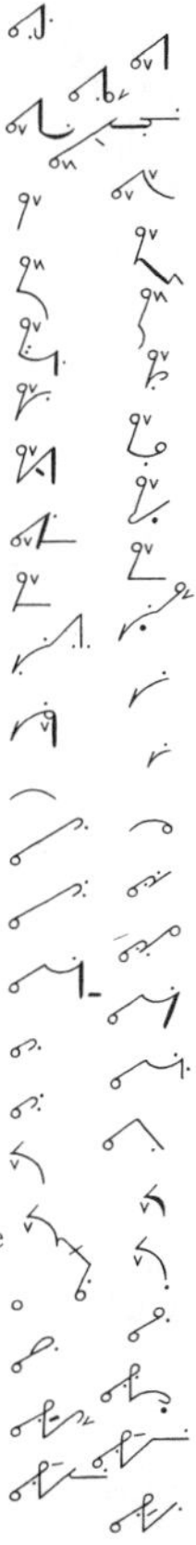

hit
hitch
hith'er
hither*to'*
hive
hoard
hoard'ed
hoard'er
hoard'ing
hoarse
hoarse'ly
hoarse'ness
hoax
hoaxed
hob'ble
hob'by
hock'ey
hod
hoe
hoed
hoes
hog
hoist
hoist'ed
hoist'ing
hold
hold'er
hold'ing
hold'up
hole
hol'iday
ho'liness
hol'low
hol'lowed
ho'ly
hom'age
home
home'coming
home'less
home'ly
home'sick
home'stead
home'ward
home'work
hom'icide
hom'ily
homoge'neous
hom'onym

hon'est
hon'estly
hon'esty
hon'ey
hon'eymoon
honora'rium
hon'orary
hon'our, hon'or
hon'ourable
hon'oured
hon'ours
hood
hood'wink
hoof
hook
hop
hope
hope'ful
hope'fulness
hope'less
hope'lessness
hop'ing
horde
hori'zon
horizon'tal
hor'mone
horn
hor'rible
hor'rid
hor'rified
hor'rify
hor'ror
hors-d'oeuv'res
horse
horse'back
Horse' Guards
horse'hair
horse'man
horse'manship
horse'-power
hort'iculture or
hose
ho'siery
hos'pitable
hos'pital
hospital'ity
host
hos'tage
hos'tel
host'ess
hos'tile
hostil'ity
hot
hotel'
hot'house
hot'ter
hot'test
hound
hour
hour'ly
house
house'hold
house'holder
house'keeper
house'keeping
house'work
hous'ing
hov'el
hov'er
hov'ering
how
howev'er
howl
howled
howsoev'er
hub
hud'dle
hue
huff
hug
huge
hulk
hull
hum
hu'man
humane'
humane'ly
humanis'tic
humanita'rian
human'ity
hu'manly
hum'ble
hum'bler
hum'blest

hum'bly
hum'bug
hu'mid
humid'ity
humil'iate
humil'iated
humilia'tion
humil'ity
hummed
hu'morist
hu'morous
hu'mour,
  hu'mor
hu'moured
hump
hunch
hun'dred
hun'dredth
hun'dred-
  weight
hung
Hunga'rian
hun'ger
hun'gered
hun'ger-strike
hun'gry
hunt
hunt'ed
hunt'er
hunt'ing
hunts'man
hur'dle
hurl
hurled
hurrah'
hur'ricane
hur'ried
hur'ry
hurt
hurt'ful

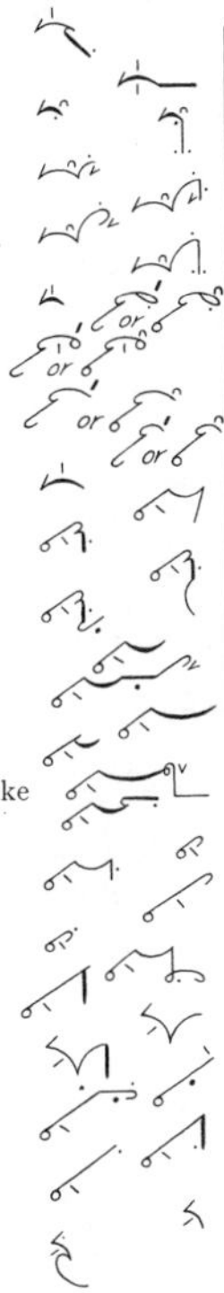

hus'band
hus'banded
hus'banding
hush
hushed
husk
husk'ily
husk'iness
husk'y
hus'tle
hus'tled
hus'tler
hut
hy'brid
hy'drant
hydraul'ic
hy'drofoil
hy'drogen
hy'drophone
hydropon'ics
hy'giene
hygien'ic
hymn
hyper'bole
hypercrit'ical
hyperson'ic
hy'phen
hypnos'is
hyp'notism
hyp'notize
hypoc'risy
hyp'ocrite
hypocrit'ical
hypothet'ical
hysterec'tomy
hyste'ria
hyster'ical
hyster'ics
hythe

I

I
ice
ice'berg
ice-cream'
iced
i'cicle
i'cing
i'cy
ide'a
ide'al
ide'alism
ide'alist
idealis'tic
iden'tical
*iden'tical*ly
identifica'tion
iden'tified
iden'tify
iden'tity
id'iocy
id'iom
idiomat'ic
idiosyn'crasy
id'iot
idiot'ic
i'dle
i'dled
i'dleness
i'dol
i'dolize
i'dyll
if
ignite'
igni'ted
igni'tion
igno'ble
ignomin'ious
ignomin'iously
ig'nominy
ignora'mus

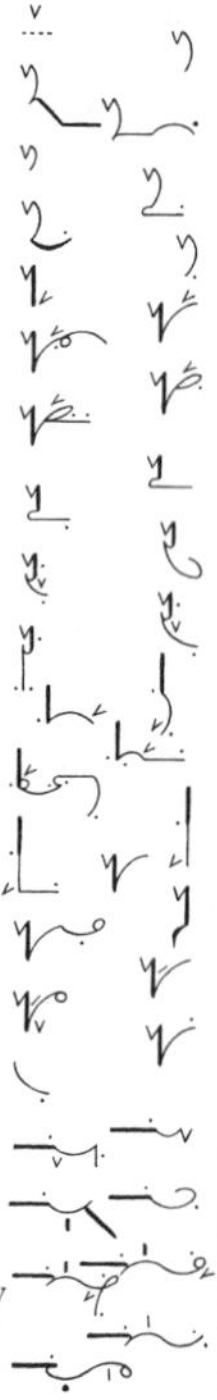

ig'norance
ig'norant
ig'norantly
ignore'
ignored'
ill
ill'-bred
ille'gal
illegibil'ity
illeg'ible
illegi'timate
illic'it
illim'itable
illit'erate
ill'ness
illog'ical
ill'-starred'
illu'minate
illu'minated
illu'minating
illumina'tion
illu'mine
ill'-used
illu'sion
illu'sive
illu'sively
illu'sory
ill'ustrate
ill'ustrated
illustra'tion
illus'trative
ill'ustrator,
ill'ustrater
illus'trious
ill-will'
im'age
imag'inable
imag'inary
imagina'tion
imag'inative

imag'ine
imag'ined
imag'ining
im'becile
imbecil'ity
imbibe'
imbibed'
imbue'
imbued'
im'itate
im'itated
im'itating
imita'tion
im'itative
im'itator
immac'ulate
immate'rial
immature'
immeas'urable
imme'diate
*imme'diate*ly
immemo'rial
immense'
immense'ly
immen'sity
immerse'
immer'sion
im'migrant
im'migrate
immigra'tion
im'minence
im'minent
immo'bile
immod'erate
immod'erately
immod'est
immod'estly
immor'al
immoral'ity
immor'tal
immortal'ity
immor'talize
immov'able
immune'
immu'nity
immu'table
imp

{im'pact, *n.*
{impact', *v.*
impair'
impaired'
impart'
impart'ed
impar'tial
impartial'ity
impas'sable
impas'sioned
impas'sive
impa'tience
impa'tient
impa'tiently
impeach'
impeach'ment
impecu'nious
impede'
imped'iment
impel'
impelled'
impend'
impend'ing
impen'etrable
impen'itent
imper'ative
imper'atively
impercep'tible
{*imper'fect*
{*imperfec'tion*
{*imper'fectly*
impe'rial
imper'il
impe'rious
imper'ishable
imper'sonal
imper'sonate
impersona'tion
imper'tinence
imper'tinent
imper'tinently
imperturb'able
imper'vious
impet'uous
impet'uously
im'petus
impinge'
im'pious

impla'cable
implant'
implant'ed
implement
im'plicate
implica'tion
implic'it
implied'
implore'
implored'
imply'
impolite'
im'port, *n.*
import', *v.*
impor'tance
impor'tant
importa'tion
import'ed
import'er
impor'tunate
importune'
impose'
imposi'tion
impossibil'ity
impos'sible
im'post
impos'tor
impos'ture
im'potence
im'potency
im'potent
im'potently
impound'
impound'ed
impov'erish
impov'erished
impov'erish-ment
im*prac'ticable*
impreca'tion
impreg'nable *or*
im'press, *n.*
impress', *v.*
impres'sion
impres'sion-able
impress'ive
impress'ively
im'print, *n.*
imprint', *v.*
imprint'ed
impris'on
impris'oned
impris'onment
im*probabil'-ity*
im*prob'able*
im*prob'ably*
impromp'tu
improp'er
improp'erly
impropri'ety
improve'
improved'
improve'-ment
improv'idence
improv'ident
improv'idently
*improv'*ing
improviza'tion
improvize'
impru'dence
impru'dent
impru'dently
im'pudence
im'pudent
im'pudently
impugn'
impugned'
im'pulse
impul'sive
impul'sively
impu'nity
impure'
impu'rity
imputa'tion
impute'
impu'ted
impu'ting
in
inabil'ity
inaccess'ible
inac'curacy
inac'curate

inac'curately
inac'tion
inact'ive
inactiv'ity
inad'equacy
inad'equate
inadmis'sible
inadvert'ent
inadvert'ently
inane'
inan'imate
inani'tion
inan'ity
inappro'priate
inapt'
inapt'itude
inartic'ulate
inartis'tic
inasmuch'
inatten'tion
inatten'tive
inaud'ible
inau'gural
inau'gurate
inaugura'tion
inauspi'cious ... or
inauspi'ciously ... or
in'born
in'bred
incal'culable
incandes'cence
incandes'cent
incapabil'ity
inca'*pable*
incapac'itate
incapac'itated
incapac'itating
incapac'ity
incar'cerate
incau'tious
incau'tiously
incen'diarism
incen'diary
in'cense
incen'tive
incep'tion
inces'sant
inces'santly
inch
in'cidence
in'cident
inciden'tal
incin'erate
incin'erator
incip'ient
inci'sion
inci'sive
incite'
incite'ment
incivil'ity
inclem'ency
inclem'ent
inclina'tion
incline'
inclined'
inclose'
inclo'sure
include'
inclu'ded
inclu'ding
inclu'sion
inclu'sive
incoher'ency
incoher'ent
in'come
*in'*coming
incom'parable
incompati-bil'ity
incompat'ible
incom'petence
incom'petent
incom'petently
incomplete'
incomprehen'-sible
inconceiv'able
inconclu'sive
inconclu'sively
incongru'ity
incon'gruous
incon'sequent
inconsequen'-tial
inconsid'erable

inconsid'erate
inconsist'ency
inconsist'ent
inconspic'-uous
inconspic'-uously
incon'stant
incontest'able
incontrovert'-ible
inconve'nience
inconve'-nienced
inconve'nient--ly
incor'porate, *adj.*
incor'porate, *v.*
incor'porated
incor'porating
incorpora'tion
incorrect'
incorrect'ly
incor'rigible
incorrupt'
incorrupt'ible
{in'crease, *n.*
{increase', *v.*
increased'
increas'ing
increas'ingly
incred'ible
incredu'lity
incred'ulous
in'crement
incrim'inate
incrim'inated
in'cubator
in'culcate
in'culcated
incum'bent
incur'
incur'able
incur'sion
indebt'ed
indebt'edness
indeci'pherable
indeci'sion
indeci'sive
indeed'
indefat'igable *or*
indefen'sible
indefin'able
indef'inite
indel'ible
indel'icacy
indel'icate
indem'nify
indem'nity
indent'
indenta'tion
inden'ture
{*independ'-ence*
{*independ'ent*
{*independ'-ently*
indescri'bable *or*
indeter'minate
in'dex
in'dexed
In'dian
in'dicate
in'dicated
indica'tion
indic'ative
in'dicator
ind'ices
indict'
indict'able
indict'ment
{in*dif'ference*
{in*dif'ferent*
in*dif'ferent*ly
in'digent
indigest'ible
indiges'tion
indig'nant *or*
indig'nantly *or*
indigna'tion *or*
indig'nity
indirect'
indirect'ly

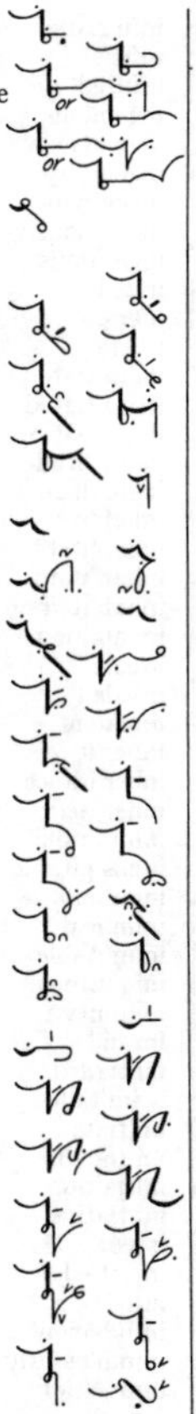

indiscreet'
indiscre'tion
indiscrim'inate
indiscrim'inately
indispen'sable
indispen'sably
indispose'
indisposed'
indisposi'tion
indispu'table
indistinct'
in*distin'guish*able
indite'
individ'ual
individ'ualist
individual'ity
individ'ually
indivis'ible
in'dolence
in'dolent
in'dolently
indom'itable
in'door
indorse'
indorse'ment
indors'er
indu'bitable
induce'
induced'
induce'ment
induct'
induc'tion
indulge'
indul'gence
indul'gent
indul'gently
indul'ging
indus'trial
indus'trialist
industrializa'tion
indus'trious
in'dustry
inebria'tion

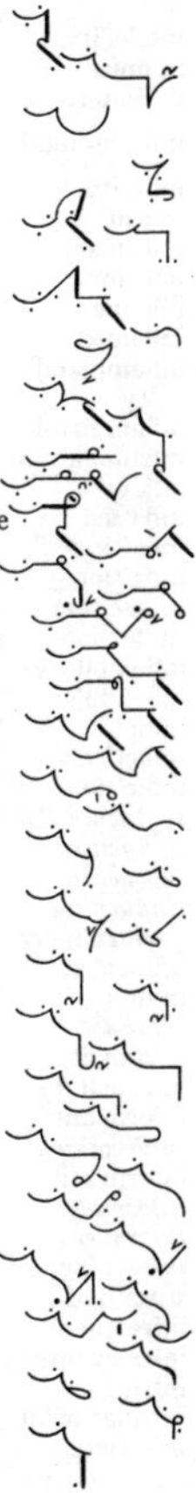

ined'ible
ineffect'ual
in*effi'ciency*
in*effi'cient*
in*effi'ciently*
inel'egant
inel'igible
in*equal'*ity
inerad'icable
inert'
iner'tia
ines'timable
inev'itable
inexact'
inexcus'able
inexhaust'ible
inex'orable
inexpe'dient
in*expen'sive*
inexpe'rience
inex'plicable
inex'tricable
infallibil'ity
infal'lible
in'famous
in'famy
in'fancy
in'fant
in'fantile
in'fantry
infat'uate
infat'uated
infatua'tion
infect'
infected'
infec'tion
infec'tious
infer'
in'ference
infe'rior
inferior'ity
infer'nal
infer'no
inferred'
infest'
infest'ed
in'fidel

infidel'ity
in'finite
in'finitely
infinites'imal *or*
infin'ity
infirm'
infir'mary
infir'mity
inflame'
inflamed'
inflammabil'-
ity
inflam'mable
inflamma'tion
inflate'
infla'ted
infla'ting
infla'tion
{inflec'tion
{inflex'ion
inflexibil'ity
inflex'ible
inflict'
inflict'ed
inflic'tion
in'fluence
in'fluenced
*in'fluenc*ing
{*influen'tial*
{*influen'tially*
influen'za
in'flux
inform'
inform'al
informal'ity
inform'ant
informa'tion
inform'ative
informed'
inform'er
*inform'*ing
infra'-red
infre'quent
infre'quently
infringe'
infringe'ment
infu'riate
infu'riated
infuse'
infused'
inge'nious
inge'niously
ingenu'ity
ingen'uous
ingen'uously
inglo'rious
in'got
ingrain'
in'grate
ingra'tiate
ingra'tiated
ingra'tiating
ingrat'itude
ingre'dient
inhab'it
inhab'itable
inhab'itant
inhab'ited
inhala'tion
inhale'
inhaled'
inher'ent
inher'it
inher'itance
inher'ited
inhibi'tion
inhos'pitable
inhu'man
inim'ical
inim'itable
iniq'uitous
iniq'uity
ini'tial
ini'tialled,
ini'tialed
ini'tiate
ini'tiated
initia'tion
ini'tiative
inject'
inject'ed
injec'tion
injudi'cious
injudi'ciously
injunc'tion

in'jure
in'jured
inju'rious
inju'riously
in'jury
injus'tice
ink
inlaid
in'land
in'let
in'mate
in'most
inn
innate'
in'ner
in'ner*most*
in'nocence
in'nocent
in'nocently
innoc'uous
innova'tion
innuen'do
innu'merable
inoc'ulate
inoc'ulated
inocula'tion
inopportune'
inopportune'ly
inor'dinate
inorgan'ic
in'-patient
in'quest
inquire'
inquired'
inquir'er
inquir'y
inquis'itive
inquis'itively
in'road
insane'
insan'itary
insan'ity
insa'tiable
inscribe'
inscribed'
*inscrib'*ing
inscrip'tion
inscru'table
in'sect
insecure'
insecu'rity
in*sensibil'ity*
in*sen'sible*
in*sen'sibly*
insep'arable
insert'
insert'ed
inser'tion
in'set, *n.*
inset', *v.*
in'side
insid'ious
in'sight
insig'nia
in*signif'icance*
in*signif'icant*
insincere'
insincere'ly
insincer'ity
insin'uate
insin'uated
insin'uating
insinua'tion
insip'id
insist'
insist'ed
insist'ence
insist'ent
insist'ently
insobri'ety
in'solence
in'solent
in'solently
insol'uble
insolv'ency
insolv'ent
insom'nia
inspect'
inspect'ed
*inspect'*ing
inspec'tion
inspec'tor
inspira'tion
inspire'
inspired'

inspir'ing
instabil'ity
install'
installa'tion
installed'
instal'ment
in'stance
in'stanced
in'stant
instanta'neous
instanta'neously
in'stantly
instead'
in'step
in'stigate
in'stigated
in'stigator
instil', instill'
in'stinct
instinc'tive
instinc'tively
in'stitute
in'stituted
institu'tion
instruct'
instruct'ed
instruc'tion
instruc'tive
instruct'or
in'strument
instrumen'tal
insubor'dinate
insubordina'tion
insuf'ferable
{*insuffi'ciency*
insuffi'cient
insuffi'ciently
in'sular
in'sulate
in'sulated
insula'tion
in'sulator
in'sulin
{in'sult, *n.*
insult', *v.*
insult'ed

insult'ing
insu'perable
insupport'able
insur'able
insur'ance
insure'
insured'
insur'gent
insurmount'able
insurrec'tion
intact'
intan'gible
in'tegral
in'tegrate
integ'rity
in'tellect
intellec'tual
intel'ligence
{*intel'ligent*
intel'ligently
intel'ligent'sia
{*intel'ligible*
intel'ligibly
intem'perance
intem'perate
intem'perately
intend'
intend'ed
intense'
intense'ly
inten'sify
inten'sity
inten'sive
intent'
inten'tion
inten'tional
intent'ly
inter'
intercede'
intercept'
intercept'ed
{in'terchange, *n.*
interchange', *v.*

interchange'-
able
in'tercom
in'tercourse
interdepend'-
ence
interdepend'-
ent
in'terest
in'terested
*in'terest*ing
interfere'
interfered'
interfer'ence
in'terim
inte'rior
interject'
interjec'tion
interlock'ing
in'terloper
in'terlude
interme'diary
interme'diate
inter'ment
inter'minable
intermin'gle
intermis'sion
intermit'tent
intern'
inter'nal
interna'tional
intern'ment
inter'polate
interpose'
interposed'
inter'pret
interpreta'tion
inter'preted
inter'preter
interred'
inter'rogate
interroga'tion
interrog'atory
interrupt'
interrup'tion
intersect'

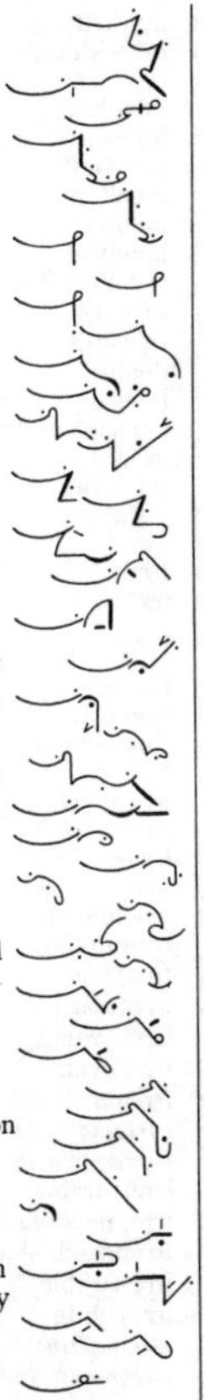

intersect'ed
intersec'tion
intersperse'
interspersed'
intertwine'
in'terval
intervene'
interven'tion
in'terview
interwov'en
intes'tate
intes'tine
in'timacy
in'timate, *n.*, *adj.*
in'timate, *v.*
in'timately
in'timating
intima'tion
intim'idate
intim'idated
intimida'tion
in'to
intol'erable
intol'erance
intol'erant
intona'tion
intox'icant
intox'icate
intox'icated
intoxica'tion
intrep'id
in'tricacy
in'tricate
intrigue'
intrin'sic
intrin'sically
introduce'
introduced'
introduc'tion
introduc'tory
introspec'tion
introspec'tive
in'trovert
intrude'
intru'ded
intru'sion

intui'tion
intu'itive
intu'itively
in'undate
in'undated
inunda'tion
inure'
invade'
in'valid
inval'id
inval'idate
inval'uable
inva'riable
inva'sion
invec'tive
inveigh'
invei'gle
invent'
invent'ed
inven'tion
invent'ive
invent'or
in'ventory
inverse'
inver'sion
invert'
invert'ed
invest'
invest'ed
inves'tigate
inves'tigated
investiga'tion
inves'tigator
invest'ing
invest'ment
invest'or
invet'erate
invid'ious
invigila'tion
invig'orate
invig'orated
invin'cible
invi'olable
invi'olate
invis'ible
invita'tion
invite'

invi'ted
invoca'tion
in'voice
in'voiced
invoke'
invoked'
invol'untary
involve'
involved'
invul'nerable
*in'*ward
*in'*wardly
i'odine
i'onize
ion'osphere
io'ta
iras'cible
irate'
ire
I'rish
irk'some
i'ron
iron'ic
iron'ical
i'ronmonger
i'rony
irra'tional
irrecov'erable
irrecov'erably
irredeem'able
irredu'cible
irrefu'table
irreg'ular
irregular'ity
irrel'evancy
irrel'evant
irreme'diable
irremov'able
irremov'ably
irrep'arable
irrepres'sible
irreproach'able
irresist'ible
irres'olute
irrespec'tive
irrespec'tively

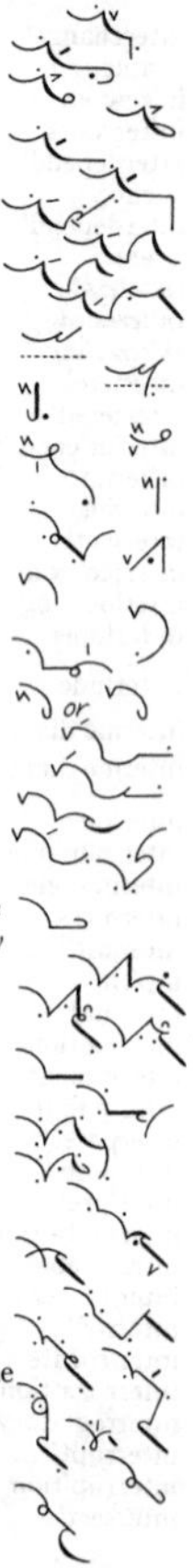

irrespon-sibil'ity
irrespon'sible
irretriev'able
irrev'erent
irrev'erently
irrev'ocable
ir'rigate
ir'rigated
irriga'tion
ir'ritable
ir'ritate
ir'ritated
irrita'tion
is
is'land
is'lander
isle
i'solate
i'solating
isola'tion
isola'tionist
is'otope
is'sue
is'sued
is'suing
it
Ital'ian
ital'ic
ital'ics
ital'icize
itch
i'tem
i'temize
itin'erant
itin'erary
its
itself'
i'vory
i'vy

J

jack
jack'et
jack'pot
Jacobe'an
jade
ja'ded
jag
jagged
jag'ged
jail
jail'er
jail'or
jam
jamb
jammed
jan'gle
jan'gled
jan'itor
Jan'uary
Japan'
Japanese'
jar
jar'gon
jar'ring
jar'ringly
jaun'dice
jaunt
jaun'tily
jaw
jay'wa'lker
jeal'ous
jeal'ousy
jeer
jeered
jel'ly
jeop'ardize
jeop'ardy
jerk
jerked
jer'ry

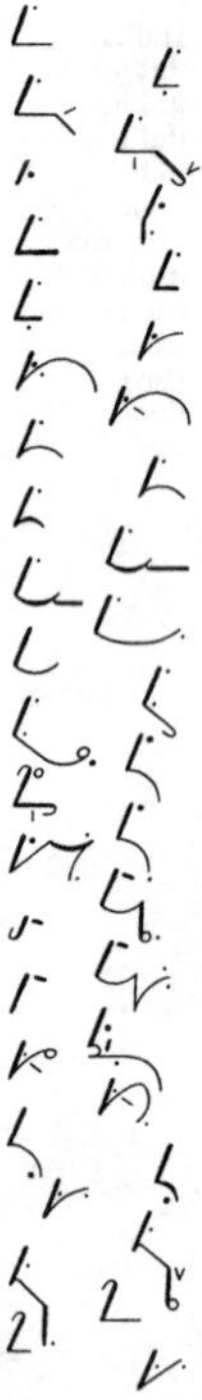

jer'sey
jest
jest'ed
jest'er
jest'ing
jest'ingly
jet
jet'sam
jet'tison
jet'ty
Jew
jew'el
jew'eller,
jew'eler
jew'ellery
jew'elry
Jew'ess
Jew'ish
jibe
jig'saw
jin'gle
jitt'ery
job
job'ber
job'bery
jock'ey
jocose'
joc'ular
jog
join
join'er
join'ing
joint
joint'ed
joint'ly
joke
jo'kingly
jol'lity
jol'ly
jolt

jos'tle
jos'tled
jot
jot'ted
jot'ting
jour'nal
journalese'
jour'nalism
jour'nalist
journalis'tic
jour'ney
jour'neyed
jo'vial
jovial'ity
joy
joy'ful
joy'ous
joy'ously
ju'bilant
jubila'tion
ju'bilee
judge
judged
judg'ing
judg'ment
ju'dicature
judi'cial
judi'cious
judi'ciously
jug
jug'gle
jug'gler
ju'gular

juice
juke'-box
July'
jum'ble
jum'bo
jump
jumped
jump'er
junc'tion
junc'ture
June
jun'gle
ju'nior
junk
jurisdic'tion
ju'rist
ju'ror
ju'ry
ju'ryman
just
jus'tice
jus'tifiable
justifica'tion
jus'tified
jus'tify
just'ly
just'ness
jut
jute
jut'ted
ju'venile
juxtaposi'tion

K

kangaroo'
keel
keen
keen'er
keen'est
keen'ly
keen'ness
keep
keep'er
keep'ing
keg
ken'nel
kept
kerb
kerb'stone
ker'nel
ker'osene
ket'tle
key
key'board
keyed
key'hole
key'note
kha'ki
kick
kicked
kick'er
kick'ing
kid
kid'nap
kid'napped
kid'napper
kid'ney
kill
kill'joy
kiln
kil'ogramme,
kil'ogram
kil'ometre,
kil'ometer

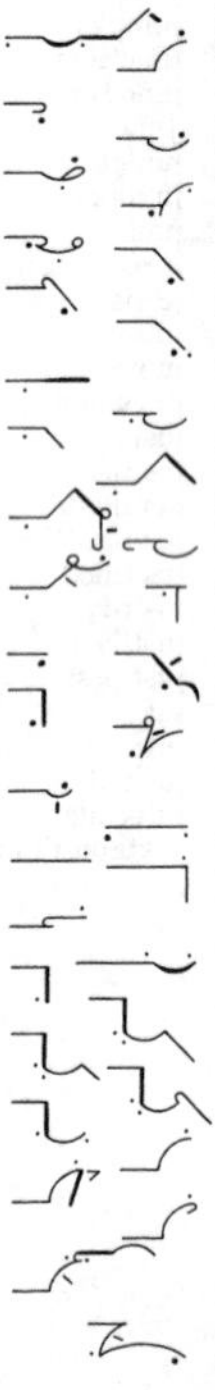

kil'owatt
kilt
kin
kinaesthet'ic
kind
kind'er
kin'dergarten
kind'est
kind'-hearted
kin'dle
kin'dled
kind'ly
kind'ness
kin'dred
king
king'dom
king'-pin
kink
kin'ship
kins'man
kiosk'
kiss
kit
kitch'en
kitchenette'
kite
kith
kit'ten
knack
knap'sack
knave
knead
knee
kneel
kneeled
kneel'ing
knell
knelt
knew
knife

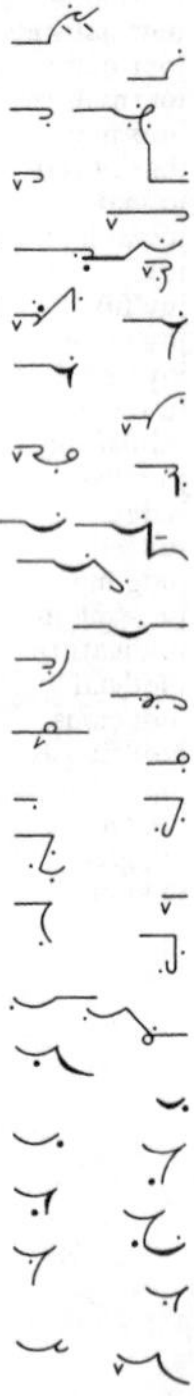

knight
knight'hood
knit
knit'wear
knives
knob
knock
knocked
knock'er
knoll
knot
knot'ted
knot'ting

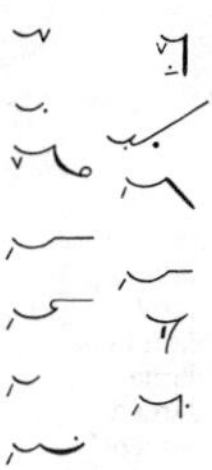

knot'ty
know
know'-how
know'ing
know'ingly
knowl'edge
known
knuck'le
knuck'led
knuck'ling
ko'dak
ku'dos

L

la'bel
la'belled,
  la'beled
la'belling,
  la'beling
lab'oratory
labo'rious
labo'riously
la'bour, la'bor
la'bourer
labur'num
lab'yrinth
lace
lac'erate
lac'erated
lacera'tion
lach'rymose
la'cing
lack
lackadai'sical
lacked
lacon'ic
lac'quer,
  lack'er
lad
lad'der
la'den
la'dle
la'dy
la'dyship
lag
la'ger
lag'gard
lagged
laid
lain
lair
la'ity

lake
lamb
lam'bent
lame
lamed
lament'
lam'entable
lamenta'tion
lament'ed
lament'ing
lam'inate
lamp
lance
lan'cet
land
land'ed
land'holder
land'ing
land'lady
land'*lord*
land'mark
land'owner
land'-rover
land'scape
land'slide
lane
lan'guage
lan'guid
lan'guish
lan'gour
lank'y
lan'tern
lap
lapel'
lapse
lapsed
laps'ing
lar'ceny

larch
lard
lard'er
large
large'ly
larg'er
larg'est
lark
lar'va
lar'vae
laryngi'tis
lar'ynx
las'car
la'ser
lash
lashed
lash'ing
lass
las'situde
last
last'ed
last'ing
last'ingly
last'ly
latch
late
late'ly
la'tent
la'ter
lat'eral
la'test
lath
lathe
lath'er
Lat'in
lat'itude
lat'ter
lat'terly
lat'tice
laud
laud'able
laud'anum
laud'atory
laugh
laugh'ingly
laugh'ter
launch

launched
launch'ing
laun'dry
lau'reate
lau'rel
la'va
lav'atory
lav'ender
lav'ish
lav'ished
lav'ishly
law
law'ful
law'fully
law'fulness
law'less
law'lessness
lawn
law'suit
law'yer
lax
lax'ative
lax'ity
lay
lay'by
lay'er
lay'ing
lay'man
lay'out
laze
la'zier
la'zily
la'ziness
la'zy
lea
lead (a metal)
lead (to conduct)
lead'en
lead'er
lead'ership
lead'ing
leaf
leaf'let
leaf'y
league
leagued
leak

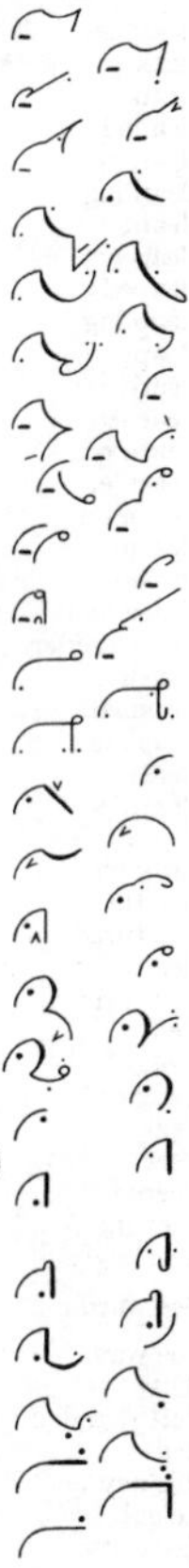

leak'age
leak'y
lean
leaned
lean'est
lean'ing
leant
leap
leaped
leap'ing
leapt
learn
learned
learn'ed
learn'er
learn'ing
learnt
lease
lease'hold
lease'holder
leash
leashed
leas'ing
least
leath'er
leave
leav'en
lec'ture
lec'tured
lec'turer
lec'turing
led
ledge
ledg'er
leek
leer
leered
leer'ing
leer'ingly
lee'ward
lee'way
left
left'-handed
leg
leg'acy
le'gal
legal'ity

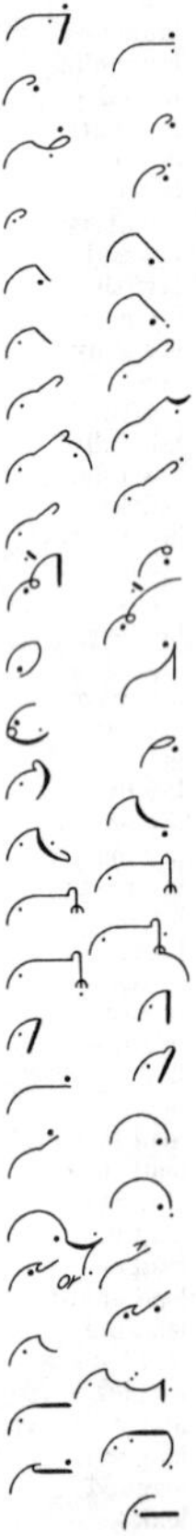

le'galize
le'gally
legatee'
lega'tion
leg'end
leg'endary
leg'erdemain
legibil'ity
leg'ible
le'gion
leg'islate
leg'islated
legisla'tion
leg'islative
leg'islator
leg'islature
legit'imacy
legit'imate, *adj.*
legitimate', *v.*
lei'sure
lei'surely
lem'on
lemonade'
lend
lend'er
lend'ing
length
length'en
length'ening
length'wise
length'y
le'nience
le'niency
le'nient
le'niently
lens
Lent, lent
leop'ard
lep'er
lep'rosy
les'bian
less
lessee'
les'sen
les'sened
les'sening
les'ser

les'son
lessor'
lest
let
le'thal
lethar'gic
leth'argy
let'ter
let'terhead
let'terpress
let'ting
let'tuce
leukaem'ia
lev'ee
lev'el
lev'elled,
lev'eled
lev'elling,
lev'eling
le'ver
le'verage
levi'athan
lev'ity
lev'y
liabil'ity
li'able
liais'on-officer
li'ar
li'bel
li'bellous,
li'belous
lib'eral
liberal'ity
lib'erally
lib'erate
lib'erated
lib'erating
libera'tion
lib'erty
libra'rian
li'brary
li'cence, *n.*
li'cense, *v.*
li'censed
licensee'
licen'tious
li'chen

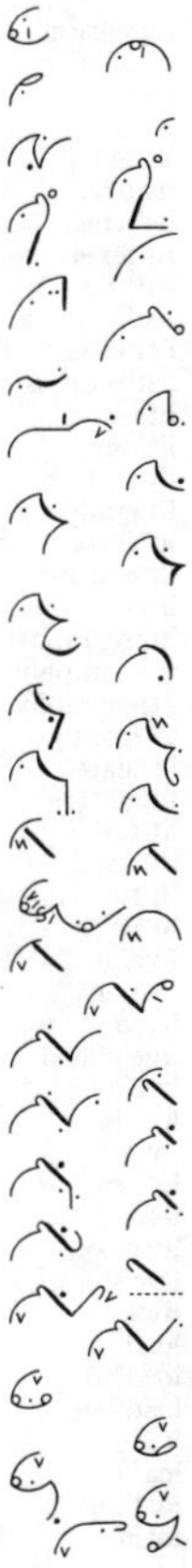

lick
licked
lid
lid'o
lie
lied
li'en
lieu
lieuten'ant
life
life'boat
life'*guard*
life'-*insurance*
life'less
life'-preserver
lifesav'er
life'-size
life'time
lift
lift'ed
lift'ing
lig'ament
lig'ature
light
light'ed
light'ening
light'er
light'erage
light'hearted
light'house
light'ing
light'ning
like
like'able
liked
like'lihood
like'ly
li'ken
li'kened
like'ness
like'wise
li'lac
lil'y
limb
lim'ber
lim'bo
lime

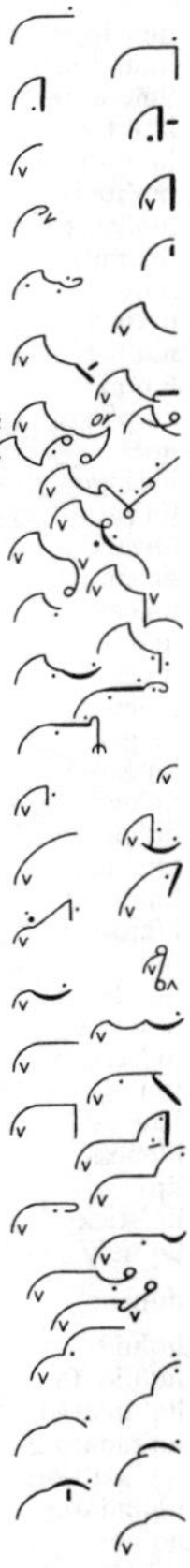

lime'light
lime'stone
lime'water
lim'it
limita'tion
lim'ited
lim'iting
lim'ousine
limp
limped
lim'pet
lim'pid
limp'ing
line
lin'eage
lin'eal
lineal'ity
lin'eament
lin'ear
lined
lin'en
li'ner
lin'ger
lin'gered
lin'gerie
lin'guist
linguis'tic
lin'iment
li'ning
link
lino'leum
li'notype
lin'seed
lint
li'on
li'oness
lip
lip'stick
liq'uefy
liqueur' *or*
liq'uid
liq'uidate
liq'uidated
liq'uidating
liquida'tion
liq'uidator
liq'uor

liq'uorice,
lic'orice
lisp
list
list'ed
lis'ten
lis'tened
lis'tener
list'ing
list'less
list'lessly
list'lessness
lit
lit'any
lit'eral
lit'erally
lit'erary
lit'erature
lithe
lithog'rapher
lithograph'ic
lithog'raphy
lit'igant
lit'igate
litiga'tion
lit'ter
lit'tered
lit'tle
lit'urgy
live, *v.*
live, *a.*
lived
live'lihood
live'long
live'ly
liv'er
liv'ery
lives
lives, *pl.*
live'stock
liv'id
load
load'ed
load'ing
loaf
loaf'er
loaf'ing
loam

loan
loan'ing
loath, loth
loathe
loath'some
loaves
lob'by
lob'ster
lo'cal
local'ity
lo'calize
lo'cally
locate'
loca'ted
loca'ting
loca'tion
loch
lock
locked
lock'er
lock'et
lock'out
lock'smith
lo'como'tion
lo'comotive
lo'cum-te'nens
lo'cust
lodge
lodged
lodg'ing
loft
loft'ier
loft'iest
loft'ily
loft'y
log
log'ic
log'ical
logi'cian
loin
loi'ter
loi'tered
loll
lolled
lone
lone'liness
lone'ly
lone'some
long
longed
long'er, *n.*
lon'ger, *adj.*
lon'gest
longev'ity
long'*hand*
lon'gitude
longitu'dinal
long'lived
long'suffering
loo'fah
look
looked
look'ing
look'out
loom
loomed
loom'ing
loop
loop'hole
loose
loosed
loose'ly
loos'en
loos'ened
loos'er
loqua'cious
loquac'ity
lord
lord'ship
lore
lor'ry
lose
los'er
los'ing
loss
lost
lot
lo'tion
lot'tery
loud
loud'er
loud'speaker
lounge
lov'able

love
love'lier
love'liest
love'liness
love'ly
lov'er
low
low'er
low'ered
low'est
low'land
low'ly
loy'al
loy'alty
loz'enge
lu'bricant
lu'bricate
lu'bricated
lubrica'tion
lu'bricator
lu'cid
lucid'ity
luck
luck'ier
luck'iest
luck'y
lu'crative
lu'dicrous
lug'gage
luke'warm
lull
lull'aby

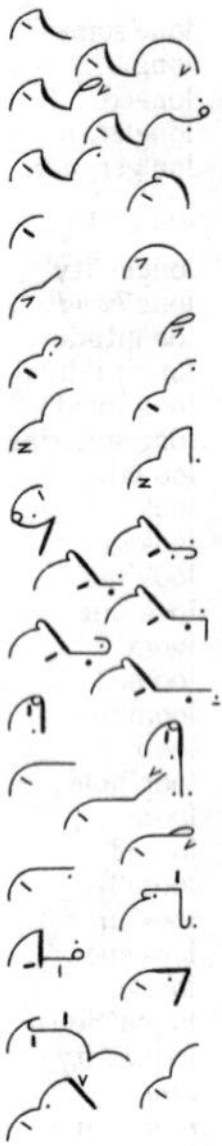

lulled
lumba'go
lum'ber
lu'minous
lump
lu'nacy
lu'nar
lu'natic
lunch
lunch'eon
lung
lunge
lurch
lure
lured
lu'rid
lurk
lus'cious
lus'tre
lus'trous
lust'y
lute
luxu'riance
luxu'riant
luxu'rious
luxu'riously
lux'ury
ly'ing
lynch
lynx
lyr'ic
lyr'ical

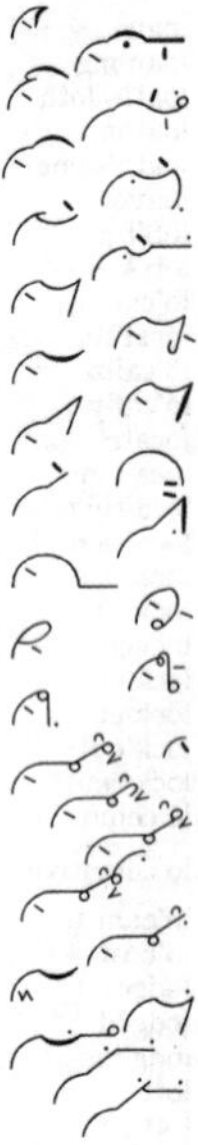

M

maca'bre
macad'amize
mace
machina'tion
machine'
machin'ery (or)
machine'-tool
machin'ist
mack'erel
mack'intosh
macrobiot'ics
mac'ron
mad
mad'am
mad'den
mad'dening
made
maes'tro
magazine'
mag'ic
mag'ical
magi'cian
magiste'rial
mag'istrate
magnanim'ity
magnan'imous
mag'nate
magne'sia
mag'net
{ *magnet'ic*
{ *mag'netism*
mag'netize
mag'netized
magnet'o
magnif'icence
magnif'icent
magnif'icently
mag'nified
mag'nify
mag'nitude
mahog'any
maid
maid'en
mail
mail'able
mailed
maim
maimed
main
main'land
main'ly
main'spring
main'stay
maintain'
maintain'ed
main'tenance
maize
majes'tic
maj'esty
ma'jor
major'ity
make
ma'ker
make'shift
make'-up
mak'ing
maladjust'ment
mal'ady
mal'aise
mal'aprop
mala'ria
mal'content
male
malev'olent
mal'ice
mali'cious
mali'ciously
malign'

malig'nant *or*
maligned'
malin'ger
malin'gerer
mal'leable
mal'nutri'tion
malt
maltreat'
maltreat'ed
mama', mamma'
mam'mal
mam'moth
man
man'acle
man'age
man'agement
man'ager
man'ageress
manage'rial
man'date, *n.*
mandate', *v.*
man'datory
man'dolin
mane
man'ful
man'fully
man'gle
man'hood
ma'nia
ma'niac
mani'acal
man'icure
man'ifest
manifesta'tion
man'ifested
man'ifesting
man'ifestly
manifes'to
man'ifold
man'ikin
manip'ulate
manip'ulated
manipula'tion
mankind'
man'lier
man'ly
mann'equin *or*
man'ner
man'nerly
manoeu'vre
manoeu'vring
man'-of-war' *or*
man'or
man'power
man'sion
man'slaughter
man'tel
man'telpiece
mantil'la
man'tle
man'ual
manufac'ture
manufac'tured
manufac'turer
manufac'turing
manure'
man'uscript
man'y
map
ma'ple
mapped
mar
mar'ble
march (March)
marched
march'ing
mare
mar'gin
mar'ginal
marine'
mar'iner
mar'ital
mar'itime
mark
marked
mar'ket
mar'malade
ma'rocain
marred
mar'riage

mar'ried
mar'ring
mar'row
mar'ry
mar'rying
marsh
mar'shal
mar'shalled, mar'shaled
mart
mar'tial
mar'tyr
mar'tyrdom
mar'vel
mar'velled, mar'veled
mar'vellous, mar'velous
marx'ist
mascar'a
mas'cot
mas'culine
mash
mashed
mask
mas'ochism
mas'ochist
ma'son
mason'ic
ma'sonry
masquerade'
Mass, mass
mas'sacre
massage'
masseur'
masseuse'
mass'ive
mass'ively
mast
mas'ter
mas'tered
mas'terful
mas'tering
mas'terly
mas'terpiece
mas'tery
mas'ticate
mas'ticated
mastica'tion
mas'turbate
masturba'tion
mat
match
match'ing
match'less
mate
mate'rial
mate'rialist
materialis'tic
mate'rialize
mater'nal
mater'nity
mathemat'ic
mathemat - ical
mathemat'- ically
mathemati'cian
mathemat'ics
mat'inée
matric'ulate
matric'ulated
matricula'tion
matrimo'nial
mat'rimony
ma'trix
ma'tron
ma'tronly
mat'ter
mat'ting
mat'tress
mature'
matured'
matu'rity
maul
mauled
mausole'um
mauve
max'im
max'imize
max'imum
may (May)
may'*be*
mayonnaise'
may'or

may'oral
may'oralty
may'oress
maze
me
mead'ow
mea'gre
meal
meal'time
mean
mean'est
mean'ingless
meant
mean'time
mean'while
mea'sles
meas'urable
meas'ure
meas'ured
meas'urement
meat
mechan'ic
{*mechan'ical*
mechan'-
ically
mech'anism
mechaniza'tion
mech'anize
med'al
med'dle
med'dled
med'dlesome
me'dial
me'diate
media'tion
me'diator
med'ical
medic'inal
med'icine
medie'val
me'diocre
medioc'rity
med'itate
med'itated
medita'tion
med'itative
Mediterra'nean
me'dium

med'ley
meek
meek'ly
meet
meet'ing
megaloman'ia
meg'aphone
meg'aton
mel'ancholy *or*
mel'low
mel'lowed
melo'dious
melodra'ma
mel'ody
mel'on
melt
melt'ed
melt'ing
mem'ber
*mem'ber*ship
mem'brane
memen'to
mem'oir
mem'orable
memoran'da
memoran'dum
memo'rial
mem'orize
mem'orized
mem'orizing
mem'ory
men
men'ace
men'aced
men'acing
menag'erie
mend
menda'cious
mend'ed
men'dicant
mend'ing
me'nial
men'opause
men'tal
mental'ity
men'tion
men'tioned

men'tioning
men'u *or*
mer'cantile
mer'cenary
mer'chandise
mer'chant
mer'ciful
mer'cifully
mer'ciless
mer'cury
mer'cy
mere
mere'ly
merge
mer'ger
merid'ian
meri'no
mer'it
merito'rious
mer'riment
mer'ry
mesh
meshed
mes'merize
mes'merized
mess
mes'sage
mes'senger
met
metab'olism
met'al
metal'lic
metall'urgy
met'aphor
metaphor'ical
metapsych'ics
mete
me'teor
meteor'ic
me'ter
meth'ane
meth'od
method'ical
Meth'odist
metic'ulous
me'tre
met'ric
met'rical
metrop'olis
metropol'itan
met'tle
Mex'ican
mias'ma
mi'ca
mice
Mich'aelmas
mi'crobe
microb'iol'ogy
mic'rofilm
mi'crophone
mi'croscope
microscop'ic *or*
mi'crowave
mid
mid'day
mid'dle
mid'dle-aged
mid'dle-class
mid'dleman
midg'et
mid'night
midst
mid'summer
mid'way
mid'winter
mien
might
might'y
mi'grant
mi'grate
mi'grated
mil'age
mild
mild'er
mild'est
mil'dew
mild'ly
mild'ness
mile
mile'age
mile'stone
mil'ieu
mil'itant
mil'itarism

militaris'tic
mil'itary
mil'itate
mil'itated
mili'tia
milk
mill
millen'nium
mill'er
mill'ibar
mil'liner
mil'linery
mil'lion
millionaire'
mill'stone
mim'ic
mince
mind
mind'ed
mind'ful
mine
mi'ner
min'eral
min'gle
min'iature
min'imal
min'imize
min'imum
mi'ning
min'ion
min'ister
min'istered
ministe'rial
min'istering
ministra'tion
min'istry
mi'nor
minor'ity
min'ster
min'strel
mint
mint'ed
mi'nus
minus'cule
min'ute, *n.*, *v.*
minute', *adj.*
minu'tiae
mir'acle

mirac'ulous
mirage'
mire
mir'ror
mirth
mirth'ful
mi'ry
misapplied'
misapply'
misapprehend'
misapprehen'sion
misappropria'tion
misbehave'
misbeha'viour
miscal'culate
miscal'culated
miscalcula'tion
miscar'ry
miscella'neous
miscel'lany
mischance'
mis'chief
mis'chievous
misconcep'tion
{miscon'duct, *n.*
{misconduct', *v.*
misconstruc'tion
miscon'strue
misdeed'
misdemean'our
misdirect'
mi'ser
mis'erable
mis'ery
misfit'
misfor'tune
mis*giv*'ing
misguide'
misguid'ed
mishap'
{mis*inform*'
{mis*informed*'
misinter'pret

misinterpreta'tion
misinter'preted
misjudge'
misjudged'
mislaid'
mislead'
misled'
misman'age
misman'aged
misman'agement
misno'mer
misplace'
misprint'
mispronounce'
misquota'tion
misquote'
misquot'ed
mis*represent'*
mis*representa'tion*
mis*represent'ed*
mis*represent'ing*
misrule'
miss
mis'ses
mis'sile
miss'ing
mis'sion
mis'sionary
miss'ive
mis-spell'
mis'state'ment
mist
mistake'
mista'ken
mistak'enly
mis'took
mis'tress
mistrust'
mistrust'ed
mist'y
mis*under*stand'
mis*under*stand'ing
mis*under*stood'
misuse', *v.*
misuse', *n.*
mite
mit'igate
mit'igated
mitiga'tion
mix
mixed
mix'er
mix'ture
mnemon'ic
moan
mob
mobbed
mo'bile
mobil'ity
mobiliza'tion
mo'bilize
mock
mock'ery
mode
mod'el
mod'elled, mod'eled
mod'erate, *n.*, *a.*
moderate', *v.*
mod'erately
modera'tion
mod'erator
mod'ern
mod'ernist
modernis'tic
moderniza'tion
mod'ernize
mod'est
mod'estly
mod'esty
mod'icum
modifica'tion
Moham'medan
Mo'hawk
Mohi'can

moi'ety
moist
mois'ten
mois'tened
mois'ture
mo'lar
molas'ses
mold
mol'ecule
mole'hill
molest'
molesta'tion
molest'ed
molest'ing
mol'lify
mol'ten
mo'ment
mo'mentarily
mo'mentary
momen'tous
momen'tum
mon'arch
monar'chical
mon'archist
mon'astery
Mon'day
mon'etary
mon'etize
mon'ey
mon'key
mon'ogram
mon'ologue
mon'oplane
monop'olist
monop'olize
monop'oly
monot'onous
monot'ony
monox'ide
monsoon'
mon'ster
*monstros'*ity
mon'strous
mon'tage
month
month'ly

mon'ument
monumen'tal / monumen'tally
mood
mood'ily
mood'y
moon
moon'light
moon'shine
moor
moored
moor'land
mop
mope
mo'ped
mor'al
morale'
mor'alist
moral'ity
mor'alize
mor'alizing
mor'ally
morass'
morato'rium
mor'bid
morbid'ity
more
moreo'ver
mor'ibund
morn
morn'ing
moroc'co
morose'
morose'ly
mor'phia
mor'row
mor'sel
mor'tal
mortal'ity
mor'tar
mort'gage / *mort'gaged*
mortgagee'
mort'gager
mort'gaging
mort'gagor

mortifica'tion
mor'tified
mor'tify
mor'tuary
mosa'ic
mosqui'to
moss
moss'y
most
most'ly
mote
motel
moth
moth'er
mo'ther-craft
moth'erhood (or)
moth'er-in-law
mo'tion
mo'tioned
mo'tionless
mot'ivate
motiva'tion
mo'tive
mot'ley
mo'tor
mo'tor-bus
mo'tor-car
mo'tor-cy'cle
mo'torist
mot'orway
mot'tled
mot'to
mould
mould'ed
mould'er
mould'ing
mould'y
mound
mount
moun'tain
mountaineer'
moun'tainous
mount'ebank
mourn
mourn'er
mourn'ful
mourn'fully
mourn'ing
mouse
moustache'
mouth
mouth'ful
mouth'piece
mov'able, move'able
move
moved
move'ment
mov'er
mow (to grimace)
{mow (to cut)
{mow (of hay)
mowed
mow'er
Mr.
Mrs.
much
mud
mud'dle
mud'dled
mud'dy
muf'fle
muf'fled
muf'ti
mug
mulat'to
mul'berry
mulct
mulct'ed
mule
multifa'rious
mul'tiple
multiplica'tion
multiplic'ity
mult'iplied
mul'tiply
mul'titude
multitu'dinous
mum'ble
mumps
munch

mun'dane
munic'ipal
municipal'ity
munif'icence
munif'icent
munif'icently
muni'tion
mu'ral
mur'der
mur'dered
mur'derer
mur'deress
mur'derous
mur'mur
mur'mured
mur'muring
mus'cle
mus'cular
muse
mused
muse'um
mush'room
mu'sic
mu'sical
musi'cian
mus'ketry
Muslim
mus'lin
mus'quash
mus'sel
must
mus'tard
mus'ter
mus'tered
mute

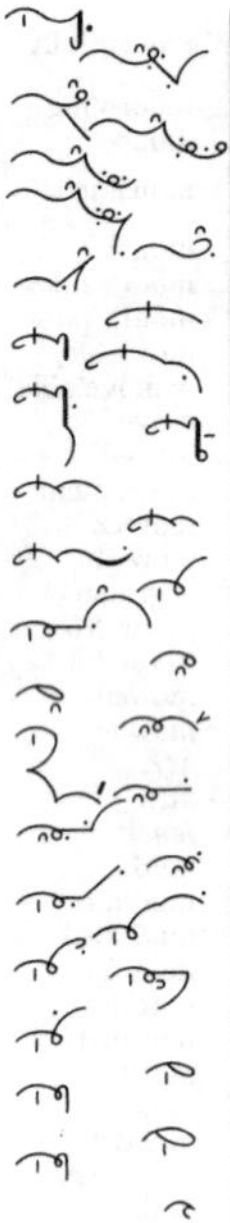

mu'tilate
mu'tilated
mutila'tion
mu'tiny
mut'ter
mut'tered
mut'tering
mut'ton
mu'tual
muz'zle
muz'zled
my
myr'iad
myrrh
myr'tle
myself'
myste'rious
myste'riously
mys'tery
mys'tic
mys'tical
mys'tically
mys'ticism
mystifica'tion
mys'tified
mys'tify
mys'tifying
mystique'
myth
myth'ical
myth'ically
mytholog'ic
mytholog'ical-
-ly
mythol'ogy

N

nag
nail
nailed
nail'ing
naïve', naive'
na'ked
name
named
name'less
name'ly
nap
naph'tha
nap'kin
narcot'ic
narrate'
narra'ted
narra'tion
nar'rative
narra'tor
nar'row
nar'rowed
nar'rower
nar'rowest
nar'rowing
nar'rowly
nar'row-minded
na'sal
nas'ty
na'tal
na'tion
na'tional
na'tionalist
national'ity
nationaliza'tion
na'tionalize
na'tionally
na'tive
nativ'ity

nat'ural
nat'uralist
naturaliza'tion
nat'uralize
nat'uralized
nat'urally
na'ture
na'turism
naught
naugh'ty
nau'sea
nau'seate
nau'tical
na'val
nave
nav'igable
nav'igate
nav'igated
naviga'tion
nav'igator
nav'vy
na'vy
nay
near
*near*ed
near'er
near'est
near'ing
near'ly
neat
neat'er
neat'est
neat'ly
neb'ulous
nec'essarily
nec'essary
neces'sitate
neces'sitated
neces'sitating
neces'sitous

neces'sity
neck
neck'lace
neck'tie
neck'wear
nec'tar
need
need'ed
need'ful
nee'dle
need'less
need'lessly
need'lessness
nee'dlework
nefa'rious
nega'tion
neg'ative
neglect',
neglect'ed
*neglect'*ful
*neglect'*ing
négligé'
neg'ligence
neg'ligent
neg'ligently
neg'ligible
negotiabil'ity
nego'tiable
nego'tiate
nego'tiated
negotia'tion
ne'gress
ne'gro
ne'groid
neigh
neigh'bour,
neigh'bor
neigh'bour-
hood
nei'ther
Nem'esis
ne'on
neph'ew
Nep'tune
nerve
nerv'ous
nerv'ously
nest
nes'tle
nes'tled
net
net'ted
net'ting
net'tle
net'tled
net'work
neural'gia
neurasthe'nia
neurasthen'ic
neuri'tis
neurot'ic
neu'ter
neu'tral
neutral'ity
neu'tralize
neut'ron
nev'er
nev'ermore
nevertheless'
new
new'comer
new'er
new'est
newfan'gled
new-fash'ioned
new'ly
news
news'agent
news'paper
news'print
next
nib
nib'ble
nib'bled
nib'bling
nice
nice'ly
ni'cest
ni'cety
niche
nick
nick'el
nick'name
nic'otine
niece
nig'gardly

nigh
night
night'gown
night'ingale
night'ly
night'mare
night'shirt
night'wear
nil
nim'ble
nine
nineteen'
nineteenth'
nine'tieth
nine'ty
ninth
nip
nip'ple
ni'trate
ni'tric
ni'trogen
nitrog'enous
nit'wit
no
nobil'ity
no'ble
no'body
noctur'nal
nod
nod'ded
nod'ding
nog'gin
noise
noise'less
noise'lessly
nois'ily
nois'y
nom'ad
nomad'ic
no'menclature
nom'inal
nom'inate
nomina'tion
nominee'
non-accep'tance
non-appear'ance
non-arri'val
non-attend'ance
non'chalance
non'chalant
non-com'batant
non-commis'sioned
non-commit'tal
non-*deliv'ery*
non'descript
none
nonen'tity
non-interven'tion
non-par'ty
nonpay'ment
non'plussed
non-res'ident
non'sense
nonsen'sical
non'-stop
nook
noon
noon'day
nor
nor'mal
Nor'man
north
north-east'
north-east'er
north-east'ern
north'erly
north'ern
north'erner
north'ward
north-west'
north-west'er
north-west'erly
north-west'ern
Norwe'gian
nose

nos'tril
not
notabil'ity
no'table
no'tary
nota'tion
notch
note
note'book
note'worthy
noth'ing
no'tice
no'ticeable
no'ticed
no'ticing
not'ifiable
notifica'tion
no'tified
no'tify
no'tion
notori'ety
noto'rious
notwithstand'-ing
nought
noun
nour'ish
nour'ished
nour'ishment
nov'el
nov'elist
nov'elty
Novem'ber
nov'ice
now
now'adays
no'where
no'wise

nox'ious
noz'zle
nucleon'ics
nu'cleus
nude
nudge
nu'dism
nu'dist
nug'get
nui'sance
null
nul'lified
nul'lify
nul'lity
numb
numbed
num'ber, num'bered
*num'ber*ing
nu'meral
numer'ical
nu'merous
nun
nup'tials
nurse
nursed
nurs'ery
nur'ture
nur'tured
nut
nu'triment
nutri'tion
nutri'tional
nutri'tious
nut'shell
nyl'on
nymph

O

O (*oh*)
oak
oar
oa'sis
oath
oat'meal
oats
ob'duracy
ob'durate
ob'durately
obe'dience
obe'dient
obe'diently
obese'
obes'ity
obey'
obey'ing
obit'uary
ob'ject, n.
object', v.
object'ed
*object'*ing
objec'tion
objec'tionable
objec'tive
*objec'tive*ly
obliga'tion
ob'ligatory
oblige'
obliged'
oblique'
oblit'erate
oblit'erated
oblitera'tion
obliv'ion
obliv'ious
ob'long
obnox'ious
obscure'

obscured'
obscu'rity
obse'quious
observ'ance
observ'ant
observa'tion
observe'
observed'
observ'er
observ'ing
obsess'
obsessed'
obses'sion
obsoles'cence
ob'solete
ob'stacle
ob'stinacy
ob'stinate
obstrep'erous
obstruct'
obstruct'ed
obstruct'ing
obstruc'tion
obstruc'tive
obtain'
obtain'able
obtained'
obtain'ing
obtrude'
obtru'ded
obtru'ding
obtru'sion
obtru'sive
obtru'sively
obtuse'
ob'viate
ob'viated
ob'viating
ob'vious

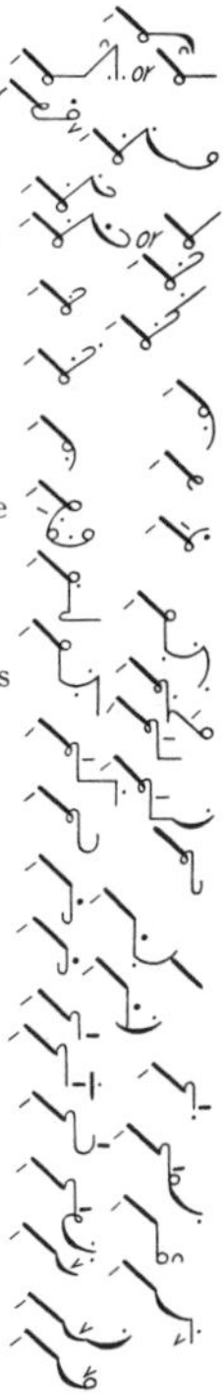

ob'viously
occa'sion
occa'sional
occa'sioned
occa'sioning
oc'cident
occiden'tal
oc'cupancy
oc'cupant
occupa'tion
oc'cupied
oc'cupier
oc'cupy
oc'cupying
occur'
occurred'
occur'rence
occur'ring
o'cean
o'clock'
oc'tagon
octag'onal
oc'tane
oc'tave
Octo'ber
oc'ulist
odd
o'dious
o'dium
o'dorous
o'dour, o'dor
oes'trogen
oes'trum
of
off
offence'
offend'
offend'ed
offend'er
offend'ing
offen'sive
of'fer
off'*hand*
of'fice
of'ficer
offi'cial
offi'cially
offi'ciate

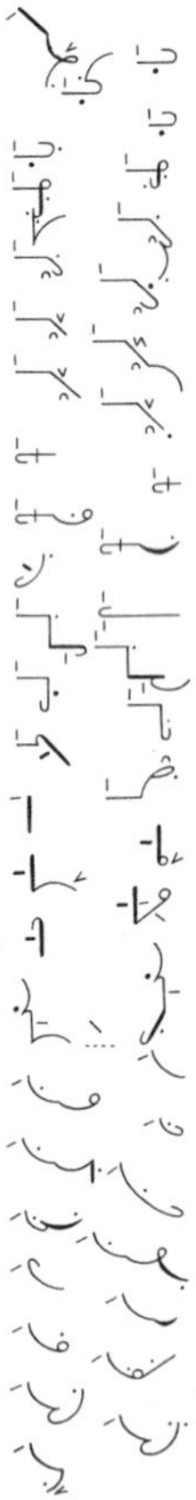

offi'ciated
offi'cious
offi'ciously
{off'set, *n.*
{offset', *v.*
off'spring
oft'en
oft'entimes
oh
oil
oil'cloth
oiled
oil'skin
oil'y
oint'ment
old
old'er
old'est
old-fash'ioned
ol'ive
om'elet,
om'elette
o'men
om'inous
om'inously
omis'sion
omit'
omit'ted
omit'ting
om'nibus
omnip'otence
omnip'otent
omnis'cience
omnis'cient
omniv'orous
on
once
on'cost
one
on'erous
oneself'
one'sided
one'-way
on'ion
on'looker
on'ly
on'set
on'slaught

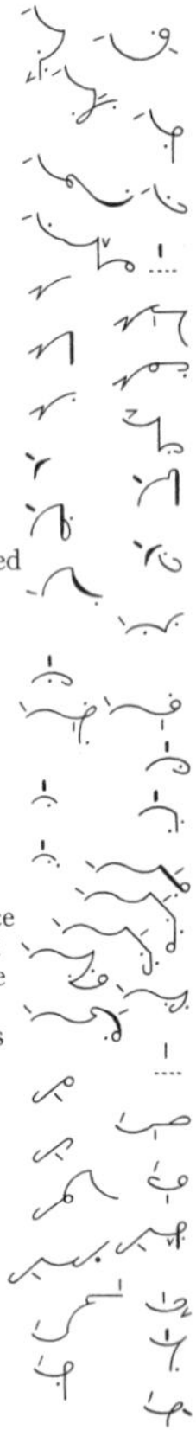

o'nus
*on'*ward
on'yx
ooze
o'pal
opaque'
o'pen
open-air'
o'pened
o'pener
o'pening
o'penly
op'era
op'erate
operat'ic
opera'tion
opera'tional
op'erative
op'erator
operet'ta
opin'ion
o'pium
oppo'nent
opportune'
opportu'nity
oppose'
op'posite
opposi'tion
oppress'
oppressed'
oppres'sion
oppress'ive
oppress'ively
oppress'or
op'tic
op'tical
opti'cian
op'timism
op'timist
optimis'tic
op'timum
op'tion
op'tional
op'ulence
op'ulent
op'us
or
or'acle

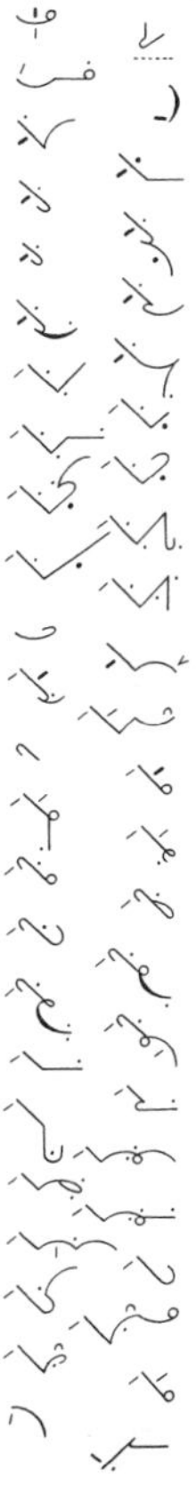

o'ral
or'ange
ora'tion
or'ator
or'atory
orb
or'bit
or'chard
or'chestra
orches'tral
or'chestrate
or'chid
ordain'
ordained'
or'deal
or'der
or'dered
or'dering
or'derliness
or'derly
or'dinance
or'dinarily
or'dinary
ord'nance
ore
or'gan
organ'ic
organ'ically
or'ganism
or'ganist
organiza'tion
or'ganize
or'ganized
or'ganizer
*or'ganiz*ing
or'gy
o'rient
orien'tal
or'igin
orig'inal
original'ity
orig'inate
orig'inated
orig'inating
origina'tion
orig'inator

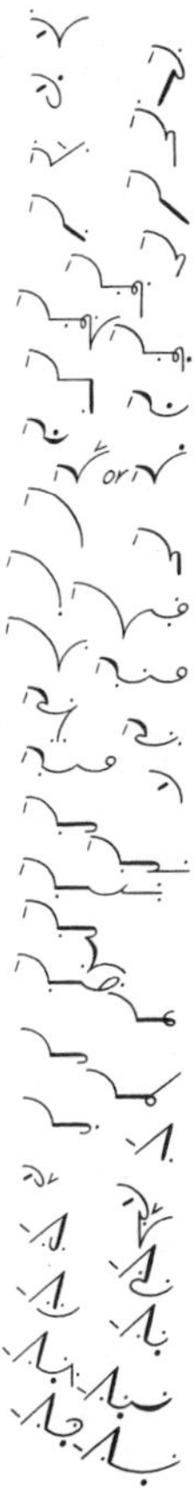

or'nament
ornamen'tal
ornamenta'-tion
ornate'
or'phan
or'thodox
os'cillate
oscilla'tion
os'cillograph
osten'sibly
ostenta'tion
ostenta'tious
os'teopath
os'tracize
os'trich
oth'er
oth'erwise
ought
ounce
our
ours
ourselves'
oust
oust'ed
oust'ing
out
out'board
out'break
out'burst
out'cast
out'*come*
out'cry
out'dated'
outdoors'
out'er
out'fit
out'fitter
out'going
out'ing
outland'ish
out'law
out'lay
out'let
out'line
out'look
out'lying
out*num'ber-ed*
out*num'ber*ing
out-of-date'
out-of-doors'
out'put
out'rage
outra'geous
out'right
out'set
out'side
outsi'der
out'size
out'skirts
outstand'ing
outstretch'
outstrip'
outvote'
out'ward
out'wardly
out'wards
outwit'
o'val
ova'tion
ov'en
o'ver
*o'ver*alls
overbal'ance
overbal'anced
*over*bear'ing
*o'ver*board
*over*bur'dened
*over*came'
*o'ver*cast
*o'ver*charge, *n.*
*over*charge', *v.*
*o'ver*coat
overcome'
*over*com'ing
*over*con'fident
*over*crowd'ed
*over*do'
*o'ver*dose, *n.*
*over*dose', *v.*
*o'ver*draft
*over*drawn'
*over*due'

{*o'ver*flow, *n.*
{*over*flow', *v.*
*over*grown'
*over*hang'
*over*haul'
*over*hauled'
over-head'
*o'ver*heads
*over*hear'
*over*heard'
*over*joyed'
*o'ver*land
{*o'ver*load, *n.*
{*over*load', *v.*
*over*look'
*o'ver*pass
*over*pow'er
*o'ver*ride'
*over*ruled'
*over*seas'
*over*see'
*o'ver*seer
*over*shad'ow
*o'ver*shoes
*o'ver*sight
o'ver-staffed'
*over*step'
*over*strain'
*over*take'
{*o'ver*tax, *n.*
{*over*tax', *v.*
*over*throw'

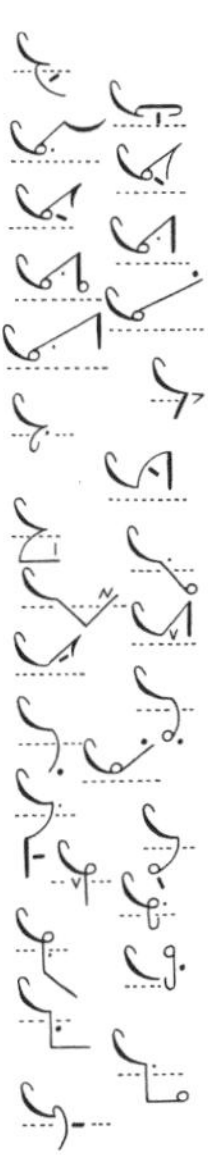

*over*thrown'
*o'ver*time
*over*took'
o'verture
*over*turn'
{*o'ver*weight, *n.*
{*over*weight', *v.*
*over*whelm'
{*o'ver*work, *n.*
{*over*work', *v.*
owe
owed
owes
ow'ing
owl
own
owned
*own'*er
*own'*ership
*own'*ing
ox
ox'en
ox'ide
oxidiza'tion
ox'idize
ox'ygen
oys'ter
oys'ter-shell
o'zone

P

pa
pace
paced
pacif'ic
pac'ified
pa'cifism
pa'cifist
pac'ify
pack
pack'age
pack'er
pack'et
pact
pad
pad'ded
pad'ding
pad'dle
pad'lock
pad'locked
paediat'rics
pa'gan
page
pag'eant
pag'eantry
paid
pail
pain
pained
pain'ful
pain'fully
pain'less
pains
pains'taking
paint
paint'ed
paint'er
paint'ing
pair
pal
pal'ace

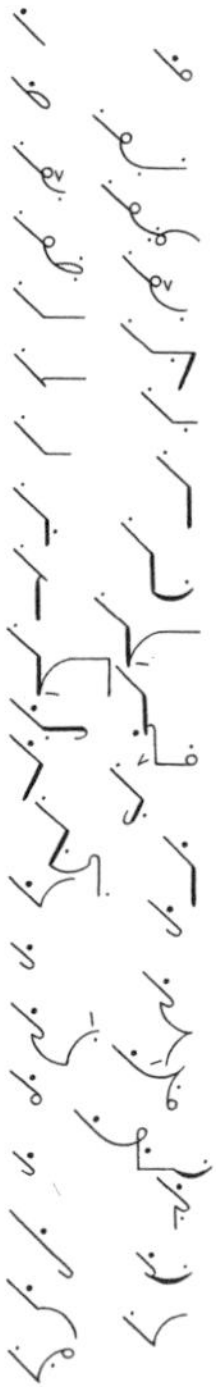

pal'atable
pal'ate
pala'tial
pale
pal'ette
palisade'
pall
pal'liate
pallia'tion
pal'liative
pal'lid
pal'lor
palm
palm'ist
pal'mistry
palm'-oil
pal'pable
pal'pitate
pal'pitated
palpita'tion
pal'try
pam'per
pam'pered
pam'pering
pam'phlet
pan
panace'a
panama'
pandemo'nium
pan'der
pan'dered
pane
pan'el
pang
pan'ic
pan'ic-stricken
panora'ma
panoram'ic

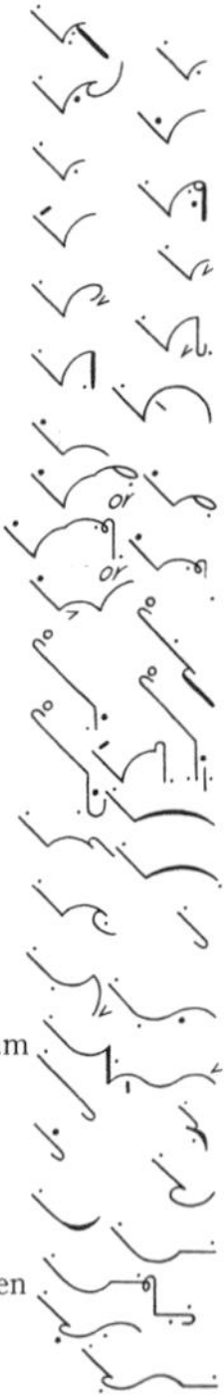

pant
pantech'nicon
pant'ed
pan'tomime
pan'try
papa'
pa'pal
pa'per
papy'rus
par
par'able
par'achute
parade'
par'adise
par'adox
paradox'ical
par'affin
par'agon
par'agraph
par'allel
par'alleled
par'alyse
par'alysed
par'alysing
paral'ysis
paralyt'ic
par'amount
paranoi'a
par'apet
paraphernal'lia
par'aphrase
par'asite
pa'rasites
parasol'
par'cel
par'cel(l)ed
parch
parch'ment
par'don
par'donable
pare
pa'rent
pa'rentage
paren'tal
paren'thesis
parenthet'ic
parenthet'ical

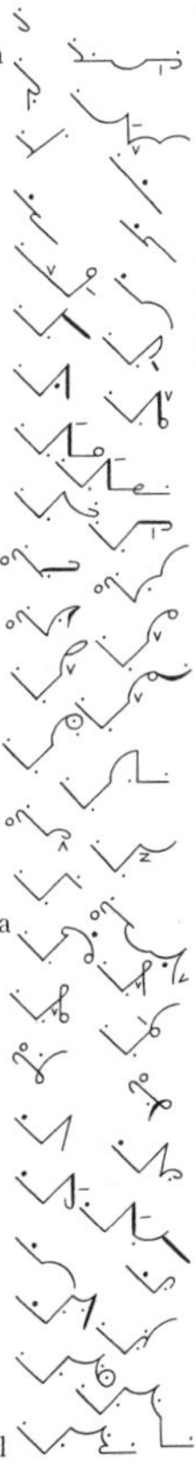

par'ish
parish'ioner
Paris'ian
par'ity
park
par'king
par'lance
par'ley
par'liament
parliamen'tary
par'lour
par'lous
paro'chial
par'ody
parole'
par'oxysm
(parquet', *n.*, *a.*
(par'quet, *v.*
par'ried
par'rot
par'ry
pars'ec
parsimo'nious
par'simony
pars'ley
pars'nip
par'son
part
partake'
part'ed
par'tial
partial'ity
partic'ipant
partic'ipate
partic'ipated
partic'ipating
participa'tion
par'ticle
partic'ular
partic'ularize
*partic'ular*ly
part'ing
par'tisan
parti'tion
parti'tioned
parti'tionist

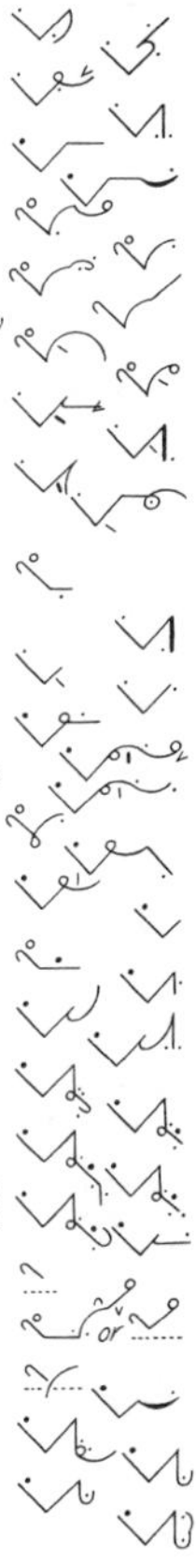

part'ly
part'ner
part'nership
part'-time
par'ty
pass
pass'able
pas'sage
passed
pas'senger
pas'sion
pas'sionate
pas'sive
pas'sively
pass'port
pass'*word*
past
paste
paste'board
pa'sted
pas'tel
pastiche'
pastille'
pas'time
past'mas'ter
pas'tor
pas'toral
pa'stry
pas'ture
pat
patch
pat'ent
pat'ented
patentee'
pater'nal
path
pathet'ic
pathet'ically
pa'thos
pa'tience
pa'tient
pa'tiently
pa'triarch
pat'riot
patriot'ic
pat'riotism
patrol'
patrolled'

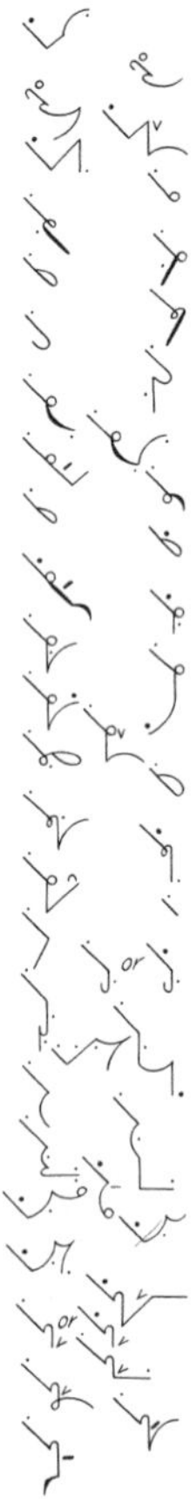

pa'tron
pat'ronage
pat'ronize
pat'ter
pat'tern
pau'city
pau'per
pause
paused
paus'ing
pave
pave'ment
pavil'ion
pav'ing
paw
pawn
pawn'broker
pawned
pawn'shop
pay
pay'able
payee'
pay'er
pay'ing
pay'master
pay'ment
pea
peace
peace'able
peace'ful
peace'fully
peach
peak
peal
pealed
pear
pearl
peas'ant
peas'antry
peb'ble
peck
pecula'tion
{*pecu'liar*
{*peculiar'ity*
*pecu'liar*ly
pecu'niary
ped'agogic
ped'agogy

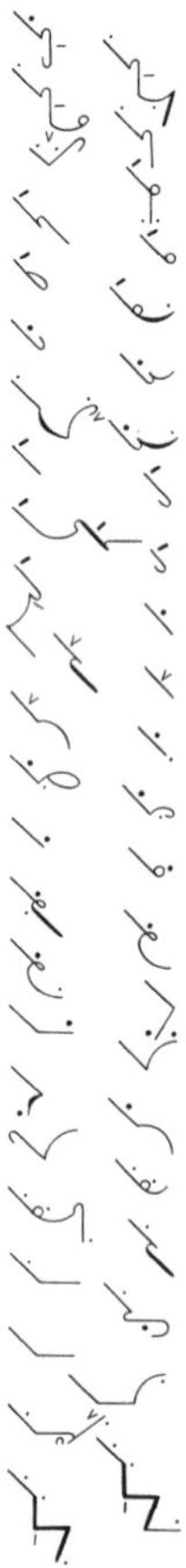

ped'al
ped'ant
pedan'tic
ped'dle
ped'estal
pedes'trian
ped'igree
ped'lar
peek
peel
peeled
peel'ing
peep
peeped
peep'ing
peer
peer'age
peer'ing
pee'vish
pee'vishly
peg
pel'let
pellu'cid
pelt
pelt'ed
pen
pe'nal
pe'nalize
pen'alty
pen'ance
pence
pen'cil
pen'cil(l)ed
pend'ant
pend'ent
pend'ing
pen'dulous
pen'dulum
pen'etrate
pen'etrated
penetra'tion
penicill'in
penin'sula
pe'nis
pen'itence
pen'itent
peniten'tiary
pen'manship

pen'niless
pen'ny
pen'sion
pen'sioned
pen'sioner
pen'sioning
pen'sive
pent
penu'rious
pen'ury
peo'ple
peo'pled
pep
pep'per
pep'sin
per
peram'bulate
peram'bulator
per an'num
perceive'
per cent'
percent'age
percep'tible
percep'tion
perch
per'colate
per'colator
percus'sion
perdi'tion
per'emptory
peren'nial
per'fect
per'fected
perfec'tion
per'fectly
per'fidy
per'forate
perfora'tion
perform'
perform'ance
performed'
perform'er
*perform'*ing
{per'fume, *n.*
{perfume', *v.*
perfunc'tory

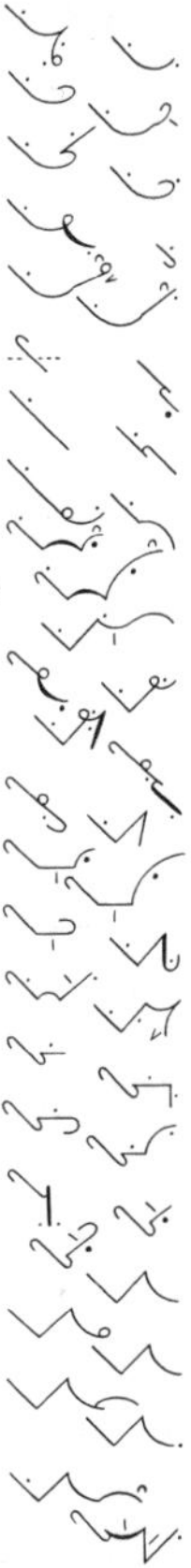

perhaps′
per′il
per′ilous
pe′riod
period′ical
per′iscope
per′ish
per′ishable
per′ished
per′jure
per′jurer
per′jury
per′manency
per′manent
per′manently
per′meate
permis′sible
permis′sion
{per′mit, *n.*
{permit′, *v.*
per′mutate
perni′cious
perox′ide
perpendic′ular
per′petrate
per′petrated
perpet′ual
perpet′uate
perpet′uated
perpetu′ity
perplex′
perplex′ity
per′quisite
per′secute
persecu′tion
per′secutor
persever′ance
persevere′
persevered′
perseve′ringly
Per′sian
persist′
persist′ence
persist′ent
persist′ently
persist′ing
per′son

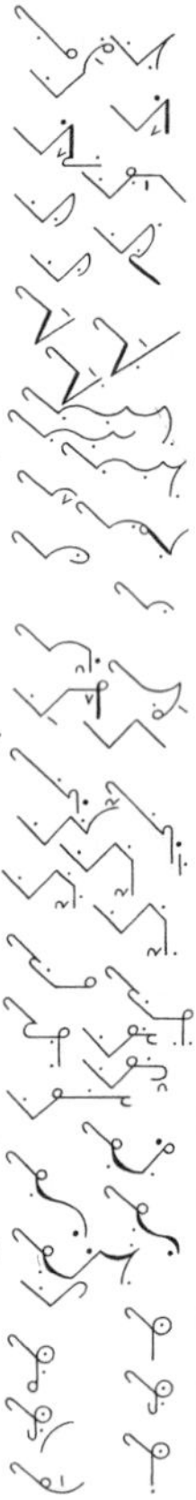

per′sonal
personal′ity
personifica′-
tion
personnel′
perspec′tive
perspicac′ity
perspicu′ity
perspira′tion
perspire′
persuade′
persua′ded
persua′sion
persua′sive
pert
pertain′
pertained′
pertain′ing
pertinac′ity
per′tinent
perturb′
peru′sal
peruse′
pervade′
perva′ded
perverse′
{per′vert, *n.*
{pervert′, *v.*
pes′simism
pes′simist
pessimis′tic
pest
pes′ter
pes′tered
pes′tilence
pes′tilent
pet
pet′al
peti′tion
peti′tioned
peti′tioner
pet′rified
pet′rify
pet′rol
petro′leum
pet′ted
pet′ticoat
pet′ty

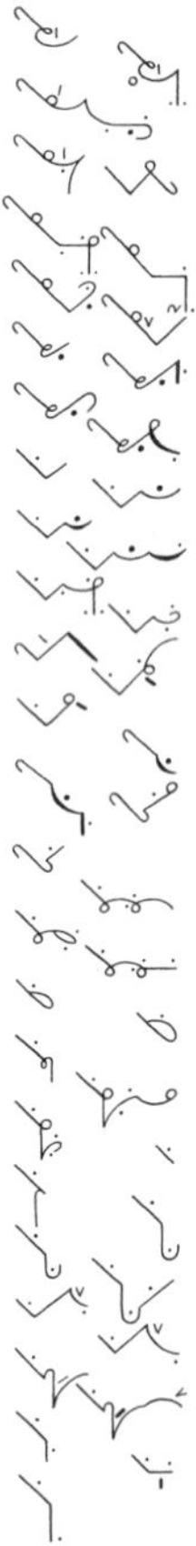

pet'ulance
pet'ulant
pew
pew'ter
phan'tasy
phan'tom
pharmaceu'-tical
phar'macist
phar'macy
phase
phenobar'-bitone
phenom'ena
phenom'enal
phenom'enon
phi'al
philanthrop'ic
philan'thropist
philan'thropy
philat'elist
philat'ely
philharmon'ic
philos'opher
philosoph'ic
philosoph'ical
philos'ophy
phlegmat'ic
phob'ia
phonet'ic
phonet'ics
phon'ograph
phos'phate
phos'phide
phos'phorus
pho'to
pho'tograph
photog'rapher
photograph'ic
photog'raphy
photogravure'
pho'ton
phrase
phys'ic

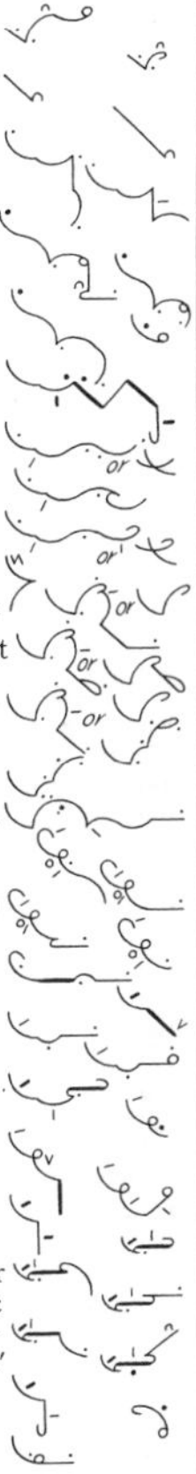

phys'ical
physi'cian
phys'icist
phys'ics
physiog'raphy
physiolog'ical
physiol'ogy
physiothe'rapist
physiothe'rapy
physique'
pi'anist
pian'o
pianofor'te
piaz'za
pick
pick'et
pick'le
pic'nic
picto'rial
pic'ture
picturesque'
pie
piece
piece'meal
piece'-work
pier
pierce
pierced
pi'ety
pig
pig'eon
pig'eonhole
pig'iron
pig'ment
pig'my
pile
pil'fer
pil'ferage
pil'fered
pil'ferer
pil'fering
pil'grim
pil'grimage
pill
pil'lage
pil'lar
pil'lion

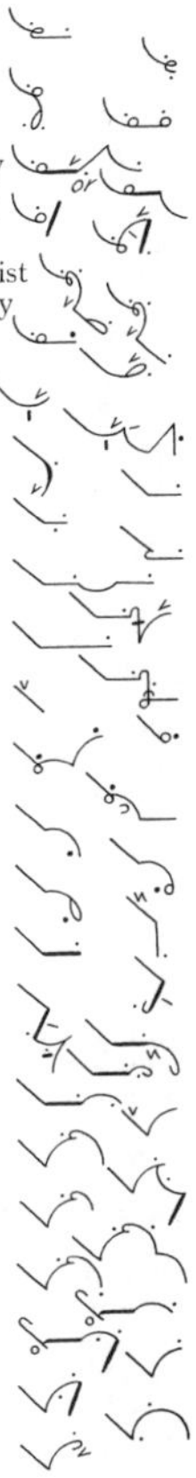

pil'low
pi'lot
pin
pin'cers
pinch
pine
pine'apple
pin'ion
pin'ioned
pink
pin'nacle
pint
pin'-up
pioneer'
pi'ous
pi'ously
pip
pipe
pi'per
pi'quancy
pi'quant
pique
pi'racy
pi'rate
pis'tol
pis'ton
pit
pitch
pitch'er
pit'eous
pit'fall
pith
pit'iable
pit'iful
pit'iless
pit'man
Pitman'ic
Pit'manite
pit'tance
pit'y
piv'ot
piv'otal
plac'ard, *n.*
placard', *v.*
placard'ed
placate'
place
placed

plac'id
pla'giarism
pla'giarize
plague
plaid
plain
plain'est
plain'ly
plain'tiff
plain'tive
plait
plait'ed
plan
plane
plan'et
plank
planned
plant
planta'tion
plant'ed
plant'er
plas'ter
plas'tered
plas'terer
plas'tic
plate
plateau'
plat'form
plat'inum
plat'itude
plausibil'ity
plau'sible
play
played
play'er
play'ful
play'fulness
play'ground
play'ing
play'mate
play'room
play'thing
plea
plead
pleas'ant
pleas'antly
please

*pleas'ur*able
pleas'ure
pleat
plea'ted
plebe'ian
pledge
ple'nary
plen'teous
plen'tiful
plen'ty
pli'able
pli'ant
plied
pli'ers
plight
plod
plot
plough
ploughed
plough'ing
pluck
plug
plum
plu'mage
plumb
plumb'er
plumb'ing
plumb'-rule
plume
plumed
plump
plun'der
plun'dered
plunge
plu'ral
plus
plush
ply
pneumat'ic
pneumo'nia
poach
pock'et
pock'et-book
po'em
po'et
po'etess
poet'ic
poet'ical
po'etry
poign'ancy
poign'ant
point
point'ed
point'er
point'ing
point'less
poise
poi'son
poi'sonous
poke
po'lar
pole
police'
police'-court
police'man
pol'icy
pol'io
pol'ish
pol'ished
polite'
pol'itic
polit'ical
politi'cian
pol'itics
poll
pollute'
pollu'tion
pol'tergeist
polytech'nic
pol'ythene
pomp
pom'pous
pond
pon'der
pon'dered
pon'derous
pongee'
pontoon'
po'ny
pool
pooled
pool'ing
poop
poor
poor'er
poor'est

poor'house
pop
pope
pop'lar
pop'lin
pop'pycock
pop'ulace
pop'ular
popular'ity
popula'tion
pop'ulous
porce'lain
porch
pore
pork
por'ous
por'poise
por'ridge
port
port'able
port'al
portend'
por'tent
porten'tous
port'er
portfo'lio
port'hole
port'ico
port'ière
por'tion
portman'teau
por'trait
por'traiture
portray'
portray'al
portrayed'
Portuguese'
pose
poseur'
posi'tion
pos'itive
pos'itively
possess'
possessed'
posses'sion
possess'ive
possess'or

possibil'ity *or*
pos'sible
post
post'age
post'al
post'card
post'date
post'dated
post'er
poster'ity
post'-free
post-haste'
post'humous
post'ing
post'man
post'mark
post'master
post'-office
postpone'
postponed'
postpone'ment
postpon'ing
post'script
pos'ture
pot
pot'ash
potas'sium
pota'to
pota'toes
po'tency
po'tent
poten'tial
po'tion
pot'ter
pot'tery
pouch
poul'tice
poul'try
pounce
pounced
pounc'ing
pound
pour
poured
pov'erty
pow'der
pow'ders

pow'er
pow'erful
pow'erless
*practic*abil'ity
prac'ticable
prac'tical
prac'tice
prac'tise
prac'tised
*prac'tis*ing
practi'tioner
prai'rie
praise
praised
praise'worthy
prance
pranced
prank
pray
prayed
prayer
pray'ing
preach
preach'er
preach'ing
pream'ble
preca'rious
precau'tion
precau'tionary
precede'
prece'dence
prece'dent, *a.*
prec'edent, *n.*
pre'cept
pre'cinct
pre'cious
prec'ipice
precip'itate, *n., a.*
precip'itate, *v.*
precise'
precise'ly
precis'ion
preclude'
preco'cious
precoc'ity
preconceive'

predeces'sor
predic'ament
predict'
predict'able
predict'ed
predic'tion
predispose'
predom'inance
predom'inant
predom'inantly
predom'inate
pre-em'inence
pre-em'inent
pre'fab
pref'ace
pref'aced
prefer'
pref'erable
pref'erence
preferen'tial
preferred'
pre'fix, *n.*
prefix', *v.*
preg'nant
prehistor'ic
prej'udice
prej'udiced
prejudi'cial
prejudi'cially
*prej'udic*ing
prel'ate
prelim'inary
prel'ude
premature'
premed'itate
premed'itated
premedita'tion
prem'ier
prem'ise, *n.*
premise', *v.*
pre'mium
pre-nat'al
prepaid'
prepara'tion
prepar'atory

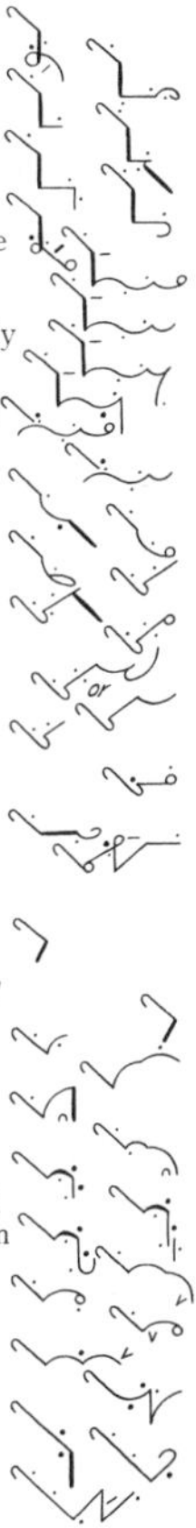

prepare'
prepared'
prepar'ing
prepon'der-
ance
prepon'derat-
ing
preposi'tion
prepossess'ing
prepos'terous
prereq'uisite
prerog'ative
Presbyte'rian
prescribe'
prescrip'tion
pres'ence
pres'ent, *n.*, *a.*
present', *v.*
present'able
presenta'tion
pres'ently
preserva'tion
preserv'ative
preserve'
preside'
pres'idency
pres'ident
presiden'tial
presi'ding
press
pressed
press'ing
pres'sure
prestige'
presu'mably
presume'
presumed'
presump'tion
presump'tive
presump'tuous
pretence'
pretend'

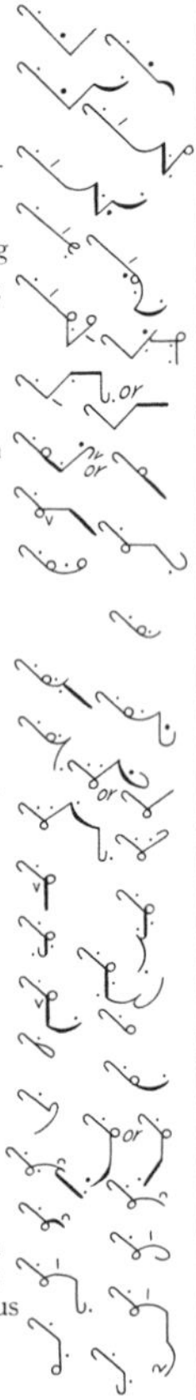

pretend'ed
pretend'ing
preten'tious
pre'text
pret'ty
prevail'
prevailed'
prevail'ing
prev'alence
prev'alent
prevar'icate
prevar'icator
prevent'
prevent'ed
prevent'ing
preven'tion
pre'view
pre'vious
pre'viously
prey
price
priced
price'less
prick
prick'ly
pride
priest
pri'marily
pri'mary
pri'mate
prime
pri'mer
prime'val, primae'val
prim'itive
prim'rose
prince
prin'cess
prin'cipal
prin'cipally
*prin'cipal*ship
prin'ciple
prin'cipled
print
print'ed
print'er
print'ing

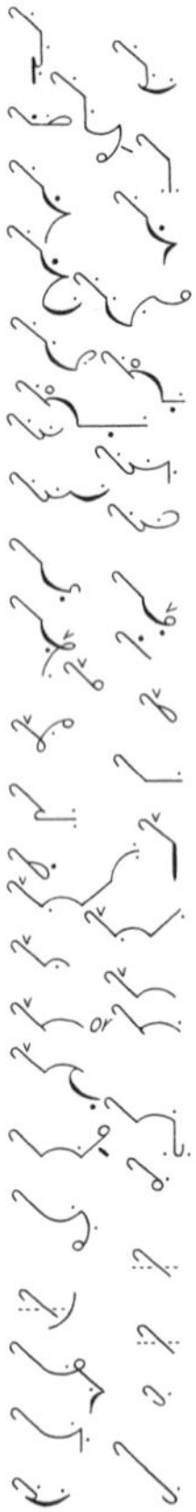

pri'or
prior'ity
pris'on
pris'oner
pri'vacy
pri'vate
priva'tion
priv'ilege
prize
{*probabil'ity*
prob'able
prob'ably
pro'bate
proba'tion
proba'tionary
probe
probed
prob'lem
problemat'ic
proce'dure
proceed'
pro'cess
pro'cessed
proces'sion
proclaim'
proclaimed'
proclama'tion
procliv'ity
procon'sul
procras'tinate
procrastina'-
tion
proc'tor
procur'able
procure'
prod
prod'igal
prodig'ious
prod'igy
prod'uce, *n.*
produce', *v.*
produ'cer
prod'uct
produc'tion
produc'tive
***produc'tive*ly**
***productiv'*ity**
profane'

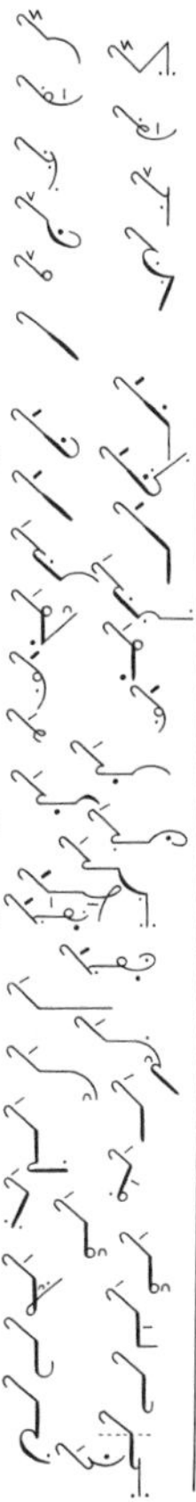

profan'ity
profess'
professed'
profess'ing
profes'sion
profes'sional
profes'sional-
ism
profes'sor
prof'fer
prof'fered
{*profi'ciency*
profi'cient
profi'ciently
pro'file
prof'it
prof'itable
prof'ited
profiteer'
prof'ligate
profound'
profuse'
profu'sion
prog'eny
proges'terone
prognos'tic
prognostica'-
tion
pro'gramme,
pro'gram
pro'gress, *n.*
progress', *v.*
progres'sive
prohib'it
prohib'ited
prohib'iting
prohibi'tion
prohibi'tive
{***pro'ject**, n.*
***project'**, v.*
project'ed
***project'*ing**
projec'tion
project'or
proleta'rian
proleta'riat
prolif'erate

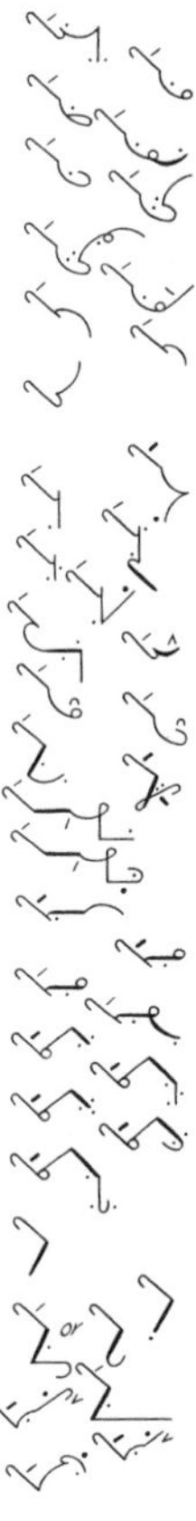

prolif'ic
pro'logue
prolong'
prolonga'tion
prolonged'
promenade'
prom'inence
prom'inent
prom'inently
promiscu'ity
prom'ise
prom'issory
promote'
promo'ted
promo'ter
promo'tion
prompt
prompt'ed
prompt'ing
prompt'itude
prone
pro'noun
pronounce'
pronounce'-
ment
pronuncia'tion
proof
prop
propagan'da
prop'agate
propaga'tion
propel'
propelled'
propel'ler
propen'sity
prop'er
prop'erly
prop'erty
proph'ecy, *n.*
proph'esied
proph'esy, *v.*
proph'et
prophet'ic
propi'tiate
propi'tiated
propi'tious
propor'tion-ed
propor'tionate-
-ly
propo'sal
propose'
proposed'
proposi'tion
propound'
propound'ed
propri'etary
propri'etor
propri'ety
propul'sion
pro ra'ta
prosa'ic
prose
pros'ecute
pros'ecuted
prosecu'tion
pros'ecutor
pros'pect, n.
prospect', v.
prospec'ted
prospec'tive
prospec'tus
pros'per
pros'pered
prosper'ity
pros'perous
pros'trate, *a.*
prostrate', *v.*
prostra'ted
prostra'tion
protect'
protec'tion
protec'tionist
protect'or
pro'test, *n.*
protest', *v.*
Pro'testant
protesta'tion
protest'ed
protest'ing
prot'on
protract'
protract'ed
protrude'
protrud'ed
proud

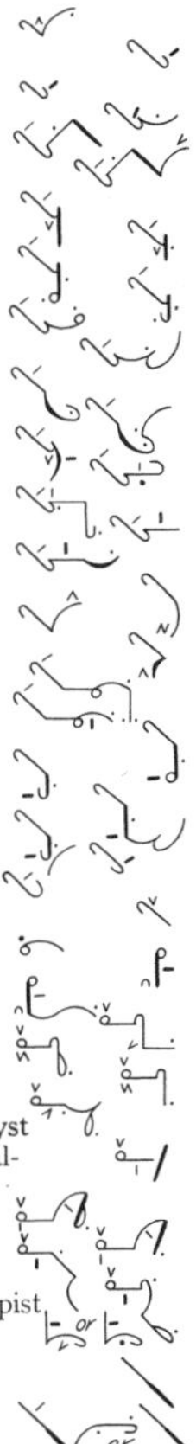

proud'ly
prove
proved
prov'en
prov'erb
prover'bial
provide'
provi'ded
prov'idence
prov'ident
prov'ince
provin'cial
provi'sion
provi'sional
provi'so
provoca'tion
provoc'ative
provoke'
provo'king
prow'ess
prowl
prowled
proxim'ity
prox'imo
pru'dence
pru'dent
pruden'tial
pru'dently
prune
Prus'sian
pry
psalm
pseu'do
pseud'onym
psychiat'ric
psychi'atrist
psychi'atry
psycho'an'alyst
psycholog'ical-
-ly
psychol'ogist
psychol'ogy
psych'opath
psychother'apist
pto'maine
pub'lic
pub'lican

publica'tion
public'ity
pub'licly
{*pub'lish*
{*pub'lished*
pub'lisher
*pub'lish*ing
pud'ding
pud'dle
pu'erile
puff
pu'gilist
pugna'cious
pugnac'ity
puis'ne
pull
pulled
pulp
pul'pit
pulsa'tion
pulse
pum'ice
pump
pumped
pump'ing
punch
punch'-card
punct'ual
punctual'ity
punct'uate
punct'uated
punctua'tion
punct'ure
pun'ish
pun'ishment
pu'nitive
pu'ny
pup
pu'pil
pup'pet
pur'chase
pur'chaser
pur'chase-tax
pure
pure'ly
purge
purifica'tion

pur'ified
pur'ify
pur'ity
purloin'
pur'ple
{pur'port, *n.*
{purport', *v.*
pur'pose
pur'poseful
pur'posely
purse
purs'er
pursu'ant
pursue'
pursued'
pursu'er

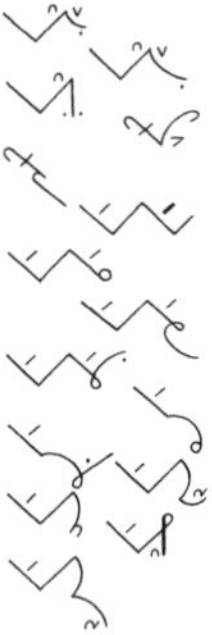

pursuit'
purvey'
push
pushed
put
pu'trefied
pu'trefy
pu'trid
put'ter
put'ting
put'ty
puz'zle
puz'zled
puz'zling
pyjam'as
pyl'on
pyr'amid

Q

quack
quacked
quad'rangle
quad'rant
quad'ruped
quad'ruple
quadru'plicate
quaff
quag'mire
quail
quaint
quake
quaked
qua'ker
qualifica'tion
qual'ified
qual'ify
qual'ity
qualm
quan'dary
quan'tify
quan'tity
qua'rantine
quar'rel
quar'reled, quar'relled
quar'relsome
quar'ry
quart
quar'ter
quar'terly
quar'termaster
quar'tern
quar'to
quartz
quash
qua'ver
qua'vered
qua'vering
quay
quay'side
queen
queen'ly
queer
quell
quelled
quench
que'ried
quer'ulous
que'ry
quest
ques'tion
ques'tionable
ques'tionably
ques'tioned
ques'tioning
ques'tionnaire
queue
quib'ble
quick
quick'en
quick'ened
quick'er
quick'ly
quick'ness
quick'sand
quick'silver
quick'witted
quies'cent
qui'et
qui'eten
qui'etly
qui'etness
qui'etude
quie'tus
quill
quilt
quinine'

quinquen'nial
quintess'ence
quip
quire
quit
quite
quits
quit'ted
quit'ter
quit'ting
quiv'er
quiv'ered
quiv'ering
quiz
quizzed
quiz'zical
quoin
quon'dam
quo'rum
quo'ta
quota'tion
quote
quo'ted
quo'ting

R

rab'bi
rab'bit
rab'ble
rab'id
race
race'course
raced
race'horse
ra'cer
ra'cial
ra'cialism
ra'cing
ra'cist
rack
rack'et
ra'dar
ra'diance
ra'diant
ra'diate
ra'diated
ra'diating
radia'tion
ra'diator
rad'ical
ra'dii
ra'dio
radioac'tive
ra'diogram
radiol'ogist
rad'ishes
rad'ium
ra'dius
raf'fle
raf'fled
raft
raft'er
rag
rage
rag'ged
ra'ging
raid
rail
rail'head
rail'ing
rail'lery
rail'road *or*
rail'way
rai'ment
rain
rain'bow
rain'drop
rain'fall
rain'ing
rain'proof
rain'-water
rain'y
raise
raised
rai'sin
rake
ral'lied
ral'ly
ral'lying
ram
ram'ble
ram'bler
ramifica'tion
rammed
ramp
rampage'
ram'pant
ram'part
ram'shackle
ran
ranch
ran'cid
ran'cour, ran'cor
rand

ran'dom
rang
range
ran'ger
rank
ranked
ran'kle
ran'kled
ran'sack
ran'som
rant
rap
rapa'cious
rapac'ity
rap'id
rapid'ity
rap'idly
ra'pier
rapped
rap'ping
rapt
rap'ture
rap'turous
rare
rare'ly
rar'ity
ras'cal
rascal'ity
rash
rash'ly
rasp
rasp'berry
rat
rat'able
rate
rate'able
rate'payer
rate'payers
rath'er
ratifica'tion
rat'ified
rat'ify
ra'ting
ra'tio
ra'tion *or*
ra'tional
rationaliza'tion

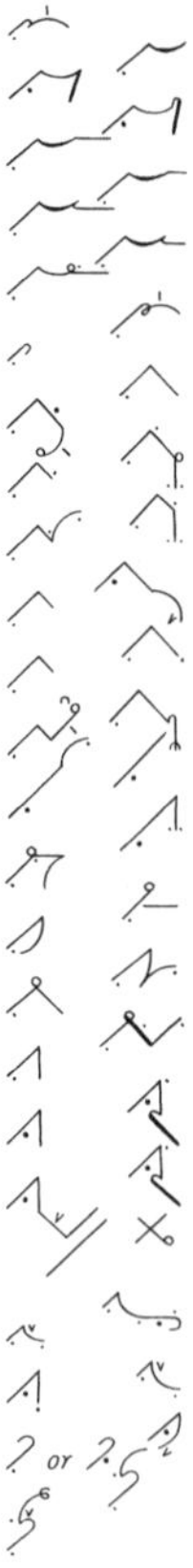

ra'tionalize
rat'tle
rau'cous
rav'age
rave
rav'el
ra'ven
rav'enous
ravine'
rav'ish
rav'ished
raw
ray
raze
ra'zor
reach
reached
reach'ing
react'
react'ed
reac'tion
reac'tionary
reac'tor
read
read, *p.t.*
read'able
readdress'
read'er
read'ier
read'ily
read'iness
read'ing
readjust'
readjust'ed
readjust'ment
readmis'sion
readmit'
read'y
read'ymade
reaffirm'
re'al
re'alism
re'alist
realist'ic
real'ity
re'alizable
realiza'tion
re'alize

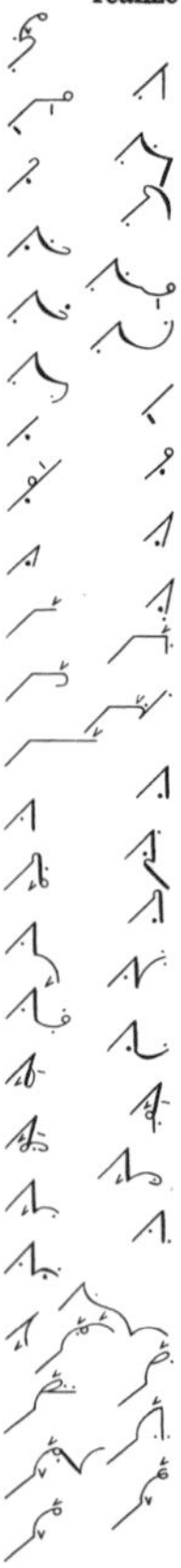

re′alized
re′alizing
re′ally
realm
ream
rean′imate
reap
reaped
reap′er
reap′ing
reappear′
reappear′ance
reappoint′
re*appoint′ment*
reappor′tion
rear
reared
re-arrange′
re-arrange′-
ment
rea′son
rea′sonable
rea′sonably
rea′soned
reassem′ble
reassert′
reassu′rance
reassure′
re′bate, *n.*
rebate′, *v.*
reb′el, *n.*
rebel′, *v.*
rebelled′
rebell′ion
rebell′ious
rebound′
rebuff′
re*build′*
re*build′ing*
rebuilt′
rebuke′
rebut′
rebut′tal
rebut′ting
recal′citrant
re*call′*
re*called′*
re*call′*ing

recant′
recapit′ulate
recapitula′tion
recap′ture
recast′
recede′
rece′ded
rece′ding
receipt′
receiv′able
receive′
received′
receiv′er
receiv′ership
re′cent
re′cently
recep′tacle
recep′tion
recep′tionist
recep′tive
receptiv′ity
recess′
reces′sion
reces′sional
re′charge′
rec′ipe
recip′ient
recip′rocal
recip′rocate
reciproca′tion
reciproc′ity
reci′tal
recita′tion
recite′
reci′ted
reci′ting
reck′less
reck′lessness
reck′on
reck′oned
reck′oning
reclaim′
reclaimed′
reclama′tion
recline′
reclined′
recli′ning
recluse′

recogni'tion
recog'nizance
rec'ognize
rec'ognized
recoil'
recoiled'
recollect'
recollec'tion
recommend'
recommenda'-tion
rec'ompense
rec'oncile
rec'onciled
reconcilia'tion
recondi'tion
reconnoi'tre
reconsid'er
reconsidera'-tion
reconsid'ered
reconsid'ering
reconstruct'
reconstruct'ed
reconstruct'ing
reconstruc'tion
rec'ord, *n.*
record', *v.*
record'er
recount'
recount'ed
recount'ing
recoup'
recourse'
recov'er
recov'erable
recov'ered
recov'ery
rec'reant
rec'reate
recrea'tion
recrim'inate
recrimina'tion
recruit'
recruit'ed
recruit'ment
rect'angle
rectan'gular
rec'tify
rec'tifying
rec'titude
rec'tor
recum'bent
recu'perate
recu'perated
recu'perating
recupera'tion
recu'perative
recur'
recurred'
recur'rence
recur'rent
recur'ring
red
redeem'
redeem'able
redeemed'
redemp'tion
redeploy'
red'-hot
redistrib'ute
red'olent
redoub'le
redound'
redound'ed
redress'
red'-tape'
reduce'
reduced'
redu'cing
reduc'tion
redun'dant
re-ech'o
re-ech'oed
reed
reef
reef'er
reek
reel
re-elect'
re-elect'ed
re'-elec'tion
reeled
re-embark'
re-enact'

re-enact'ment
re-enforce'
re-engage'
re-en'ter
re-en'tered
re-*estab'lish*
re-*estab'lished*
re-*estab'lishment*
re'-examina'tion
re-exam'ine
refer'
referee'
ref'erence
referen'dum
referred'
refer'ring *or*
refill'
refine'
refine'ment
refi'ner
refi'nery
refit'
reflect'
reflect'ed
reflec'tion
reflec'tive
reflect'or
re'flex, *n.*, *adj.*
reflex', *v.*
reform'
reforma'tion *or*
reform'atory
reformed'
reform'er
*reform'*ing
refrac'tion
refrac'tory
refrain'
refrained'
refresh'
refreshed'
refresh'ing
refresh'ment
refrig'erate
refrig'erated
refrig'erating
refrigera'tion
refrig'erator
ref'uge
refugee'
refund'
refund'ed
refund'ing
refu'sal
ref'use, *n.*, *a.*
refuse', *v.*
refuta'tion
refute'
refu'ted
refu'ting
regain'
regained'
re'gal
regale'
regaled'
rega'lia
re'gally
regard'
regard'ed
regard'ing
regard'less
re'gency
regen'erate, *n.*, *adj.*
regen'erate, *v.*
regen'erated
regenera'tion *or*
re'gent
régime'
reg'imen
reg'iment
regimen'tal
re'gion
re'gional
reg'ister
reg'istered
reg'istering
reg'istrar *or*
registra'tion
reg'istry

regret'
regret'ful
regret'table
regret'ted
regret'ting
reg'ular
regular'ity
*reg'ular*ly
reg'ulate
reg'ulated
reg'ulating
regula'tion
reg'ulator
rehabil'itate
rehabilita'tion
rehears'al
rehearse'
rehearsed'
rehears'ing
reign
reigned
reimburse'
reimbursed'
reimburse'-
ment
rein
reincarna'tion
rein'deer
reined
reinforce'
reinforced'
reinforce'ment
reinforc'ing
reinsert'
reinsert'ed
re*inspec'tion*
reinstate'
reinstat'ed
reinstate'ment
reinstat'ing
re*insur'ance*
reinsure'
reinvest'
re*invest'ment*
reis'sue
reis'sued

reit'erate
reit'erated
reitera'tion
reject'
reject'ed
rejec'tion
rejoice'
rejoiced'
rejoin'
rejoin'der
rejoined'
relapse'
relapsed'
relate'
rela'ted
rela'tion
rela'tionship
rel'ative
rel'atively
relativ'ity
relax'
relax'ation
relaxed'
relay', *n.*
re-lay', *v.*
release'
released'
releas'ing
rel'egate
relega'tion
relent'
relent'ed
relent'ing
relent'less
rel'evancy
rel'evant
reliabil'ity
reli'able
reli'ance
reli'ant
rel'ic
relied'
relief'
relieve'
relieved'
relig'ion *or*

relig'ious
relig'iously
relin'quish
relin'quished
*relin'quish*ing
rel'ish
rel'ished
reluc'tance
reluc'tant
reluc'tantly
rely'
rely'ing
remain'
remain'der
remained'
remain'ing
remand'
remand'ed
remark'
remark'able
remark'ably
remarked'
*remark'*ing
reme'dial
rem'edy
remem'ber
remem'bered
*remem'b*ering
*remem'b*rance
remind'
remind'ed
remind'er
remind'ing
reminis'cence
reminis'cent
remiss'
remis'sion
remit'
remit'tance
rem'nant
remod'el
remon'strance
remon'strant
remon'strate
*remon'strat*ed
*remon'strat*ing

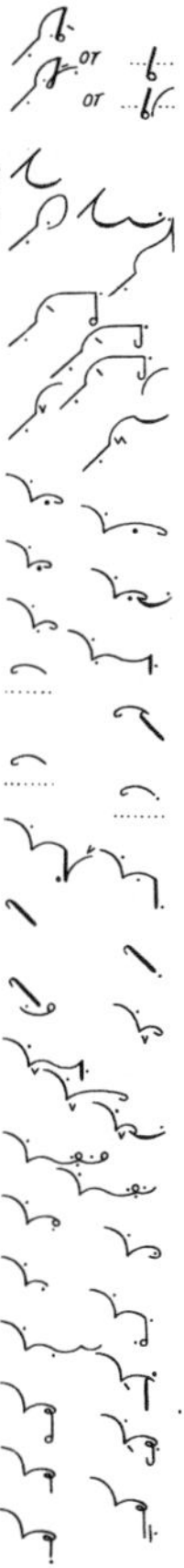

remorse'
remorse'ful
remorse'less
remote'
remote'ly
remov'able
remov'al
remove'
removed'
remov'ing
remu'nerate
remu'nerated
remunera'tion
remu'nerative
rend
ren'der
ren'dered
ren'dering
ren'dezvous
ren'egade
renew'
renew'al
renewed'
renew'ing
renounce'
renounced'
ren'ovate
renova'tion
renown'
renowned'
rent
rent'al
rent'ed
re*num'ber-ed*
renuncia'tion
reoc'cupy
reop'en
re*organiza'tion*
reor'*ganize*
reor'*ganized*
reor'*ganiz*ing
reorienta'tion
repaid'
repair'
repaired'
repair'er
repair'ing
repara'tion

repartee'
repass'
repast'
repay'
repay'able
repay'ment
repeal'
repealed'
repeat'
repeat'edly
repeat'ing
repel'
repelled'
repel'lent
repent'
repent'ance
repent'ant
repent'ed
repent'ing
repercus'sion
repertoire'
rep'ertory
repeti'tion
repeti'tious
repet'itive
repine'
repined'
repi'ning
replace'
replace'able
replace'ment
replen'ish
replen'ished
replen'ishing
replete'
reple'tion
rep'lica
replied'
reply'
reply'ing
report'
report'ed
report'er
report'ing
repose'
repos'itory
reprehend'
reprehensible
reprehen'sion
represent'
representa'tion
represent'ative
represent'ed
*represent'*ing
repress'
repressed'
repres'sion
reprieve'
reprieved'
repriev'ing
rep'rimand, *n.*
reprimand', *v.*
re'print, *n.*
reprint', *v.*
reprint'ed
repri'sal
reproach'
reproached'
reproach'ful
reproach'fully
reproach'ing
rep'robate
reproduce'
re*produc'tion*
re*produc'tive*
reproof'
reprove'
reproved'
rep'tile
repub'lic
repub'lican
re*publica'tion*
re*pub'lish*
re*pub'lished*
repu'diate
repu'diated
repu'diating
repudia'tion
repug'nance
repug'nant
repulse'
repulsed'
repuls'ing
repul'sion

repul'sive
repul'sively
rep'utable
reputa'tion
repute'
repu'ted
request'
request'ed
request'ing *or*
req'uiem
require'
required'
require'ment
requir'ing
req'uisite
requisi'tion
requisi'tioned
requisi'tioning
requi'tal
requite'
re-read'
re-read', *p.t.*
rescind'
rescind'ed
res'cue
res'cued
res'cuer
res'cuing
research'
resem'blance
resem'ble
resem'bled
resent'
resent'ed
resent'ful
resent'ing
resent'ment
reserva'tion
reserve'
reserved'
reserv'ing
res'ervoir
reset'
reship'ment
reside'
resi'ded
res'idence
res'idency
res'ident
residen'tial
resid'ual
resid'uary
res'idue
resign'
resigna'tion *or*
resigned'
resign'ing
resil'ience
resil'iency
resil'ient
res'in
resist'
resist'ance
resist'ed
res'olute
res'olutely
resolu'tion
resolve'
resolved'
resolv'ing
res'onance
res'onant
resort'
resort'ed
resound'
resound'ed
resource'
resource'ful
respect'
*respect*abil'ity
*respect'*able
*respect'*ably
respect'ed
*respect'*ful
*respect'*fully
*respect'*ing
respect'ive
*respect'*ively
respira'tion
res'pirator
respir'atory
res'pite
resplen'dent

respond'
respond'ed
respon'der
respond'ing
response'
responsibil'-ities
{*responsibil'-ity*
respon'sible}
respon'sive
rest
res'taurant *or*
restau'rateur
rest'ed
rest'ful
rest'fully
rest'fulness
rest'ing
restitu'tion
rest'ive
rest'less
rest'lessly
rest'lessness
restora'tion
restor'ative
restore'
restored'
restrain'
restrained'
restrain'ing
restraint'
restrict'
restrict'ed
restrict'ing
restric'tion
result'
result'ant
result'ed
resume'
résumé'
resumed'
resu'ming
resump'tion
resurrec'tion *or*
resus'citate
resuscita'tion
re'tail, *n., a.*
retail', *v.*
retail'er
retain'
retained'
retal'iate
retal'iated
retal'iating
retalia'tion
retard'
retard'ed
reten'tion
reten'tive
ret'icence
ret'icent
ret'ina
ret'inue
retire'
retired'
retire'ment
retir'ing
retort'
retort'ed
retouch'
retrace'
retraced'
retra'cing
retract'
retreat'
retreat'ed
retreat'ing
retrench'
retrench'ment
retribu'tion
retrieve'
retrieved'
retriev'er
retriev'ing
ret'rograde
ret'rograded
ret'rospect
retrospec'tion
retrospec'tive
retrospec'tively
return'
return'able
returned'

return'ing
reu'nion
reunite'
re*valua'tion*
reveal'
revealed'
reveal'ing
rev'el
revela'tion
rev'elry
revenge'
revenged'
revenge'ful
rev'enue
rever'berate
rever'berated
rever'berating
reverbera'tion
reverb'erator
revere'
revered'
rev'erence
rev'erend
rev'erent
rev'erie
revers'al
reverse'
reversed'
revers'ible
revert'
revert'ed
revert'ing
review'
reviewed'
review'er
review'ing
revile'
revise'
revised'
revi'sing
revi'sion
revi'sionary
revi'sionist
revis'it
revi'val
revive'
revived'
revoke'
revolt'
revolt'ed
revolt'ing
revolu'tion
revolu'tionary
revolu'tionize
revolve'
revolved'
revolv'er
revul'sion
reward'
reward'ed
reward'ing
rewrite'
rewrit'ten
rhap'sody
rhe'ostat
rhes'us
rhet'oric
rhetor'ical
rheumat'ic
rheum'atism
rheu'matoid
rhinoc'eros
rhu'barb
rhyme
rhythm
rhyth'mic
rhyth'mical
rib
rib'ald
rib'bon
rice
rich
rich'er
rich'es
rich'est
rich'ly
rid
rid'dance
rid'dle
ride
ri'der
ridge
rid'icule
rid'iculed
ridic'ulous

ridic'ulously
rid'ing
rife
riff'raff
ri'fle
ri'fled
ri'fling
rift
rig
right
right'-angle
right'-angled
right'eous
right'eousness
right'ful
right'fulness
right'-*hand*
right'ing
right'ly
rig'id
rigid'ity
rig'or
rig'orous
rig'our
rile
riled
ri'ling
rim
rime
rind
ring
ringed
ring'er
ring'ing
ring'leader
ring'let
ring'-road
rink
rinse
rinsed
rins'ing
ri'ot
ri'oter
ri'otous
ri'otously
rip
ripe
ri'pen
ri'pened
ri'pening
ripped
rip'ping
rip'ple
rise
ris'en
risibil'ity
ris'ible
ri'sing
risk
risked
risk'ing
risk'y
ris'qué
rite
rit'ual
ri'val
ri'val(l)ed
ri'val(l)ing
ri'valry
riv'er
riv'et
riv'eted
riv'eting
road
road'hog
road'side
road'ster
road'way
road'worthy
roam
roamed
roam'er
roan
roar
roared
roast
roast'ed
roast'er
roast'ing
rob
rob'ber
rob'bery
robe
rob'in
rob'ot
robust'

robust'ly
rock
rock'er
rock'ery
rock'et
rock'ing
rod
rode
ro'dent
rode'o
roe
rogue
rogu'ish
rogu'ishly
rôle
roll
rolled
roll'er
roll'ing
roll'ing-stock
ro'man, Ro'man
romance'
roman'tic
romp
romped
romp'ing
rood
roof
roof'ing
roof'less
room
room'y
roost
roost'er
root
root'ed
rope
ro'sary
rose
ro'seate
ros'in
ros'ter
ros'trum
ro'sy
rot
Rotar'ian
ro'tary

rotate'
rota'ted
rota'tion
rote
rot'ted
rot'ten
rot'ting
rotund'
rotund'ity
rou'ble
rouge
rough
rough'en
rough'er
rough'ly
round
round'about
round'ed
round'ing
round'ly
rouse
roused
rous'ing
rout
route
routine'
rove
ro'ver
ro'ving
row (a rank)
row (a tumult)
row'diness
row'dy
row'dyism
rowed
row'lock
roy'al
roy'alist
roy'ally
roy'alty
rub
rubbed
rub'ber
rub'bing
rub'bish
ru'by
ruc'tion
rudder

rude
rude'ness
ru'diment
rudimen'tal
rudimen'tary
rue
rued
rue'ful
rue'fully
ruf'fian
ruf'fle
ruf'fled
ruf'fling
rug
rug'ged
ru'in
ruina'tion
ru'ined
ru'ining
ru'inous
rule
ruled
ru'ler
ru'ling
rum
rumble
ru'minate
rum'mage
ru'mour,
ru'mor
rump
rum'ple
rum'pled

run
run'away
run'-down'
run'way
rung
run'ner
run'ning
rupee'
rup'ture
rup'tured
ru'ral
ruse
rush
rushed
rush'ing
rusk
rus'set
Rus'sian
rust
rus'tic
rus'ticate
rust'ing
rus'tle
rus'tled
rus'tling
rust'y
rut
ruth
ruth'less
ruth'lessly
ruth'lessness
rye

S

Sab'bath
sa'ble
sabotage'
sa'bre
sack
sack'ing
sac'rament
sa'cred
sac'rifice
sac'rificed
sac'rilege
sacrile'gious
sad
sad'den
sad'der
sad'dest
sad'dle
sad'dled
sad'dler
sa'dism
sad'ly
safa'ri
safe
safe-con'duct
safe'-depos'it
safe'*guard*
saf'er
saf'est
safe'ty
saga'cious
sagac'ity
sage
said
sail
sailed
sail'ing
sail'or
saint
saint'ly
sake
sal'ad
sal'aried
sal'ary
sale
sale'able
sales'man
sales'manship
sales'woman
sa'lient
salin'ity
sal'low
sall'y
salm'on
saloon'
salt
salt'ed
salt'ing
salu'brious
sal'utary
saluta'tion
salute'
salu'ted
sal'vage
salva'tion
salve
salved
Samar'itan
same
sam'ple
sanato'rium
sanc'tified
sanc'tify
sanc'tion
sanc'tioned
sanc'tioning
sanc'tity
sanc'tuary
sanc'tum
sand
san'dal

sand'stone
sand'wich
sand'y
sane
sang
san'guine
san'itary
sanita'tion
san'ity
sank
sap
sap'per
sap'phire
sar'casm
sarcas'tic
sarcas'tically
sardine'
sa'ri
sarong'
sarsaparil'la
sartor'ially
sash
sat
satch'el
sate
sa'ted
sateen'
sa'tiate
sa'tiated
sati'ety
sat'in
sat'ire
satir'ical
sat'irist
satisfac'tion
satisfac'torily
satisfac'tory
sat'isfied
sat'isfy
sat'urate
sat'urated
sat'urating
satura'tion
Sat'urday
sauce
sauce'pan
sau'cer
saun'ter
saun'tered
saun'tering
sau'sage
sav'age
sav'agely
save
sa'viour
sa'vour, sa'vor
sa'voury
savoy'
saw
saw'dust
sawed
saw'ing
saw'mill
sawn
saw'yer
Sax'on
sax'ophone
say
say'ing
says
scab'bard
scaf'fold
scaf'folding
scald
scale
scaled
scalp
scamped
scam'per
scam'pered
scam'pering
scam'pi
scan
scan'dal
scan'dalous
scan'ner
scant
scant'ily
scant'ly
scant'y
scar
scarce
scarce'ly
scarce'ness
scar'city

scare
scare'monger
scarf
sca'ring
scar'let
scarred
scathe
sca'thing
scat'ter
scat'tered
scat'tering
scenar'io
scene
sce'nery
sce'nic
scent
scent'ed
scep'tic, skep'tic
scep'tical
scep'ticism
scep'tre
sched'ule or (U.S.)
sched'uled
scheme
sche'mer
schizophren'ia
schnör'kel
schol'ar
schol'arly
schol'arship
scholas'tic
school
school'boy
schooled
school'fellow
school'girl
school'house
school'master
school'mistress
school'room
school'teacher
schoon'er
sciat'ica
sci'ence
scientif'ic
scientif'ically
sci'entist
scin'tillating
scis'sors
scoff
scoffed
scoff'er
scoff'ing
scold
scone
scoop
scoot'er
scope
scorch
score
scored
scor'er
scor'ing
scorn
scorn'ful or
scorn'fully or
scorn'ing
Scot
Scotch, scotch
Scots'man
Scot'tish
scoun'drel
scour
scourge
scout
scowl
scowled
scowl'ing
scram'ble
scram'bled
scram'bling
scrap
scrape
scratch
scrawl
scrawled
scream
screamed
screech
screen
screened
screw

screwed
scrib'ble
scrib'bled
scrim'mage
scrip
script
Scrip'ture
scroll
scrounge
scrub
scrubbed
scru'ple
scru'pulous
scru'pulously
scru'pulous-
ness
scru'tinize
scru'tiny
scuf'fle
scuf'fled
scull
scull'er
scull'ery
sculp'tor
sculp'ture
scum
scur'ried
scur'rilous
scur'ry
scut'tle
scythe
sea
sea'board
sea'borne
sea'-coast
sea'faring
seal
sealed
sea'-level
seal'skin
seam
sea'man
sea'manship
seamed
sea'plane
sea'port
search

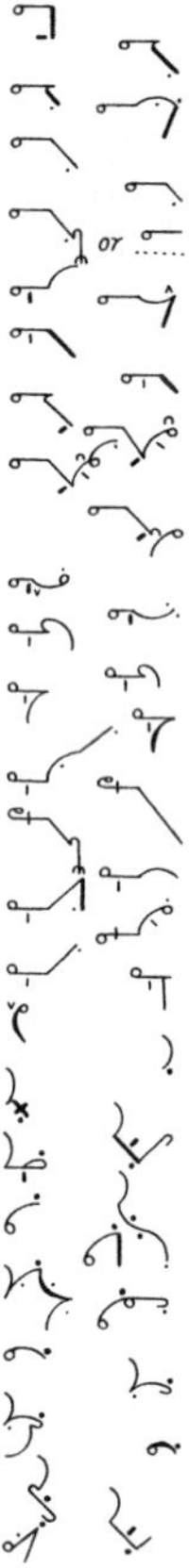

search'er
search'ing
search'light
sea'shore
sea'side
sea'son
sea'sonable
sea'sonal
sea'soned
seat
seat'ed
seat'ing
sea'ward
sea'weed
sea'worthy
secede'
seclude'
seclu'sion
seclu'sive
Sec'onal
sec'ond
sec'ondary
sec'onded
sec'onder
sec'ond-*hand*
sec'ondly
sec'ond-rate
sec'onds
se'crecy
se'cret
secreta'rial
secreta'riat
sec'retary
secrete'
secre'ted
secre'tion
se'cretive
sect
secta'rian
sec'tion
sec'tional
sec'tionalize
sec'tor
sec'ular
secure'
secured'
secure'ly
secu'ring

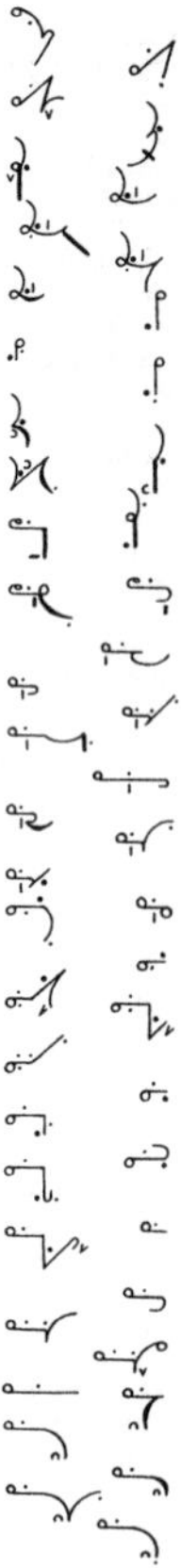

secu'rity
sedate'
sed'entary
sed'iment
sedi'tion
sedi'tious
see
seed
see'ing
seek
seem
seemed
seem'ingly
seen
seethe
seeth'ing
seg'ment
seg'regate
segrega'tion
segrega'tionist
seismol'ogy
seize
seized
seiz'ing
sei'zure
sel'dom
select'
select'ed
select'ing
selec'tion
select'ive
select'or
self
self-addressed'
self'-assur'ance
self-con'fidence
self-con'scious
self-contained'
self-control'
self-defence'
self-determina'-
tion
self-esteem'
self-ev'ident
self-explan'-
atory
self-***in'terest***
self'ish
self'ishly
self'ishness
self-possessed'
self-posses'sion
self-reli'ance
self-*respect'*
self-service'
self-willed'
sell
sell'er
Sel'lotape
selves'
sem'aphore
sem'blance
sem'ibreve
sem'icircle
sem'icolon
sem'inar
sem'inary
sen'ate
sen'ator
send
send'er
send'ing
se'nile
senil'ity
se'nior
senior'ity
sensa'tion
sensa'tional
sense
sense'less
sense'lessly
sense'lessness
sensibil'ity
sen'sible
sen'sibly
sen'sitive
sen'sitively
sen'sitiveness
sen'sual
sent
sen'tence
sen'tenced
sen'tient
sen'timent
sentimen'tal-ly
sen'tinel

sen'try
sep'arate, *adj.*
sep'arate, *v.*
sep'arated
sep'arating
separa'tion
sep'arator
Septem'ber
sep'tic
sepul'chral
sep'ulchre
se'quel
se'quence
seques'tered
serenade'
serene'
serene'ly
seren'ity
serge
ser'geant
se'rial
seria'tim
se'ries
se'rious
se'riously
se'riousness
ser'jeant
ser'mon
serv'ant
serve
served
serv'ice
serv'iceable
serv'ile
servil'ity
serv'ing
serv'itude
ses'sion
set
set'back
set'ting
set'tle
set'tled
set'tlement
set'tler
set'tling
sev'en
seventeen
seventeenth'
sev'enth
sev'entieth
sev'enty
sev'er
{*sev'eral*
{*sev'erally*
sev'erance
severe'
sev'ered
severe'ly
sev'ering
sever'ity
sew
sew'age
sewed
sew'er
sew'erage
sew'ing
sewn
sex
sex'ton
sex'y
shab'by
shack
shack'le
shack'led
shade
shad'ow
shad'owy
sha'dy
shaft
shaft'ing
shake
sha'ken
sha'ker
sha'ky
shall
shal'low
shal'lower
sham
shame
shamed
shame'ful
shame'fully
shame'less
shampoo'
shampooed'

shampoo'ing
sham'rock
shape
shape'less
share
shared
share'holder
sha'ring
shark
sharp
sharp'en
shar'pened
shar'pening
sharp'er
sharp'est
sharp'ly
shat'ter
shat'tered
shave
shaved
shav'ing
shawl
she
sheaf
shear
sheared
shear'ing
shears
sheath
sheathe
sheaves
shed
sheen
sheep
sheep'ish
sheep'ishly
sheer
sheet
sheet'ing
shelf
shell
shellac'
  shell'-lac
shelled
shell'fish
shel'ter
shel'tered
shel'tering

shelve
shemoz'zle
shep'herd
sher'bet
sher'iff
sher'ry
shield
shield'ed
shield'ing
shift
shift'ed
shift'ing
shift'less
shift'y
shil'ling
shim'mer
shim'mered
shim'mering
shin
shine
shin'gle
shi'ning
shi'ny
ship
ship'builder
ship'*building*
ship'ment
ship'*owner*
ship'per
ship'ping
ship'yard
shire
shirk
shirked
shirk'er
shirk'ing
shirt
shiv'er
shiv'ered
shiv'ering
shoal
shock
shod
shod'dy
shoe
shoe'maker
shone

shook
shoot
shoot'ing
shop
shop'keeper
shop'ping
shop'-stew'ard
shore
shorn
short
short'age
short'bread
short'-circ'uit
short'coming
short'en
short'er
short'est
short'hand
short'ly
shorts
short'sighted
short'-term
shot
should
shoul'der
shout
shout'ed
shout'ing
shove
shov'el
shov'el(l)ed
show
show'down
showed
show'er
show'ered
show'ering
show'ing
show'manship
shown
show'room
show'y
shrank
shrap'nel
shred
shrewd
shriek
shrill
shrine
shrink
shrink'age
shrink'ing
shriv'el
shroud
shroud'ed
shrub
shrug
shrunk
shrunk'en
shud'der
shud'dered
shuf'fle
shuf'fled
shun
shunt
shunt'ed
shunt'ing
shut
shut'ter
shut'tle
shy
shy'ly
sick
sick'en
sick'le
side
side'board
side'-car
side'-effect
side'light
si'ding
si'dle
siege
sieve
sift
sift'ed
sigh
sighed
sigh'ing
sight
sight'seeing
sight'seer
sign
sig'nal
sig'natory
sig'nature

sign'board
signed
sign'er
signif'icance
signif'icant
*signif'icant*ly
significa'tion
sig'nified
sig'nify
*sig'nify*ing
sign'ing
sign'post
sign'*writ'er*
si'lence
si'lencer
si'lent
si'lently
silhouette'
silicos'is
silk
sil'ly
sil'ver
sil'verware
sim'ilar
similar'ity
sim'ilarly
sim'ile
simil'itude
sim'mer
sim'mered
sim'mering
sim'per
sim'pered
sim'ple
sim'pler
simplic'ity
simplifica'tion
sim'plify
sim'ulate
sim'ulated
simulta'neous
sin
since
sincere'
sincere'ly
sincer'ity
si'necure
sin'ew
sin'ewy
sin'ful
sin'fully
sing
singe
singed
singe'ing
sing'er
sing'ing
sin'gle
sin'gle-handed
sin'gular
singular'ity
sin'ister
sink
sin'ner
sip
si'phon
sip'ping
sir
sire
si'ren
sir'loin
sis'al
sis'ter
sis'ter-in-law
sit
site
sit'ter
sit'ting
sit'uate
sit'uated
situa'tion
six
six'pence
six'penny
sixteen'
sixteenth'
sixth
six'ty
size
size'able
skate
ska'ted
ska'ter
ska'ting
skel'eton
sketch

sketched
sketch'ily
sketch'ing
sketch'y
skew
skew'er
ski
skid
skid'ding
skiff
skil'ful
skill
skilled
skim
skimmed
skimp
skin
skinned
skin'ning
skip
skipped
skip'per
skir'mish
skir'mished
skirt
skull
sky
sky'lark
sky'light
sky'scraper
sky'way
slab
slack
slack'en
slack'ened
slag
slain
sla'lom
slam
slan'der
slan'dered
slan'dering
slan'derous
slang
slant
slant'ed
slant'ing
slap

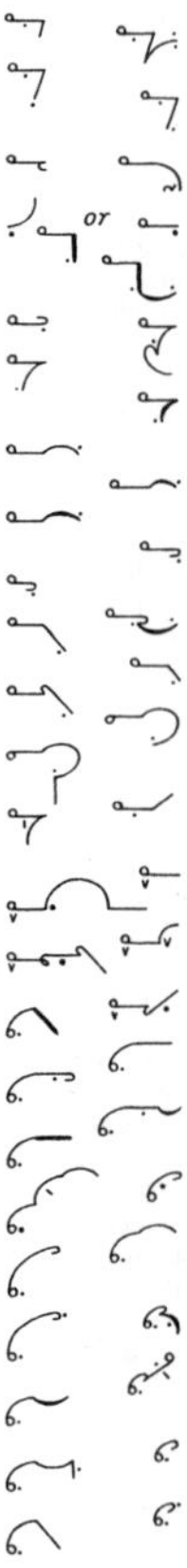

slapped
slap'ping
slash
slashed
slash'ing
slate
slaugh'ter
slaugh'tered
slaugh'ter-house
slave
sla'very
sla'vish
sla'vishly
slay
slay'er
sledge
sleek
sleep
sleep'er
sleep'ily
sleep'ing
sleep'less
sleep'lessness
sleep'y
sleet
sleeve
sleigh
sleight
slen'der
slept
sleuth
slew
slice
sliced
slick
slid
slide
slide'-rule
sli'ding
slight
slight'est
slight'ly
slim
slime
sling
slink
slip

slip'per
slip'pery
slip'ping
slip'road
slip'shod
slit
slo'gan
slope
slot
sloth
sloth'ful
slot'ted
slouch
slough (a bog)
slough (a cast skin)
slov'enly
slow
slow'ly
slow'ness
slug
slug'gard
slug'gish
slug'gishly
sluice
slum
slum'ber
slum'bered
slum'bering
slump
slung
slur
slurred
slur'ring
slush
sly
smack
small
small'er
small'est
smart
smart'en
smart'er
smart'est
smart'ly
smash
smashed
smat'ter

smat'tering
smear
smeared
smear'ing
smell
smelled
smelt
smelt'ed
smelt'er
smile
smiled
smi'lingly
smith
smog
smoke
smo'ker
smooth
smooth'er
smote
smoth'er
smoth'ered
smoul'der
smoul'dered
smudge
smug'gle
smug'gled
smug'gler
snack'-bar
snag
snail
snake
snap
snapped
snap'shot
snare
snared
sna'ring
snarl
snarled
snatch
snatched
snatch'ing
sneak
sneer
sneered
sneer'ing
sneeze
sniff

sniv'el
snob
snob'bery
snob'bish
snoop
snoop'er
snore
snort
snow
snow'drift
snowed
snow'fall
snow'shoes
snow'storm
snub
snuff
snug
so
soak
soaked
soap
soar
soared
sob
so'ber
sobri'ety
so'-called
socc'er
sociabil'ity
so'ciable
so'cial
so'cialism
so'cialist
socialist'ic
soci'ety
sociol'ogy
sociom'etry
sock
sock'et
sod
so'da
so'fa
soft
sof'ten
sof'tener
soft'ly
soft'wood
soil

soiled
soj'ourn
sol'ace
so'lar
sold
sol'der
sol'dered
sol'dier
sole
sole'ly
sol'emn
solem'nity
solemniza'tion
sol'emnize
sol'emnly
solic'it
solicita'tion
solic'ited
solic'itor
solic'itous
solic'itude
sol'id
solidar'ity
solid'ified
solid'ify
solid'ity
sol'idly
solil'oquize
solil'oquized
solil'oquy
sol'itary
sol'itude
so'lo
so'loist
solubil'ity
sol'uble
solu'tion
solve
solved
solv'ency
solv'ent
som'bre
some
some'body
some'*how*
some'one
som'ersault

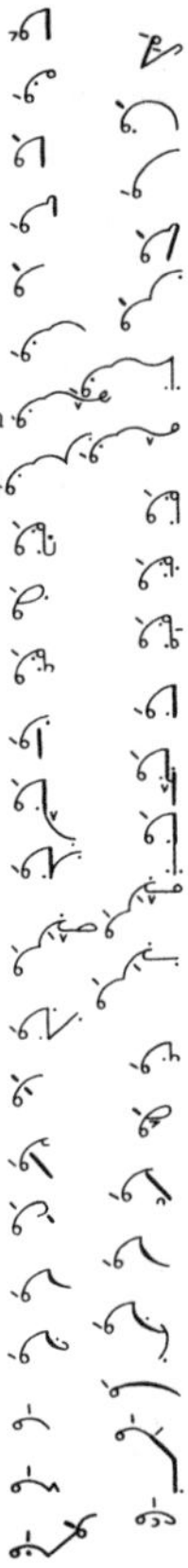

some'thing
some'time
some'what
some'where
son
song
song'ster
son'ic
son'-in-law
son'net
sonor'ity
sono'rous
sono'rously
soon
soon'er
soot
soothe
soothed
sooth'ing
sop
sophis'ticated
sophistica'tion
soporif'ic
sopra'no
sor'did
sor'didness
sore
sor'row
sor'rowful
sor'rowfully
sor'rowing
sor'ry
sort
sort'ed
sort'er
sort'ing
sought
soul
sound
sound'ed
sound'er
sound'est
sound'ing
sound'proof
sound'track
soup
sour
source

soured
south
south-east'
south-east'ern
south'erly
south'ern
south'erner
south'ward
south-west'
south-west'ern
souvenir'
sov'ereign
sov'ereignty
Sov'iet
sow (pig)
sow (to scatter)
sowed
sow'er
sow'ing
sown
space
spaced
space'-man
space'-ship
space'-station
space'-suit
spa'cious
spa'ciously
spade
span
span'gle
Span'iard
span'iel
Span'ish
spanned
spar
spare
spared
spar'ing
spar'ingly
spark
spark'le
spark'led
spark'ling
spar'row
sparse
sparse'ly
spar'sity

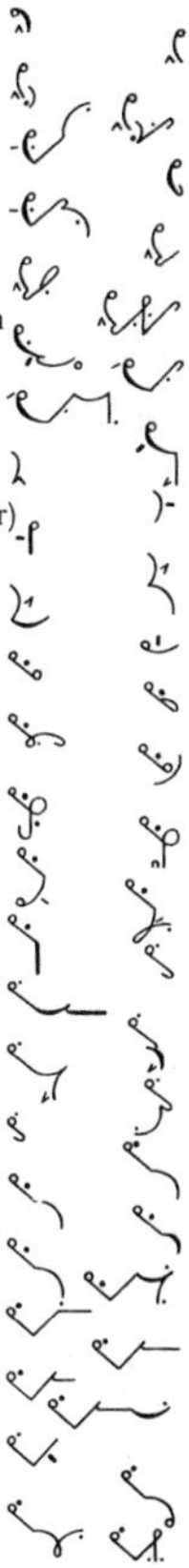

Spar'tan
spasm
spasmod'ic
spasmod'ically
spat
spate
spat'ter
speak
speak'er
speak'ing
spear
spe'cial
spe'cialist
special'ity
specializa'tion
spec'ialize
spe'cially
spec'ialty
spe'cie
spe'cies
specif'ic
specif'ically
specifica'tion
spec'ified
spec'ify
spec'ifying
spec'imen
spe'cious
speck
spec'tacle
spectac'ular
specta'tor
spec'tre
spectrom'eter
spec'ulate
spec'ulated
spec'ulating
specula'tion
spec'ulative
spec'ulator
sped
speech
speed
speed'ily
speedom'eter
speed'way
speed'y
spell

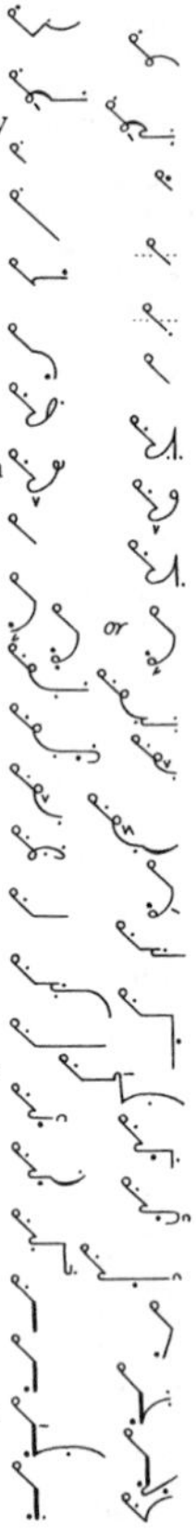

spell'bound
spelled
spell'ing
spelt
spend
spend'ing
spend'thrift
spent
sphere
spher'ical
sphinx
spice
spi'der
spike
spill
spilled
spilt
spin
spin'ach
spi'nal
spin'dle
spine
spin'ster
spi'ral
spire
spir'it
spir'ited
*spir'it*ual
spit
spite
spite'ful
spite'fulness
splash
splashed
splash'ing
spleen
splen'did
splen'didly
splen'dour
splice
splint
splin'ter
splin'tered
splin'tering
split
splutter'
splut'tered
splut'tering

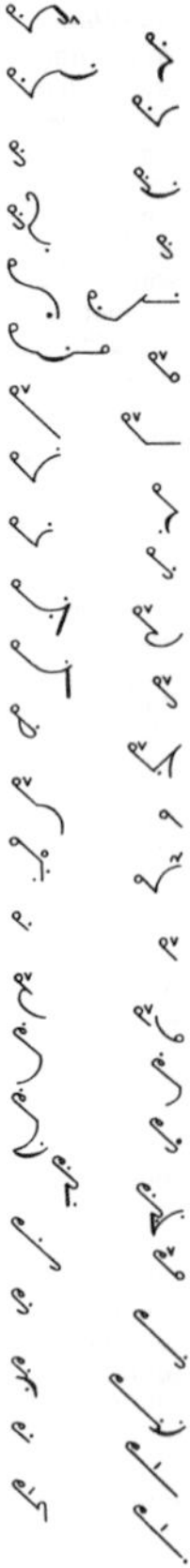

spoil
spoiled
spoilt
spoke
spo'ken
spokes'man
sponge
spon'sor
spon'sored
spontane'ity
sponta'neous
spool
spoon
sporad'ic
sport
sport'ing
sports'man
sports'manship
sports'wear
spot
spot'-check
spot'less
spouse
spout
sprain
sprained
sprain'ing
sprang
sprawl
sprawled
sprawl'ing
spray
spread
spread'ing
sprig
spright'ly
spring
spring'ing
spring'time
sprin'kle
sprin'kled
sprint
sprout
sprout'ed
spruce
sprung
spry
spun

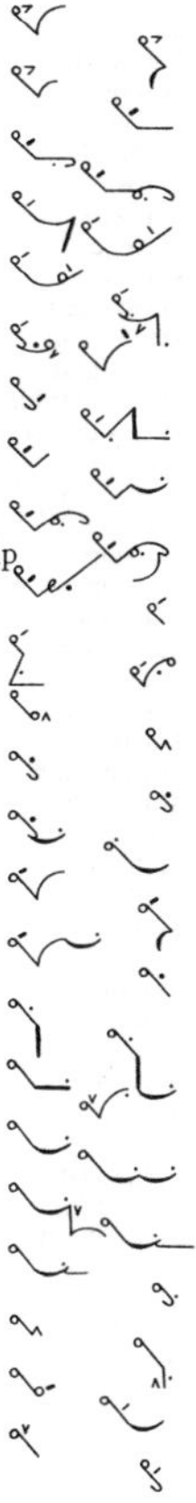

spur
spu'rious
spurn
spurned
spurn'ing
spurred
spurt
spy
spy'ing
squab'ble
squad
squad'ron
squal'id
squall
squall'y
squal'or
squan'der
squan'dered
squan'dering
square
squash
squaw
squeak
squeal
squeam'ish
squeeze
squint
squire
squirm
squir'rel
squirt
stab
stabbed
stabil'ity
sta'bilize
sta'bilizer
sta'ble
stack
sta'dium
staff
stag
stage
stage'craft
stag'ger
stag'gered
stag'gering
stag'nant
stagna'tion

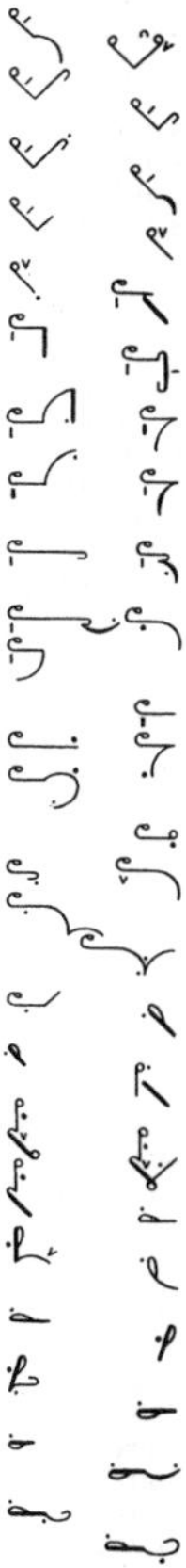

staid
stain
stained
stain'less
stair
stair'case
stair'way
stake
staked
stale
stalk
stalked
stalk'er
stall
stal'wart
stam'ina
stam'mer
stam'mered
stam'mering
stamp
stamped
stampede'
stanch
stand
stand'ard
standardiza'-tion
stand'ardize
stand'-by'
stand'-*in*
stand'ing
stand'point
stand'still
sta'ple
star
starch
starch'iness
stare
stared
sta'ring
stark
star'ring
star'ry
start
start'ed
start'er
start'le
start'led
start'ling
starva'tion
starve
starved
starv'ing
state
sta'ted
state'less
state'ly
state'ment
state'room
states'man
states'manlike
states'manship
stat'ic
stat'ically
sta'ting
sta'tion
sta'tionary
sta'tioned
sta'tioner
sta'tionery
statis'tical
statis'tically
statisti'cian
statis'tics
stat'ue
stat'ure
sta'tus
stat'ute
stat'utory
staunch
stave
stay
stayed
stay'ing
stead
stead'fast, sted'fast
stead'fastly
stead'ied
stead'ier
stead'iest
stead'ily
stead'y
steak
steal
stealth

stealth'y
steam
steam'boat
steamed
steam'er
steam'roller
steam'ship
steed
steel
steel'yard
steep
stee'ple
steer
steer'age
steered
steer'ing
stem
stench
sten'cil
stenog'rapher
stenograph'ic
stenog'raphy
sten'otypist
stento'rian
step
step'-ladder
stepped
step'ping
step'ping-stone
ster'eotyped
ster'ile
steril'ity
steriliza'tion
ster'ilize
ste'rilizer
ster'ling
stern
stern'er
stern'est
stern'ly
stet
steth'oscope
ste'vedore
stew
stew'ard
stew'ardess
stew'ardship
stich, stick
stiff
stiff'en
stiff'ened
sti'fle
sti'fled
sti'fling
stig'ma
stig'matize
still
stim'ulant
stim'ulate
stim'ulated
stim'ulating
stimula'tion
stim'ulus
sting
stint
stint'ed
stint'ing
sti'pend
stip'ulate
stip'ulated
stip'ulating
stip'ulation
stir
stirred
stir'ring
stir'rup
stitch
stitched
stitch'ing
stock
stock'broker
stock'holder
stock'ing
stock'ist
stock'pile
stock'piling
stock'taking
stodg'y
stoic
sto'ical
sto'icism
stoke

stok'er
stok'ing
stole
sto'len
stol'id
stom'ach
stone
stood
stooge
stool
stoop
stop
stop'page
stop'ping
stor'age
store
stored
store'keeper
stor'ing
storm
stor'y
stout
stout'er
stout'est
stout'heart'ed
stout'ly
stove
stow
stow'age
stow'away
stowed
stow'ing
strad'dle
strag'gler
straight
straight'away
straight'en
straight'ened
straight'ening
straight'er
straight'est
straightfor'-
ward
strain
strained
strain'er
strain'ing
strait

strait'en
strait'ened
strand
strand'ed
strange
strange'ly
stran'ger
stran'gle
stran'glehold
strap
straphang'er
stra'ta *or*
strat'agem
strateg'ic
strat'egy
strat'osphere
stra'tum *or*
straw
straw'berry
straw'board
stray
strayed
streak
stream
streamed
stream'ing
stream'line
street
strength
strength'en
strength'ened
strength'ening *or*
stren'uous
stren'uously
streptococ'cus
streptomy'cin
stress
stretch
stretch'er
stretch'ing
strew
strewed
strick'en
strict
strict'er
strict'est
strict'ly
stric'ture

stride
stri'dent
strife
strike
stri'ker
stri'king
string
strin'gency
strin'gent
strip
stripe
strip'tease
strive
strode
stroke
stroll
strolled
strong
stron'ger
stron'gest
strong'hold
strong'ly
strong'minded
strong'room
strop
strove
struck
struc'tural
struc'ture
strug'gle
strug'gled
strug'gling
strung
strut
strut'ted
strych'nin,
strych'nine
stub'born
stub'bornness
stuc'co
stuck
stud
stud'ded
stu'dent
stud'ied
stu'dio
stu'dious
stud'y

stud'ying
stuff
stum'ble
stum'bled
stum'bling
stum'bling-block
stump
stumped
stun
stunned
stung
stunt
stunt'ed
stupefac'tion
stu'pefy
stupen'dous
stu'pid
stupid'ity
stu'pidly
stu'por
stur'dy
stut'ter
stut'tered
stut'tering
style
styled
styl'i
sty'lish
sty'lishly
sty'lo
suave
subal'tern
subaquat'ic
subcommit'tee
subdivide'
subdivi'sion
subdue'
subdued'
subed'it
sub'hu'man
sub'ject, a.
subject', v.
subject'ed, p.p.
*subject'*ing
subjec'tion
subjec'tive

*subjec'tive*ly
subjoin'
subjoined'
sublet'
sublime'
sublim'ity
sub'marine
submerge'
submers'ible
submis'sion
submiss'ive
submit'
submit'ted
submit'ting
subnor'mal
subor'dinate, *n., a.*
subor'dinate, *v.*
subordina'tion
subpoe'na
subscribe'
subscribed'
subscri'ber
*subscrib'*ing
subscrip'tion
sub'sequent
sub'sequently
subserv'ient
subside'
subsi'ded
subsi'dence
subsid'iary
sub'sidize
sub'sidized
sub'sidizing
sub'sidy
subsist'
subsist'ed
subsist'ence
subson'ic
sub'stance
substan'tial
substan'tially
substan'tiate
substan'tiated
substantia'tion
sub'stitute
sub'stituted
substitu'tion
subsume'
sub'terfuge
subterra'nean
sub'tle
sub'tlety
subtract'
subtract'ed
subtrac'tion
sub'urb
subur'ban
suburb'ia
sub'urbs
sub'way
succeed'
succeed'ed
succeed'ing
success'
success'ful
success'fully
succes'sion
succes'sive
succes'sively
success'or
succinct'
suc'cour, suc'cor
succumb'
succumbed'
such
suck
suck'le
suc'tion
sud'den
sud'denly
sud'denness
sue
sued
suède
su'et
suf'fer
suf'ferance
suf'fered
suf'ferer

suffice'
sufficed'
suffi'ciency
suffi'cient
suffi'ciently
suf'fix, *n.*
suffix', *v.*
suf'focate
suf'focated
suf'focating
suffoca'tion
suf'frage
sug'ar
suggest'
suggest'ed
suggest'ing
sugges'tion
suggest'ive
suici'dal
su'icide
su'ing
suit
suitabil'ity
suit'able
suite
suit'ed
suit'ing
sulk'y
sul'len
sul'lenness
sul'phate
sul'phide
sul'phur
sulphu'ric
sul'tan
sul'try
sum
sum'marily
sum'marize
sum'mary
summed
sum'mer
sum'mit
sum'mon
sum'moned
sum'mons
sump'tuous
sump'tuously
sun
sun'bathe
sun'beam
sun'burn
sun'burnt
Sun'day
sun'der
sun'dry
sung
sunk
sunk'en
sun'light
sun'lit
sun'rise
sun'set
sun'shine
sun'spot
sup
su'per
su'perable
superabun'dance
superabun'dant
superan'nuate
superan'nuated
superannua'tion
superb'
supercil'ious
superfi'cial
su'perfine
superflu'ity
super'fluous
superhu'man
superintend'
superintend'ed
superintend'ence
superintend'ent
supe'rior
superior'ity
super'lative
super'latively
su'permarine
su'permarket

supernat'ural
supersede'
superse'ded
superse'ding
superson'ic
supersti'tion
supersti'tious
supervise'
supervised'
supervi'sion
supervi'sor
sup'per
supplant'
supplant'ed
supplant'ing
sup'ple
sup'plement
supplemen'tal
supplemen'-tary
sup'pliant
sup'plicant
sup'plicate
supplica'tion
supplied'
supply'
support'
support'able
support'ed
support'er
support'ing
suppose'
supposed'
suppo'sing
supposi'tion
suppress'
suppressed'
suppress'ing
suppres'sion
suprem'acy
supreme'
supreme'ly
sur'charge, *n.*
surcharge', *v.*
sure
sure'ly
sur'est
sure'ty

surf
sur'face
surf'-board
sur'feit
sur'feited
surge
surged
sur'geon
sur'gery
sur'gical
sur'ly
surmise'
surmised'
surmount'
surmount'able
surmount'ed
surmount'ing
sur'name
surpass'
surpassed'
sur'plus
surprise'
surprised'
*surpri'*sing
surre'alism
surren'der
surren'dered
surrepti'tious
surround'
surround'ed
surround'ing
sur'tax, *n.*
surtax', *v.*
sur'vey, *n.*
survey', *v.*
surveyed
survey'ing
survey'or
survi'val
survive'
survived'
survi'ving
survi'vor
susceptibil'ity
suscep'tible
sus'pect, *n.*

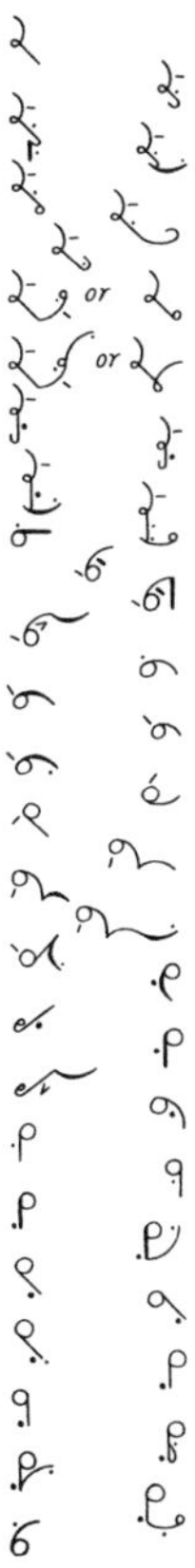

suspect', v.
suspect'ed
suspend'
suspend'ed
suspend'ing
suspense'
suspen'sion
suspi'cion
suspi'cious
suspi'ciously
sustain'
sustained'
sustain'ing
sus'tenance
swag'ger
swal'low
swal'lowed
swal'lowing
swam
swamp
swamped
swamp'y
swan
swap
swarm
swarmed
swarm'ing
swarth'y
swathe
sway
swayed
sway'ing
swear
sweat
sweat'er
Swede
Swe'dish
sweep
sweep'er
sweep'ing
sweet
sweet'er
sweet'est
sweet'ly
sweet'ness
swell

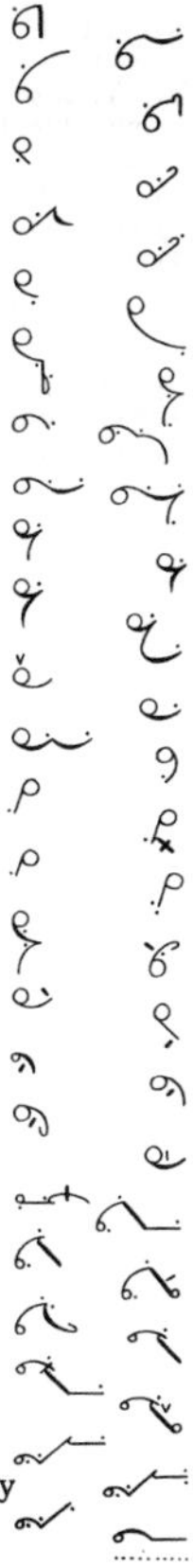

swelled
swell'ing
swel'ter
swel'tered
swept
swerve
swerved
swerv'ing
swift
swift'er
swift'est
swift'ly
swim
swim'mer
swim'ming
swim'mingly
swin'dle
swin'dled
swin'dler
swin'dling
swine
swing
swing'ing
Swiss
switch
switch'bōard
switched
switch'ing
swiv'el
swoll'en
swoon
swoop
sword
swore
sworn
swung
syc'amore
syllab'ic
syl'lable
syl'labus
syl'van
sym'bol
symbol'ic
sym'bolize
symmet'rical
symmet'rically
sym'metry
sympathet'ic

sympathet'-
ically
sym'pathize
sym'pathized
sym'pathy
sym'phony
sympo'sium
symp'tom
syn'agogue
synchroniza'-
tion
syn'chronize
syn'chronized
syn'chronizing

syn'dicate
syn'onym
synon'ymous
synop'sis
syn'thesis
synthet'ic
synthet'ically
syn'thetize
syr'inge
syr'up
sys'tem
systemat'ic
systemat'ical
systemat'ically

T

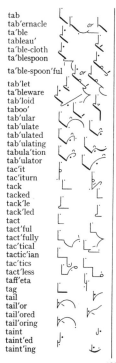

tab
tab'ernacle
ta'ble
tableau'
ta'ble-cloth
ta'blespoon
ta'ble-spoon'ful
tab'let
ta'bleware
tab'loid
taboo'
tab'ular
tab'ulate
tab'ulated
tab'ulating
tabula'tion
tab'ulator
tac'it
tac'iturn
tack
tacked
tack'le
tack'led
tact
tact'ful
tact'fully
tac'tical
tactic'ian
tac'tics
tact'less
taff'eta
tag
tail
tail'or
tail'ored
tail'oring
taint
taint'ed
taint'ing

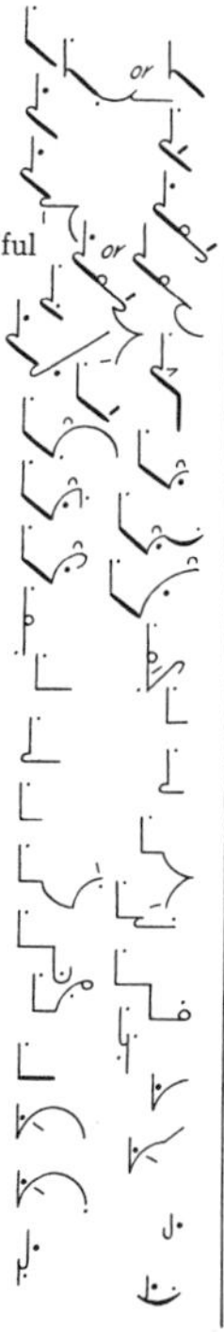

take
ta'ken
take'-over
ta'king
talc
tale
tal'ent
tal'ented
tal'isman
talk
talk'ative
talk'er
talk'ing
tall
tall'er
tallest
tal'lied
tal'low
tal'ly
tame
tamed
ta'mer
tam'per
tam'pered
tam'pering
tan
tan'dem
tan'gent
tan'gible
tan'gle
tang'o
tank
tank'ard
tan'ker
tan'ner
tan'nery
tan'nic
tan'nin
tan'talize
tan'talizing

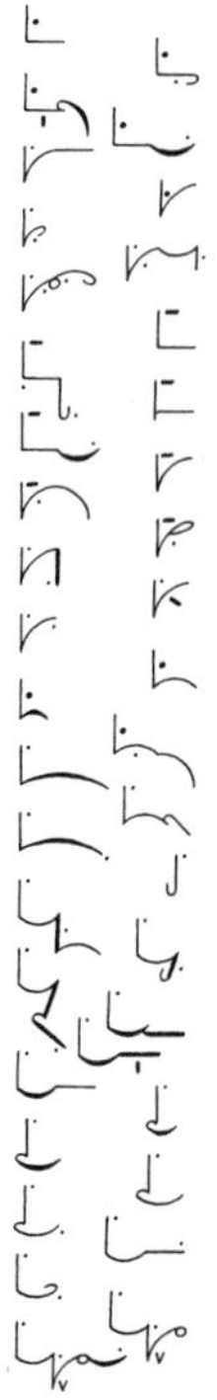

tan'tamount
tan'trum
tap
tape
ta'per
tape'-record'er
ta'pering
tap'estry
tapio'ca
tapped
tap'ping
tar
tar'dily
tar'diness
tar'dy
tare
tar'get
tar'iff
tar'mac
tar'nish
tar'nished
tarpau'lin
tar'ried
tar'ring
tar'ry, *adj.*
tar'ry, *v.*
tart
tar'tan
tar'tar
tartar'ic
task
tas'sel
taste
ta'sted
taste'ful
taste'fully
taste'less
taste'lessness
ta'sting
ta'sty
tat'ter
tat'tered
tat'tle
tattoo'
tattooed'
taught
taunt
taunt'ed

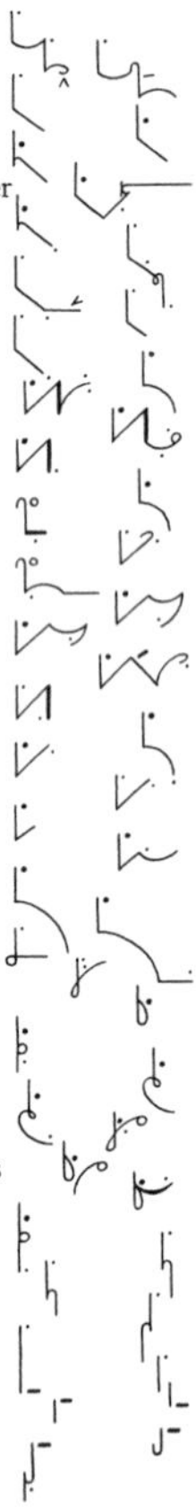

taunt'ing
taut
tav'ern
taw'dry
taw'ny
tax
tax'able
taxa'tion
taxed
tax'-free
tax'i
tax'icab
tax'payer
tea
teach
teach'er
teach'ing
tea'cup
teak
team
tea'pot
tear, *n.*
tear, *v.*
tear'ful
tear'ing
tease
tea'spoon
tea'spoonful
tech'nical
technical'ity
tech'nically
technique'
technol'ogist
technol'ogy
te'dious
te'diously
te'dium
tee
teem
teemed
teem'ing
teen'age
teen'ager
teeth
teethe
teeto'tal
teeto'taler,
teeto'taller

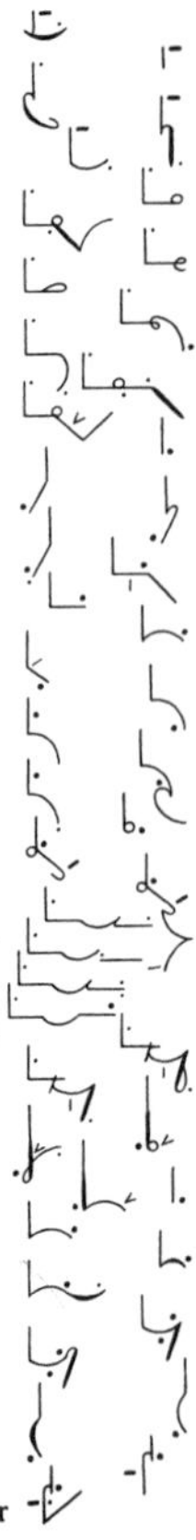

tel'ecast
telegen'ic
tel'egram
tel'egraph
telegraph'ic
teleg'raphist
teleg'raphy
telep'athy
tel'ephone
telephon'ic
teleph'onist
teleph'ony
tele'photo
tel'eprinter
teleprompt'ter
tel'escope
telescop'ic
tele'type
tel'eview
tele'vise
tel'evision
tell
*tell'*er
*tell'*ing
tell'-tale
temer'ity
tem'per
tem'perament
tempera-men'tal
tempera-men'tally
tem'perance
tem'perate
tem'perately
tem'perature
tem'pered
tem'pering
tem'pest
tempes'tuous
tem'ple
tem'poral
tem'porarily
tem'porary
tempt
tempta'tion
tempt'ed

tempt'ing
ten
ten'able
tena'cious
tena'ciously
tenac'ity
ten'ancy
ten'ant
tend
tend'ed
ten'dency
ten'der
ten'dered
ten'dering
ten'derly
tend'ing
ten'don
ten'ement
ten'et
ten'fold
ten'nis
ten'or
tense
tense'ly
ten'sion
tent
ten'tacle
ten'tative
ten'tatively
tenth
ten'ure
tep'id
term
termed
ter'minable
ter'minal
ter'minate, *a.*
ter'minate, *v.*
ter'minated
termina'tion
ter'minus
ter'race
ter'ra-cot'ta
terrain'
ter'rible
ter'ribly
ter'rier
terrif'ic

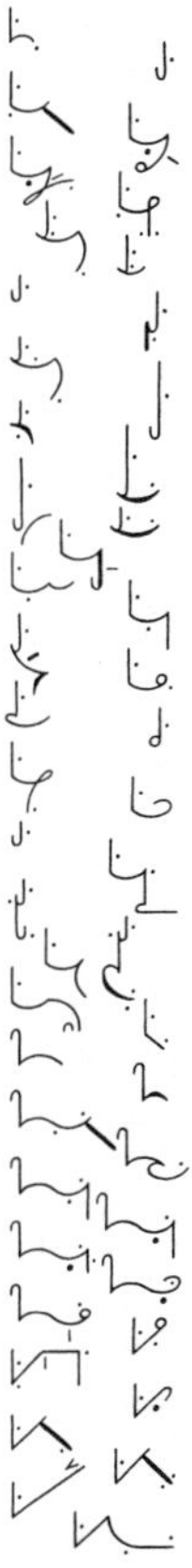

ter'rified
ter'rify
territo'rial
ter'ritory
ter'ror
ter'rorism
ter'rorize
terse
terse'ly
terylene'
test
tes'tament
testamen'tary
testa'tor
testa'trix
test'ed
test'er
tes'tified
tes'tify
testimo'nial
tes'timony
test'ing
tes'ty
teth'er
teth'ered
text
text'book
tex'tile
tex'ture
than
{*thank*
{*thanked*
{*thank'ful*
{*thank'fully*
*thank'*fulness
*thank'*ing
*thank'*less
thanks
thanks'giving
that
thatch
thatched
thaw
thawed
the
the'atre,
the'ater
theat'rical

theft
their
theirs
them
theme
themselves'
then
thence
thenceforth'
thencefor'ward
{theolog'ical
{theolog'-
ically
theol'ogist
theol'ogy
the'orem
theoret'ical
theoret'ically
the'orist
the'orize
the'ory
there
*there'*about
*there*af'ter
*there*at'
*there*by'
*there'*for
there'fore
*there*from'
*there*in'
*there*of'
*there*on'
*there*out'
*there*to'
*there*upon'
*there*with'
therm
thermion'ic
thermom'eter
ther'mos
ther'mostat
these
the'sis
they
thick
thick'en
thick'ened
thick'ening

thick'er
thick'et
thick'ly
thick'ness
thief
thieves
thigh
thim'ble
thin
thine
thing
think
think'er
think'ing
thin'ly
thinned
thin'ner
third
third'ly
third'-rate'
thirds
thirst
thirst'ed
thirst'ing
thirst'y
thirteen'
thirteenth'
thir'tieth
thir'ty
this
this'tle
thorn
thorn'y
thor'ough
thor'oughbred
thor'oughfare
thor'oughly
thor'oughness
those
thou
though
thought
thought'ful
thought'fully
thought'ful-
ness
thought'less
thought'lessly
thought'less-
ness
thou'sand
thou'sandfold
thrash
thrashed
thrash'ing
thread
thread'bare
thread'ed
thread'ing
threat
threat'en
threat'ened
three
three-
quarters
thresh
thresh'old
threw
thrice
thrift
thrift'y
thrill
thrilled
thrill'er
thrill'ing
thrive
thri'ving
throat
throb
throbbed
throb'bing
throne
throng
thronged
throng'ing
throt'tle
through
throughout'
throw
throw'back
throw'ing
thrown
thrust
thrust'ing
thud
thumb

thump
thumped
thun'der
thun'dered
Thurs'day
thus
thwart
thwart'ed
tick'et
tick'le
ti'dal
tide
ti'ded
ti'dings
ti'dy
tie
tied
tier
ti'ger
tight
tight'en
tight'ened
tight'ening
tight'ly
tight'ness
tile
tiled
till, *n.* and *v.*
till, prep.
tilt
tilt'ed
tilt'ing
tim'ber
time
time'keeper
time'table
tim'id
timid'ity
tim'idly
tim'orous
tin
tinc'ture
tinge
tin'gle
tin'kle
tinned
tin'plate
tin'sel
tint
tint'ed
tint'ing
ti'ny
tip
tip'off
tipped
tip'ping
tirade'
tire
tired
tire'less
tire'some
tir'o
tis'sue
Titan'ic
tit'-bit
tithe
ti'tle
tit'ter
tit'ular
to
toast
toast'ed
toast'ing
tobac'co
tobac'conist
tobog'gan
*to*day'
toe
tof'fee,
tof'fy
togeth'er
toil
toiled
toi'let
tok'en
told
tol'erable
tol'erably
tol'erance
tol'erant
tol'erate
tol'erated
tol'erating
tolera'tion
toll
tolled

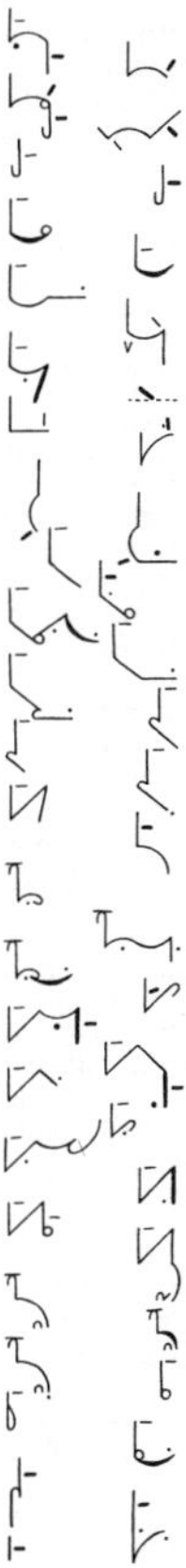

toma'to
tomb
tomb'stone
*to*mor'row
ton
tone
tongs
tongue
ton'ic
tonight'
ton'nage
too
took
tool
tooth
tooth'ache
top
to'paz
top'-heavy
top'ic
top'ical
top'ple
top'pled
top'pling
torch
tore
{tor'ment, *n.*
{torment', *v.*
torment'ed
torment'ing
torn
torna'do
torpe'do
tor'pid
tor'rent
torren'tial
tor'rid
tor'toise
tor'tuous
tor'ture
tor'tured
tor'turing
toss
tossed
toss'ing
to'tal
to'tally
tote

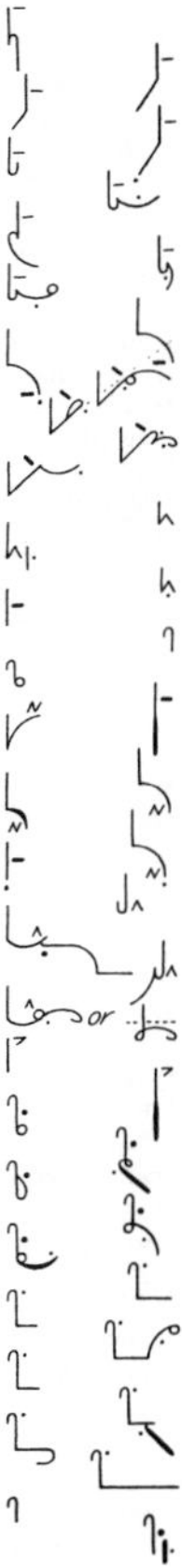

tot'ter
touch
touched
touch'ing
tough
tough'en
tough'er
tough'est
tough'ness
tour
tour'ing
tour'ism
tour'ist
tour'nament
tour'ney
tout
tout'ed
tout'ing
tow
to'ward
to'wards
towed
tow'el
tow'er
tow'ered
tow'ering
tow'ing
town
town'-clerk'
town'ship
towns'man (or)
toy
toyed
trace
trace'able
traced
tra'cer
tra'cing
track
tracked
track'less
tract
tract'able
trac'tion
trac'tor
trade
tra'ded

trade'-mark
tra'der
*trades'*man
trades-u'nion
trades-u'nion-ism
trade-u'nion
*tra'd*ing
tradi'tion
tradi'tional
tradi'tionally
traf'fic
trag'edy
trag'ic
trag'ically
trail
trail'er
trail'ing
train
trainee'
train'er
train'ing
trait
trai'tor
tram
tramp
tramped
tramp'ing
tram'ple
tram'pled
tram'pling
trance
tran'quil
tranquil'lity
transact'
transact'ed
transact'ing
transac'tion
transatlan'tic
transcend
transcend'ed
transcend'ent
transcribe'
tran'script
transcrip'tion

{trans'fer, *n.*
{transfer', *v.*
trans'ferable
trans'ference
transferred'
transfix'
transform'
transforma'-tion
transform'er
transgress'
transgressed'
transgress'ing
transgres'sion
tranship'
tranship'ment
tran'sient
transist'or
trans'it
transi'tion
transi'tional
trans'itory
translate'
transla'ted
transla'ting
transla'tion
transla'tor
transmis'sion
transmit'
transmit'ted
transmit'ter
transmit'ting
transpa'rent
transpire'
transpired'
transpi'ring
transplant'
{trans'port, *n.*
{transport', *v.*
transporta'-tion
transport'ed
transpose'
transship'
transship'ment
trap

trap'-door'
trapeze'
trapped
trap'ping
trash
trav'el
trav'elled,
trav'eled
trav'eller,
trav'eler
trav'elogue
trav'erse
trav'ersed
treach'erous
treach'ery
treac'le
tread
tread'ing
trea'son
treas'ure
treas'urer
treas'ury
treat
treat'ed
treat'ing
trea'tise
treat'ment
trea'ty
treb'le
tree
trel'lis
trem'ble
trem'bled
trem'bling
tremen'dous
trem'or
trem'ulous
trench
trench'ant
trend
tres'pass
tres'passed
tres'passer
tres'passing
tress
tri'al
tri'angle
trian'gular
tri'bal
tribe
tribula'tion
tribu'nal *or*
trib'une
trib'utary
trib'ute
trick
tricked
trick'ery
trick'le
trick'led
trick'y
tried
trien'nial
tri'fle
tri'fled
tri'fling
trig'ger
trim
trim'ly
trimmed
trin'ity
trin'ket
tri'o
trip
tripe
trip'le
trip'lex
trip'licate, *n.*, *a.*
trip'licate, *v.*
trite
trite'ly
trite'ness
tri'umph
trium'phal
trium'phant
trium'phantly
tri'umphed
triv'ial
trivial'ity
trod
trodd'en
trol'ley
troop
troop'er

tro'phy
trop'ical
trot
trot'ted
trot'ting
troub'le
troub'led
troub'lesome
troub'ling
troub'lous
trough
trou'sers
trousseau'
trout
trow'el
tru'ant
truce
truck
tru'culence
tru'culent
trudge
trudged
trudg'ing
true
tru'est
tru'ism
trump
trump'et
trump'eter
trun'dle
trunk
trunk'-*call*
truss
trust
trust'ed
trustee'
trust'ful
trust'fully
trust'ing
trust'ingly
trust'worthi-ness
trust'worthy
trust'y
truth
truth'ful
truth'fulness
truths

try
try'ing
try'-*on*
tryst
tub
tube
tuber'cular
tuberculo'sis
tuber'culous
tu'bing
tu'bular
tuck
Tu'dor
Tues'day
tuft
tug
tui'tion
tu'lip
tum'ble
tum'bled
tum'bler
tu'mult
tumul'tuous
tune
tuned
tuneful
tune'fully
tu'ner
tu'nic
tu'ning
tun'nel
tur'bine
tur'bulent
turf
Turk
tur'key
tur'moil
turn
turned
turn'er
turn'ing
turn'ing-point
tur'nip
turn'over
turn'stile
turn'table
tur'pentine
tur'ret

tur'tle
tusk
tus'sle
tu'tor
tuto'rial
tu'tors
twad'dle
tweed
twee'zers
twelfth
twelve
twen'tieth
twen'ty
twice
twig
twi'light
twill
twin
twine
twinge
twi'ning
twin'kle
twin'kled
twin'kling
twist
twist'ed
twist'ing
twitch
two
two'fold

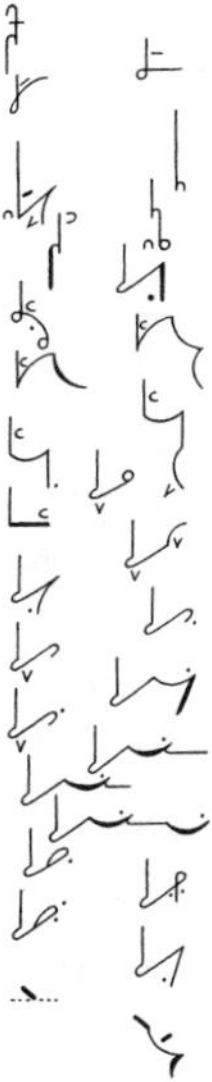

two-seater
two-some
ty'ing
type
type'script
type'writer
type'writing
type'written
ty'phoid
typhoon'
typ'ical
typ'ified
typ'ify
ty'pist
typograph'ic
typograph'ical
typog'raphy
typol'ogy
tyran'nic
tyran'nical
tyran'nically
tyr'annize
tyr'annized
tyr'annous
tyr'anny
ty'rant
tyre
ty'ro

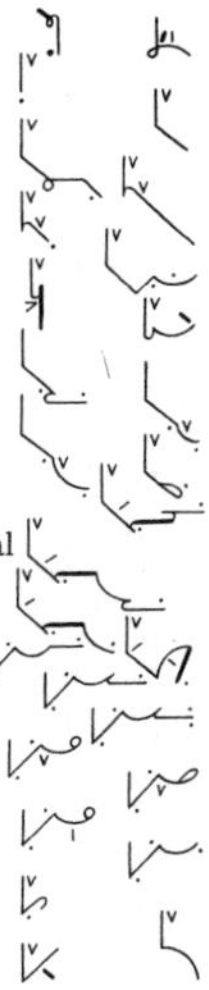

U

ubiq'uitous
ubiq'uity
ug'lier
ug'liest
ug'ly
ukule'le
ul'cer
ul'cerated
ulcera'tion
ulte'rior
ul'timate
ul'timately
ultima'tum
ul'timo
ultrason'ic
um'brage
umbrel'la
um'pire
unabashed'
unaba'ted
una'ble
unaccom'-
panied
unaccount'-
able
unaccus'tomed
unacquaint'ed
unadorned'
unaid'ed
unal'terable
unambi'guous
unanim'ity
unan'imous
unan'imous-
ly
unarmed
unassu'ming
unattached'
unattract'ive
unau'thorized
unavail'able
unavoid'able
unaware'
unbal'anced
unbear'able
unbecom'ing
unbelief'
un*believ'*able
unbeliev'er
unbeliev'ing
unbend'
unbi'assed
unblem'ished
unborn'
unbound'ed
unbrok'en
un*called'*
uncan'ny
unceas'ing
unceas'ingly
unceremo'-
nious
uncer'tain
unchal'lenged
unchanged'
unchar'itable
unciv'il
unciv'ilized
un'cle
unclean'
uncom'fortable
uncom'mon
uncom'monly
unconcern'
unconcern'edly
uncondi'tional
unconge'nial
unconnect'ed
uncon'scious

unconstitu'tional
unconstitu'tionally
uncontrol'lable
uncontrolled'
unconven'tional
uncouth'
uncov'er
uncul'tivated
uncut'
unda'ted
undaunt'ed
undeci'ded
undefend'ed
undefiled'
undefined'
undeliv'ered
undeni'able
un'der
*un'der*carriage
*und'er*coat
*un'der*current
*un'der*dog
under-es'timate, *n.*
under-es'timate, *v.*
under-es'timated
*under*go'
*under*grad'uate
*un'der*ground
*un'der*growth
un'derhand
*un'der*line
*under*ly'ing
*under*neath'
un'der-nourished
*un'der*pass
un'der-pri'vileged
*under*rate'
under-sec're-tary
*un'der*staffed
*under*stand'
*under*state'ment
*under*stood'
*un'der*study
*under*take'
*un'der*tone
*un'der*wear
*un'der*world
un'derwriter
undeserved'
undesir'able
undeterred'
undisclosed'
undisturbed'
undivi'ded
undo'
undoubt'ed
undoubt'edly
undress'
undue'
un'dulating
undu'ly
unearned'
uneas'ily
uneas'y
uneconom'ic
unemploy'able
unemployed'
unemploy'ment
une'*qual*
une'*qualled*
une'*qually*
uner'ring
uner'ringly
une'ven
une'venly
unevent'ful
unexam'pled
un*expect'ed*
un*expect'ed*ly
unfail'ing
unfair'
unfaith'ful
un*famil'iar*
unfash'ionable
unfa'vourable
unfeel'ing
unfeigned'

unfert'ilized
unfin'ished
unfit'
unflag'ging
unflat'tering
unfold'
unforeseen'
unforgett'able
unfor'tunate
unfor'tunately
unfound'ed
unfriend'ly
unfulfilled'
unfurl'
unfurled'
unfur'nished
un*gen'tleman*ly
un*gov'ern*able
ungra'cious
ungrate'ful
unguard'ed
unhap'pily
unhap'py
unharmed'
unhealth'y
unhes'itatingly
unhook'
unhurt'
unhygien'ic
uni'fied
{*u'niform*
uniform'ity
u'niformly}
u'nify
unilat'eral
unimpaired'
un*impor'tant*
un*in'fluenced*
un*informed'*
un*intel'ligible*
uninten'tional
uninterrupt'ed
u'nion
U'nionist
unique'

u'nison
u'nit
unite'
uni'ted
u'nity
univer'sal
universal'ity
univer'sally
u'niverse
univer'sity
unjust'
unjust'ifiable
unjus'tified
unkind'
unknown'
unlaw'ful
unless'
unlike'
unlike'ly
unlim'ited
unload'
unlock'
unluck'ily
unluck'y
unman'nerly
unmind'ful
unmista'kable
unmit'igated
unmoved'
unnat'ural
unnec'essarily
unnec'essary
unno'ticed
unobtain'able
unoffi'cial
un*or'ganized*
unorth'odox
unpaid'
unpal'atable
unpar'alleled
unpleas'ant
unpleas'antly
unpop'ular
unprec'edented
un*prej'udiced*
unpremed'ita-
ted
unprepared'

un*prin'cipaled*
un*produc'tive*
unprof'itable
unprotect'ed
unprovoked'
un*pub'lished*
unqual'ified
{un*ques'tionable*
{un*ques'tionably*
unrav'el
unre'alizable
unrea'sonable
unrelat'ed
unreli'able
unremu'nerative
un*represent'ed*
unreserv'edly
unrest'
unrestrict'ed
unru'ly
unsafe'
un*satisfac'tory*
unscrew'
unscrewed'
unscru'pulous
unseen'
un*self'ish*
un*self'ish*ly
un*self'ishness*
unset'tle
unset'tled
unsight'ed
unsight'ly
unskil'ful
unskilled'
unso'ciable
unsoiled'
unsold'
unsolic'ited
unsophis'ticated
unsound'
unsound'ly
unspa'ring

unspa'ringly
unspe'cified
unsta'ble
unstead'ily
unstead'y
unstud'ied
unsuccess'ful
unsuccess'fully
unsuit'able
unsurpassed'
un*suspect'ed*
un*suspect'*ing
unswerv'ing
un*sympathet'ic*
untaxed'
unti'diness
unti'dy
untie'
untied'
until'
untime'ly
untir'ing
un'to
un*told'*
unto'ward
un*tried'*
untrod'den
untrue'
untruth'
{unu'*sual*
{unu'*sually*
unva'rying
unveil'
unveiled'
unwar'rantable
unwar'ranted
unwea'ried
unwel'come
unwell'
unwhole'some
unwield'y
unwil'ling
unwil'lingly
unwise'
unwise'ly
unwit'tingly
unwork'able
unwor'thy

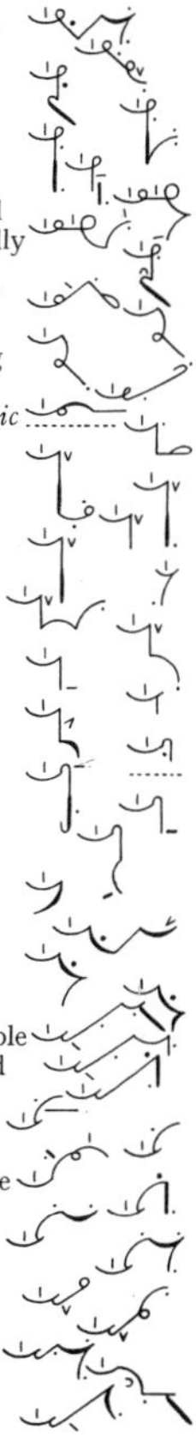

unwrit'ten
unyield'ing
up
up'bringing
upheav'al
upheave'
upheld'
uphill'
uphold'
uphold'ing
uphol'ster
uphol'sterer
uphol'stery
uplift'
upon'
up'per
up'per*most*
up'right'
up'roar
uproar'ious
uproot'
upset'
up'surge
up'swing
up'wards
ur'ban
urbane'
urban'ity
ur'chin
urge
ur'gency
ur'gent
ur'gently
urn
us

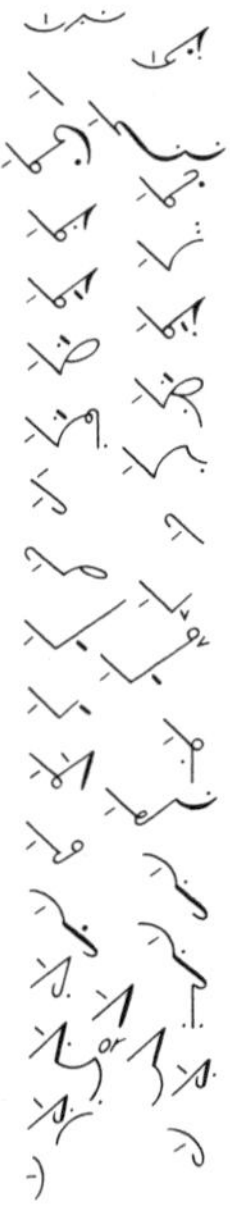

u'sable
u'sage
use
used
use'ful
use'fully
use'fulness
use'less
use'lessly
use'lessness
u'ser
ush'er
ush'ered
usherette'
u'sing
u'sual,
u'sually
u'surer
usurp'
u'sury
uten'sil
util'ity
utiliza'tion
u'tilize
u'tilized
u'tilizing
ut'*most*
Uto'pia
ut'ter
ut'terance
ut'tered
ut'tering
ut'terly
ut'ter*most*

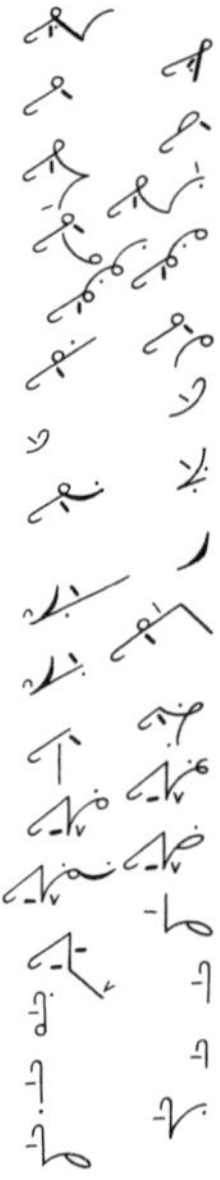

V

va'cancy
va'cant
vacate'
vaca'ted
vaca'ting
vaca'tion
vac'cinate
vac'cinated
vaccina'tion
vac'cine
vac'illate
vac'illated
vac'illating
vacilla'tion
vac'uous
vac'uum
vag'abond
vaga'ry
va'grancy
va'grant
vague
vague'ly
vain
vain'ly
vale
valedic'tory
val'ency
val'et
val'iant
val'iantly
val'id
valid'ity
valise'
val'ley
val'orous
val'our
val'uable
valua'tion
val'ue

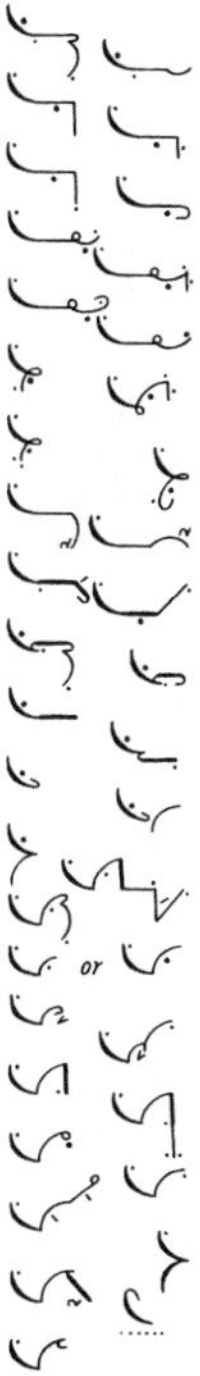

val'ued
valve
valv'ular
vamp
vam'pire
van
vanil'la
van'ish
van'ished
van'ishing
van'ity
van'quish
van'tage
vap'id
vap'orizer
va'pour,
va'por
va'riable
va'riance
va'riant
varia'tion
va'ried
vari'ety
va'rious
var'nish
var'nishing
va'ry
va'rying
vase
Vas'eline
vas'sal
vast
vast'ly
vat
Vat'ican
vaude'ville
vault
vault'ed
vault'ing
vaunt

vaunt'ed
veal
veer
veered
veer'ing
veg'etable
vegeta'rian
vegeta'rianism
vegeta'tion
ve'hemence
ve'hement
ve'hemently
ve'hicle
vehic'ular
veil
veiled
vein
vel'lum
veloc'ity
velour'
vel'vet
velveteen'
vend'er, vend'or
vendet'ta
vend'or (*legal term*)
veneer'
ven'erable
ven'erate
venera'tion
Vene'tian
ven'geance
ve'nial
ven'ison
ven'om
ven'omous
vent
ven'tilate
ven'tilated
ventila'tion
ven'tilator
ven'ture
ven'tured
ven'turesome
ven'turing

ven'ue
vera'cious
verac'ity
veran'dah
verb
ver'bal
verba'tim
ver'biage
verbose'
verbos'ity
ver'dant
ver'dict
ver'dure
verge
verifica'tion
ver'ified
ver'ify
ver'ily
ver'itable
vermil'ion
ver'min
ver'satile
versatil'ity
verse
ver'sion
ver'sus
ver'tebrae
ver'tical
ver'y
ves'sel
vest
vest'ed
ves'tibule
ves'tige
vest'ment
ves'try
ves'ture
vet'eran
vet'erinary
ve'to
vex
vexa'tion
vexa'tious
vexed
vi'a
vi'aduct
vi'al
vi'brant

vi′brate
vi′brated
vibra′tion
vic′ar
vica′rious
vice
vice-*chair′*man
vice-pres′ident
vice-*prin′cipal*
vice′roy
vic′e ver′sa
vicin′ity
vic′ious
vic′iously
vicis′situde
vic′tim
victimiza′tion
vic′tor
victo′rious
vic′tory
vict′uals
vid′eo
vie
view
viewed
vig′il
vig′ilance
vig′ilant
vig′orous
vig′our
vile
vil′la
vil′lage
vil′lain
vil′lainous
vil′lainy
vim
vin′dicate
vin′dicated
vindica′tion
vindic′tive
vindic′tively
vine
vin′egar
vine′yard
vin′tage
vi′olate
vi′olated

viola′tion
vi′olence
vi′olent
vi′olently
vi′olet
violin′
violin′ist
vi′per
vir′gin
vir′ile
viril′ity
vir′tual
vir′tue
virtuos′ity
vir′tuous
vir′ulence
vir′ulent
vi′sa
vis′age
vis′cous
vi′sé
visibil′ity
vis′ible
vi′sion
vi′sionary
vis′it
visita′tion
vis′ited
vis′iting
vis′itor
vis′ta
vis′ual
visualiza′tion
vis′ualize
vi′tal
vital′ity
vi′tally
vi′tamin
vi′tiate
vi′tiated
vitriol′ic
vitu′perate
vitupera′tion
viva′cious
vivac′ity
viv′id
viv′idly
vivisec′tion

vocab′ulary
vo′cal
vo′calist
vocaliza′tion
voca′tion
voca′tional
vocif′erous
vod′ka
vogue
voice
void
vol′atile
vol′-au-vent′
volcan′ic
volca′no
vol′ley
volt
volt′age
volubil′ity
vol′uble
vol′ume
volu′minous
vol′untarily
vol′untary
volunteer′
volunteered′
volunteer′ing
vora′cious
vo′tary
vote
vo′ted
vo′ter
vouch
vouch′er
vouchsafe
vow
vowed
vow′el
voy′age
vul′canite
vul′canize
vul′gar
vulgar′ity
vul′garly
vulnerabil′ity
vul′nerable
vul′ture
vy′ing

W

wad
wad'ding
wade
wa'ded
wa'ding
wa'fer
waf'fle
waft
waft'ed
wag
wage
wage'-freeze
wa'ger
wag'on,
  wag'gon
waif
wail
wailed
wain'scot
wain'scotting
waist
waist'coat
wait
wait'ed
wait'er
wait'ing-list
wait'ing-room
wait'ress
waive
wake
wake'ful
wake'fulness
wa'ken
wa'kening
walk
walked
walk'er
walk'ing
walk'ing-stick
walk'-out

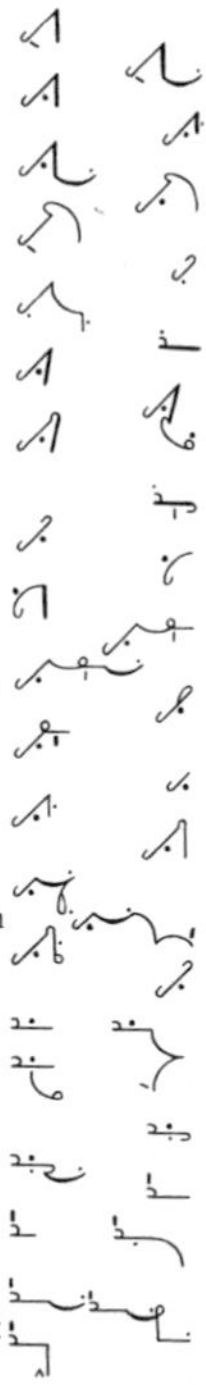

walk'-over
wall
wal'let
wal'low
wall'paper
wal'nut
wal'rus
waltz
waltzed
wan
wand
wan'der
wan'dered
wan'derer
wan'dering
wane
want
want'ed
wan'ton
war
war'ble
ward
ward'en
ward'er
ward'robe
ware'house
wares
war'fare
war'ily
war'like
warm
warmed
warm'er
warm'est
warm'-hearted
warmth
warn
warned
warn'ing
War'-Office

warp
war'rant
war'ranted
war'ranty
war'rior
war'ship
wa'ry
was
wash
wash'able
washed
wash'er
wash'ing
wash'out
wasp
waste
wast'ed
waste'ful
waste'fully
wa'sting
watch
watched
watch'er
watch'ful
watch'fulness
watch'ing
watch'man
wa'ter
wa'terfall
wa'terfront
wa'termark or
wa'termelon
wa'terproof
wa'tershed
wa'tertight
watt
wave
waved
wave'length
wa'ver
wa'vered
wa'vering
wa'ving
wa'vy
wax
way
way'farer
way'faring
way'side
we
weak
weak'en
weak'er
weak'ness
weal
wealth
wealth'ier
wealth'iest
wealth'y
weap'on
wear
wear'able
wear'er
wear'ied
wear'ing
wear'isome
wear'y
wear'ying
weath'er
weath'erproof
weave
weav'er
weav'ing
web
wed'ding
wedge
wedged
wedg'ing
Wednes'day
weed
week
week'day
week-end'
week'ly
weep
weigh
weighed
weigh'ing
weight
weight'y
weir
weird
wel'*come*
wel'comed
wel'coming

weld
weld'ed
weld'ing
wel'fare
well
well-known'
well-mean'ing
Welsh
wel'ter
went
wept
were
west
west'erly
west'ern
west'ward
wet
whale
wharf
wharf'age
what
whatev'er
*what*soev'er
wheat
wheel
wheel'-base
wheeled
when
whence
whenev'er
whensoev'er
where
where'abouts
whereas'
whereat'
whereby'
where'fore
where'*in*
whereinsoev'er
whereof'
whereon'
wheresoev'er
where*to*'
whereupon'
wherev'er
wherewithal'
wheth'er

which
*which*ev'er
whiff
while
whiled
whilst
whim
whim'per
whim'pered
whim'pering
whim'sical
whine
whined
whi'ning
whip
whirl
whirled
whirl'ing
whirl'pool
whirl'wind
whis'key,
whis'ky
whis'per
whis'pered
whis'pering
whist
whis'tle
whis'tled
whit
white
whith'er
whithersoev'er
whit'tle
whiz
who
*who*ev'er
whole
whole'heart'ed
whole-
heart'edly
whole'sale
whole'some
whol'ly
whom
whoop
whose
*who*soev'er
why

wick
wick'ed
wick'er
wick'et
wide
wide'ly
wi'den
wi'dened
wi'dening
wi'der
wide'spread
wid'ow
wid'ower
width
wield
wife
wig
wild
wild'er
wil'derness
wild'est
wild'ly
wile
wil'ful
wil'fully
wil'fulness
will
willed
will'ing
wil'lingly
wil'low
wilt
wi'ly
win
wince
winced
wind, *n.*
wind, *v.*
wind'fall
wind'ing
win'dow
win'dow-dressing
wind'screen
wind'-tunnel
wind'ward
wine
wine'-cellar
wine'-glass
wing
wink
win'ner
win'ning
win'some
win'ter
win'terly
win'try
wipe
wiped
wi'ping
wire
wired
wire'less
wir'y
wis'dom
wise
wise'ly
wi'ser
wi'sest
wish
wished
wish'ing
wist'ful
wist'fully
wit
with
withal'
withdraw'
withdraw'al
withdrawn'
withdrew'
with'er
with'ered
withheld'
withhold'
within'
without'
withstand'
withstood'
wit'ness
wit'ticism
wit'ty
wiz'ard
wob'ble
wob'bled
wob'bling

woke
wolf
wom'an
wom'anhood
wom'anly
wom'en
won
won'der
won'dered
{*won'derful*
{*won'derfully*
won'dering
won'deringly
won'drous
won'drously
won't
wont
wont'ed
wood
wood'en
wood'work
wool
wool'len
wooll'ies
wool'sack
word
word'ed
word'ing
word'y
wore
work
work'able
worked
work'er
work'ing
work'less
work'man
work'manship
work'shop
world
world'ly
world'wide
worm
worn
wor'ried
wor'ry
wor'rying
worse
wor'sen
wor'ship
worst
worst'ed
worth
wor'thier
wor'thiest
wor'thily
worth'less
worth'lessness
worthwhile'
wor'thy
would
would-be
wound, *n.*, *v.*
wound, *v.*
wound'ing
wove
wo'ven
wran'gle
wrap
wrapped
wrap'per
wrap'ping
wrath ... *or* ...
wrath'ful
wreath
wreathe
wreck
wreck'age
wrecked
wreck'ing
wrench
wrenched
wrench'ing
wrest
wres'tle
wres'tled
wrest'ling
wretch
wretch'ed
wretch'edness
wrig'gle
wright
wring
wring'er
wrin'kle
wrist

wrist'let
wrist'watch
writ
write
wri'ter
write'-up
writhe
writhed
wri'ting
writ'ten
wrong
wronged
wrong'ful
wrong'fully
wrong'ly
wrote
wroth
wrought'
wrought'-iron'
wrung
wry

X

xan'thium
xantho-
car'pous
xe'nial
xenog'amy
xenoglos'(s)ia
xen'on
xenophob'ia
xera'sia
xero'graphy
xeroph'agy
xerophthal'mia
xero'sis

xiph'oid
X-ray'
X-rays
xy'lem
xy'locarp
xy'lograph
xy'loid
xyloi'din(e)
xylom'eter
xy'lonite
xyloph'agous
xy'lophone
xys'ter
xys'tus

Y

yacht
yacht'ing
yank
yard
yarn
yawn
yawned
yawn'ing
ye
yea
year
year'book
year'ly
yearn
yearned
yearn'ing
yeast
yell
yel'low
yelp
yelped
yelp'ing
yes
yes'terday

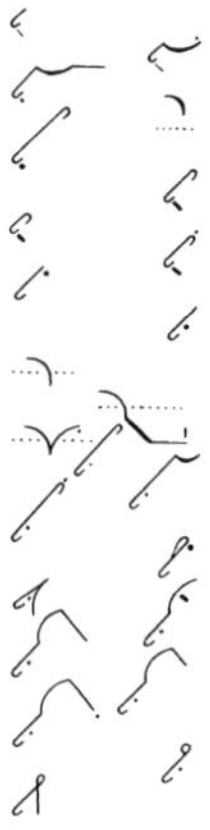

yet
yew
Yid'dish
yield
yield'ed
yo'ghourt
yoke
yo'kel
yolk
yon'der
you
young
young'er
young'est
young'ster
your
*your*self'
*your*selves'
youth
youth'ful
youth'fulness
Yule
Yule'tide

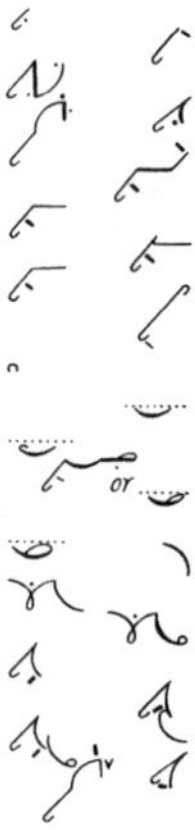

Z

za'ny
zap'tieh
zare'ba
zar'nich
zax
ze'a
zeal
zeal'ot
zeal'ous
zeal'ously
ze'bra
zed
zed'oary
zeit'geist
zen
zen'ith
zeph'yr
ze'ro
zest
zest'ful
zig'zag
zinc
zin'nia
zip
zip'-fas'tener

zir'con
zith'er
zo'diac
zo'nal
zone
zo'ning
zoolog'ical
zool'ogist
zool'ogy
zoom
Zu'lu
zy'gal
zygodac'tyl
zygo'ma
zygomat'ic
zyg'ote
zyme
zymol'ogist
zymol'ogy
zymom'eter
zy'moscope
zymo'sis
zymot'ic
zy'murgy
zy'thum